Super Stupid

— or —

Why The Educated Elite

Are So Wrong

So Often

About So Many Things

M. R. Lauer

The Pinnacle Quest series:

Pinnacle Questions

Pinnacle Reasoning

Ultrareasoning

The Structure of Truth

Super Stupid

Xiom (in progress)

3

Neither agree,

nor disagree;

explore

and

discover.

Contents

1 The Problem 1

I Normal Stupidity

2 Normal Stupidity 9

3 Core Constraints 25

Realities 26

Physical Reality, $\mathbb{R}$ 30

Limits of $\mathbb{R}$ 32

Semantic Reality, $\mathbb{SR}$, Part I 34

Cognitive Space ($\mathbb{CS}$) = Curved Space 36

Compound Curved Space 41

Semantic Reality Part II 41

Value and Meaning 48

Internal Reality 49

Evolutionary Reality 53

L0 60

L1 61

L2 64

Conclusion 69

i

ii

4   Limits   71

 Limit 1. Physical Reality, $\mathbb{R}$, is Real   72

 Limit 2. Semantic Reality, $\mathbb{SR}$, is Real   74

 Limit 3. Mortality is Real   79

 Limit 4. Cognitive Space Is Personal   79

  Corollary: We Think Inside Our Head   81

 Limit 5. The Mind Evolved in Layers   84

  Corollary 1: Layers Limit Thought   86

  Corollary 2: Intelligence Is Layer Specific   88

 Limit 6. Error Exceeds Content   91

5   Coping Tools   93

 Traditional Coping   93

 Creative Coping   98

  Lesson One: All unverified thought is personal . .   99

  Lesson Two: Error exceeds content   101

  Lesson Three: Informal vs. Formal   104

  Lesson Four: Truth is a matrix, not a scalar . . .   109

  Lesson Five: Think in Multiple Dimensions . . .   114

6   Summary   121

II Super Stupidity

7   Super Stupidity   127

 Defining Super Stupidity   129

 Limit Principles   130

 Character Flaws and Super Stupidity   132

  Disrespect   133

  Disrespect of $\mathbb{R}$ 133

Disrespect of $\mathbb{SR}$ 134

Disrespect of Tradition 136

Disrespect of Religion 137

Disrespect of the Individual 137

Disrespect of Knowledge 138

Disrespect of the Unknown 140

Hubris 141

Irresponsibility 141

Sloth 142

Inconstancy 143

Alienation 143

Cowardice 144

Conclusion 144

8   Religion 147

Supernatural Reality 161

Uncomfortable Truth of Religion 167

Reflections on Religion 170

Hypocrisy 170

Divine Origin 172

Crippled $\mathbb{S}$ 174

Future 174

9   The Source of Super Stupidity 177

Higher Education 186

Disregarding Reality 192

The Higher Education Stupidity Pump 193

10   The Power of Super Stupidity 197

Calculating Super Stupidity Power 200

iv

11 The Cost of Super Stupidity 213

    Self-Other-Ultimate Value Vector 216

    Blocking Intellectual Progress 225

    Causing Unbounded Loss 228

        Self 229

        Evil 231

III The Future

12 Solutions 247

13 Stop the Bleeding 249

    Reasoning 250

        What to Stop 252

        What to Start 255

    Identify and Respond 255

        What to Stop 255

        What to Start 256

    Opinion 257

        What to Stop 258

        What to Start 258

    Evidence 259

        What to Stop 259

        What to Start 260

    Debate 261

        What to Stop 261

        What to Start 262

    Education 262

        What to Stop 265

What to Start 265

Politics 266

What to Stop 266

What to Start 267

Postmodernism 267

14 Coping Strategies 271

Traditional Strategies 273

Religion 273

Create a Personal Code 278

Creative Strategies 282

Statement 283

Listening Perceptively 284

Questions 290

Formal and Informal Language 294

Using the Truth Matrix 296

Understanding Conversations 302

Practical Tips 306

Rules of Thumb 307

Tip 1: Solid Foundation 309

Tip 2: Knowledge-Humble 311

Tip 3: Settling 311

Tip 4: Realities 312

Tip 5: Explorer 313

15 ASPICS 315

Appendices 327

A Laws 329

vi

B   Levels 343

C   UCM: *Universal Cognition Model* 351

D   Data Objects 357

    Evacule 359

    Mentacule 361

    Situation 364

    Result 364

    Pattern 365

    Container 368

    Opinion 370

E   Fallacies 373

F   Optimization Formula 379

Index 387

List of Figures

2.1   Perception, evaluation, action process 14

2.2   Brain is made up of a finite number of elements . 18

2.3   Hubble telescope fixed by adding, not regrinding. . . 20

2.4   The mind cannot see its own boundaries... . . . 21

2.5   Boundaries do exist within our mind. 22

2.6   Visible fences are easier to jump 22

3.1   Physical reality is the set of all measurables . . . 30

3.2   All perspectives are equal in flat space. 31

3.3   Our mortality distorts reality with value 36

3.4   Reality vs. mental images 39

3.5   Compound space 42

3.6   Some inputs are followed by actions 52

3.7   Primitive layers process input first 59

3.8   L0 decides to approach, retreat, or ignore 62

3.9   L1 - Experience 62

3.10 L1 looks to past lessons to guide current actions   63

3.11 L2 - Patterns 65

3.12 L2 patterns connect 65

4.1   Ignoring limits is perilous 71

4.2   Reality is real 73

4.3   Feel free to dispute it   73

4.4   Semantic reality is asymmetrically curved   75

4.5   Internal vs. external knowledge   80

4.6   Lost in reality   81

4.7   Idea vs. Reality   82

4.8   The internal detached world.   83

4.9   Evolutionary model of the mind   84

4.10 Levels and objects   87

4.11 L1 result/experience object   89

4.12 L2 pattern object   90

5.1   Informal and formal thought 106

9.1   Epicycles in Ptolemaic astronomy 182

11.1 Ignore reality at your peril 216

11.2 Representing the maximum as the nadir of a pit. 217

11.3 Representing the maximum as a peak. 218

11.4 Semantic reality landscape 219

11.5 The radius to evil. 233

11.6 Super stupidity, ideology, and the radius to evil. . 238

15.1 ASPICS can reprogram themselves. 325

D.1   Opinion Object 371

F.1   Expanding the subjective problem into an L3 so-
      lution. 380

Most stock images are from https://pixabay.com/ or https://www.pexels.com/

Chapter 1

The Problem

Normal stupidity, super stupidity, and plain, unadorned, every-day stupidity are all legitimate but different kinds of stupidity. It may sound strange, but it turns out that stupidity really does come in different flavors that aren't equally stupid — some of them are far more serious and dangerous than others.

Plain stupidity is what causes us to make mistakes we could have avoided if only we had put a little more effort into learning, or a little more thought into our decisions, or care into our actions. We often call this on ourselves the moment we realize that we should have known better than to have done something the way we did.

In Part I, we will explain how normal stupidity is different from plain stupidity because it is built into our equipment, it is inherent. It is also not a bad thing, but more than that, it's actually a quite a good thing. Such a good thing, in fact, that our cognitive system actually is, and has to be, built on it. So, while normal stupidity does have its downsides (hence the term stupid), it brings quite a few advantages to us. We will further explain how humanity has been dealing fairly well with normal stupidity for a very long time, and then finish our discussion by explaining how we can use some new tools and concepts to manage it even better in the future.

In Part II, we will explain how super stupidity is a different order of stupidity than the others. It is neither careless, nor inherent, but on the contrary, it is the result of choices deliberately made and actions carefully taken to satisfy a person's mean little emotional needs without any concern whatsoever for the wider consequences. Super stupidity breeds on character flaws and thrives on intellectual weakness; it is a noxious concoction of arrogance and disrespect that anyone can brew on their own, but that our institutions of higher learning have made an art of breeding into their arts and humanities graduates.

In full flower, though, super stupidity is worse than a mere moral or mental flaw, it is much more serious than that, because its far-reaching effects are primarily responsible for all of the worst crimes and atrocities of the last century. Historically, super stupidity has always stunted education, but its modern variant has metastasized far enough to nurture and ripen private fantasies into public nightmares of tyranny and destruction.

While everyone is, by virtue of their organic cognitive structure, normally stupid, it is mostly the educated elite who ascend to the highest levels of super stupidity. With the one small exception of scientists, technologists, and engineers working in their respective fields, all other graduates of higher education fit into the class most afflicted by super stupidity that we call the educated elite.

If we clear the fog of reverence we were taught to have for scholars from our eyes, we might be able to see the specter of institutionalized stupidity that has been in front of us all along. To see this, try to imagine that you could bring together the most intelligent people you can think of who have different ideas about politics, philosophy, or current affairs. Now imagine that they have the best debate of their lives against each other, where they each adduce the most trenchant facts, and make their arguments with the sharpest rhetoric.

Can we predict the outcome? Certainly we can, because it will all be to no effect, since afterwards, they will still maintain their original positions, no matter what facts were cited, no matter what reasoning was employed, no matter what rhetorical flourishes were used. We all know that ideology and even personal opinions will prevail over both facts and reasoning every time. More to the point, why would we expect anything different, why would we ever think that a debate would be anything but the circus it always has been?

How often does this scenario occur? Every single time the educated elite debate anything. How long has this been happening? Certainly three, maybe five thousand years, but probably longer. How do we explain, then, why intellectuals still haven't caught onto the fact that debates cannot do what they expect them to do? The answer is simple, sad and demonstrably true: it's because intellectuals' understanding of reasoning, debate, and even reality is totally inadequate, if not completely off-base.

This farce of expecting 'rational' discussions to solve subjective or interest questions couldn't keep happening unless the educated elite had no clue about how debate and reasoning work. But, if they don't understand reasoning, then how can they understand education, the process they use to learn high-level reasoning? And, if they don't understand reasoning or education, how can they presume to have any understanding about how their own mind actually works? And, finally, if they don't understand how their mind works, how can they claim that they can use it to fully and accurately understand reality?

If intellectuals and academics actually knew anything beyond the hard sciences, then why have they spent the last four centuries duck paddling in the religious, political and ideological backwaters, just wandering this way then that, never making any real, cumulative progress, while in the same time period, the scientific and technological disciplines have produced an explosion of progress that has utterly changed our world?

How can all of the most educated people claim to know *the* answer when they all know different answers to the same problem? If intellectuals in the humanities and social sciences could actually reason, why do they now, almost as a group, reject the very notion of individual freedom and responsibility in favor of collective identity and control?

The problem is not even so much that intellectuals all seem to agree on the most idiotic ideas, as it is that they all privately think that *they alone* are, by dint of their education and high-level reasoning, objectively correct. Yet, the patent absurdity of this contradiction is barely noticed by anyone.

The fact that something is, and has long been, horribly wrong with education and educated people is crystallized in our topic question: **why are smart, educated, privileged people so very, very stupid, so very, very often?** While this stupidity admittedly concentrates most in the fields of the humanities and the social sciences, actual scientists are not exempt, since, once they get away from their hard data, their opinions are at least as stupid as their colleagues' are.

It is undeniable that, a thousand years after the university movement began, higher education is still churning out well-spoken, erudite, uneducated dolts who lack critical reasoning skills. Of course, the hallowed halls can't be belching out vapid fools without the help of incredibly dumb teachers, so it goes without saying that, in order to be able to dumb down their students, year after year, the professors have to be even dumber than the entering freshmen.

The sad fact is that, technical courses aside,[1] the average college student pursuing a soft degree in the hope of gaining entry to the ranks of the educated elite actually gets dumber the longer they stay in school. Super stupidity can be thought

---

[1] Unless otherwise stated, whenever university or college education is excoriated in this book, the target is always non-technical areas of study, not the hard sciences. The difference will be explained over the next few chapters.

of as a measure of the degree to which the ideas of the educated elite are unrealistic or off-kilter.

That the educated elite are afflicted both by a grotesque arrogance, and an excessive measure of super stupidity, is self-evident, but why this is so is not as easy to understand, or surely the problem would have been addressed long before now. What we will show in the following pages is that there are two paths that can explain the problem: the first uses traditional knowledge and values; the second is much more technical, because it uses a new theoretical framework called the `universal cognition model`[2] that allows us to create quantitative models of subjective phenomena. While the first path is surely more familiar and easier to grasp, the second is much more powerful because the model is well-defined and precise.

Given that the educated elite have been a festering sore on society's backside for millennia, an ulcer which has never been adequately addressed and treated, it should not be a surprise that the modern treatment for the ailment will be a little complex and involved. In the end, the reader will be richly rewarded for the effort they will have to expend to master the new model, but on the way, we will be navigating through several abstract and difficult discussions. Worry not, though, because you just have to remember that, whenever the going gets tough, all you have to do is recall the boxed paragraph below to bring everything back into perspective. By keeping these few ideas in mind,

---

[2] The full explanation with technical details is presented in the texts *Ultrareasoning, The Structure of Truth*, and *Xiom*. The current volume presents a higher level introduction to the subject that should be more readily accessible than the material in those works.

you will be able to confidently push forward on the right track, knowing that you don't need to master every detail to get the big picture.

> **KEEP THIS IN MIND:** We think inside of our heads, we always and only think inside of our heads. When we see a tree, our brain has to decode the sensory input and load it into an inherited data structure in our brain in order to process it, in order to understand it. Our knowledge of the tree is entirely inside our head, not outside where the tree is. This means that, in order to understand reality, we first have to have some idea about how our mind perceives and thinks about experience using mental structures that developed layer by layer over our long evolutionary history.

Everything in this book is related to this one little paragraph, to this one question: **how is the reliability of what we know affected by the evolutionary development of increasingly sophisticated data structures in our brain?** Once we understand this small, but crucial idea, then understanding the profound stupidity of the educated elite will be a breeze.

It is worth noting that the explanation of how our reasoning has evolved over time will account for both the current decline of the higher education system, as well as the abysmal state of the horde of intelligentsia being puked out of it every year. Do not, however, expect to find a nostalgia for the past, nor a deprecation of the current state of things in the answer, because the problem is not new, it is not caused by our modern age. No, the university system has been corrupt since day one, and this problem has been around forever. The ultimate cause of the super stupidity presently engulfing the enlightened, educated, privileged classes will be traced beyond facile theories about socioeconomic or pedagogical conditions all the way to the very nature of the cognitive process itself.

Finally, in Part III, we will discuss different things that we can do to start reducing the damage being done to our society by the educated elite. Then, we will examine how we can work with, and around, our natural limits and barriers so that we will finally be able to begin to develop testable solutions to our most difficult, pinnacle problems.

Our path forward can lead to a human history unlike anything we have known. It is up to us whether we will learn enough to know how to deliberately find it through exploration, or just fall back into our old, disappointing ways. To spark the imagination, a few of the many explorable paths open to us will be suggested, but which ones we choose is entirely up to each of us.

Part I

Normal Stupidity

Chapter 2

Normal Stupidity

Despite how it might sound, it's really not an insult to say that we're all inherently stupid, since the particular way our brain is stupid is not only a good thing, it's the primary miracle in all of existence. Our fundamental stupidity is an ineradicable part of us, but it is not caused by anything we do or don't do, it is not a result of any failure or mistake on our part, nor is it due to any moral or spiritual defect.

This good, built-in kind of stupidity is *structural*, not behavioral. It's structural in the sense that it was there even before our species or our immediate evolutionary ancestors appeared, not structural in the sense of an engineering or construction mistake that threatens a building's or bridge's stability. It's structural in the sense that cognition, the perceptual/reasoning ability we call *thinking*, can only successfully evolve on top of it, on top of an organic substrate that already has a bridge connecting the senses to the mind, a bridge that is built of deliberately stupid elements. In fact, if we weren't stupid in this particular way, we would never have developed the ability to think, or even to move deliberately.

In other words, the miracle of consciousness, of self-aware-ness, of reasoning and feeling, is a flower that grows on a bed of a special kind of stupidity. But, stupidity, like infinity, comes in different magnitudes or varieties: with infinity, there is count-able and uncountable; with stupidity, there is normal stupidity and super stupidity. And, just as uncountable infinity is in-finitely larger than countable infinity, so, too, super stupidity is, if not infinitely, then at least immensely and unnecessarily stupider than normal stupidity.

Normal, structural stupidity is a necessary consequence of any evolutionary process that produces an effective cognitive ability. Think about this for a second: in order for the muta-tions producing voluntary movement to survive the natural se-lection process beyond the stage where they are merely benign, they have to have a net neutral or positive effect on the surviv-ability of the affected organisms. That is, in order to survive and reproduce, organisms with the ability to move deliberately also have to have a concomitant ability to *choose* movements that tend to their benefit, over movements that increase their risk.

In other words, the capacity for deliberate movement pre-supposes the ability to evaluate perceptions well enough to choose whether to move away from, move towards, or move without regard to, external phenomena, and to do this well enough to survive more often than not. This is clear enough.

With this in mind, now consider how many entities, forces, and objects there are in the vicinity of a mobile creature, how many of them it can sense, and how many details can be found in each. The total differs, of course, depending on the size and sophistication of the creature and the acuity of its senses, but certainly, the number is way, way larger than three. Why the comparison to three? Because the fundamental purpose of base level cognition is to *reduce* perceived experience down to the three-value data structure that is used by the decision-making process. In its three dimensions (anti-self [dangerous, bad, false, etc.]; pro-self [opportunity, good, true, etc.]; and non-self [unimportant, ignorable, etc.]), this primordial data structure holds a rolled up evaluation of sensory input in a form that maps directly to the most basic movement commands: retreat, approach, ignore.

This transition from the complex (entities embedded in reality) to the simple (an actionable evaluation data structure), is an irreversible transformation because so much information is lost in the transformation down to the simple data structure that not enough remains to link back to its source. That is, we can get from facts to feelings, but since all of the feelings we have are linked to more than one fact set, there is no unique path back from feeling to perception. But, since we normally think in the direction from perception/idea to feeling, we tend not to notice this little glitch in the matrix, and live our lives convinced that the feeling is the *truth* of the thing, rather than just being a value linked to it.

Volitionally mobile creatures, such as ourselves, embody the idea that an action solution exists for every problem, that for any event/circumstance in the local biosphere an action can be chosen that will improve, or at least preserve, the organism's viability quotient as the event transpires. That is, we are the living manifestation of the bias that movement can enhance our survival potential.

The reduction of complex sensory experience down to simple, actionable thought begins right in our senses, since they do not sense most of the information available in external phenomena (dogs have 50 times more olfactory receptors than we do, an eagle's visual acuity is 5 times greater than ours, and some creatures can perceive infrared or ultraviolet light). Every species has a sensory capacity that has proven sufficient to survive in its original niche, but none has the maximum of all, and none has a sufficient sensory range to perceive all the data that exists in reality.

The loss of information in the cognitive process continues when the analog input from our senses is transmitted to our brain and converted into a range-limited, discrete digital format that the evaluation function can use to calculate an appropriate action response. That our cognitive process can so often deliver useful results despite this extreme data loss — which may well exceed 99%+ — is remarkable, and is possible because our only natural interest in external phenomena is exactly limited to just what they mean to us, to our interests, rather than in any external entity's internal reality. It is only because we interpret experience through this tightly focused interest lens that all data not directly related to our interest calculation can naturally and properly be disregarded without compromising the goal of producing actionable understanding from perception.

Why the reductive nature of the perceptual → cognitive process inescapably makes us stupid is easier to see in the formal, symbolic specification of the perception process:

$$\forall\, x \in (\mathbb{R} \cup \mathbb{I})\ \exists\, p \in \mathbf{P} : L0(p) \to e : AM(e) \to a \in \mathbf{A} \qquad (2.1)$$

In words, this expression translates as:

Perception: For all phenomena (x) in physical and cognitive reality ($\mathbb{R} \cup \mathbb{I}$), there exists a (possibly null) perception (p) in the set of all perceptions ($\mathbf{P}$) such that the first cognitive level $(L0)$ of the mind can process it into an evaluation (e) such that the mind's action module (AM) can process it into a (possibly null) action (a) from the set of possible actions ($\mathbf{A}$).

Of course, null actions are included in the set of possible responses to a perception, just as null perceptions are included in the set of possible perceptions, because there are very many cases where we simply do not perceive, for one reason or another, something that is really there, as well as the common case where we decide, for whatever reason, not to react to something.

If you stop and reflect on expression 2.1 for just a moment or two, you should see that the entire purpose of the perception

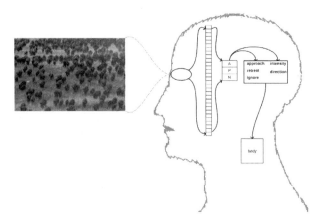

Figure 2.1: Perception, evaluation, action process

process is to produce a viability-enhancing action (the right side of the expression), *not* to see the world as it is (the left side). Cognition is a *reductive* process that distills boundless amounts of perceived sensory information down into a collection of simple bad/good/indifferent evaluations in order to answer the question, "what does **that** *mean* **to me**?" Perception is emphatically *not* an intensive process that addresses the question, "what *is* that?" Our mortality and vulnerability to injury and death in each and every moment dictates that we simply don't have time to care about whatever *that* may actually be apart from our exigent concerns.

The perception → evaluation → action process is *necessarily* a reductive process designed to take *any x* as input and produce a movement solution. The sheer number and variety of animals currently living on our planet is proof that natural selection has validated the legitimacy of this action solution strategy.

In figure 2.1, there are a specific number of animals in the herd, each of which has numerous attributes:

- type
- height, width, length
- weight
- age
- sex
- health, vigor
- vector (r, x, y, z)
- number of hairs in the coat
- number of cells in the body, etc.

Almost all of this available data is either not perceived by our sensorium, or is discarded by our brain. This data reduction step is perfectly reasonable, since we don't need to know all of that just to ascertain the very few things about the herd that will suffice to satisfy our interest, such as: their level of threat or edibility, their comparative number (few, many), speed (slow, fast), and the direction of their movement relative to our position.

This example is being used to illustrate that all perceptions, no matter how simple or complex, are converted from analog sensory signals carrying huge amounts of data to discrete digital values that use very little of the available data to form an impression in our mind that we can evaluate for risk, opportunity, and importance, an evaluation that is then passed to the action module. In the universal cognition model, the action module is a primordial structure that converts evaluations into action commands. These action commands are then transmitted to the body that implements them in its own particular way (e.g., any particular command, such as *flee fast*, will be implemented differently by crawlers, flyers, and swimmers).

This process of reducing any and all perceivable phenomena to movement solutions in four dimensions is thus stupid at its core, since it deliberately excludes most available information in order to achieve its purpose of producing a time-sensitive action solution to whatever problem is perceived in the encompassing reality. The perceptive process makes *no* attempt to investigate the external phenomenon for what it actually is in its own terms, but that does not mean that this reductive process is ineffective. The fact that the process of natural selection culls unsuccessful survival strategies frees biology and genetics to evolve through mutation without the need for, or expense of, an internal editor or correction mechanism.

The action of natural selection thus opens the door for biological entities to implement *partial functions*, functions that only solve part of a problem, effectively outsourcing the remaining part of the solution to exogenous forces. Reproduction is an example of such a partial function: in most cases, organisms reproduce in numbers that would far exceed their environment's available resources, thus leaving the problem of overpopulation to be solved by predation, disease, or starvation. The perceptual/cognition process is another example of a partial function: the question of how radical a reductive process can be in its elimination of data, of how much input data can be ignored in calculating responses, is answered, not by an internal mechanism, but by natural selection, for when a species discards too much information, it will eventually cease to propagate in numbers sufficient to ensure its survival.

First level cognition is the process of reducing everything in physical and cognitive reality to *me-relevant* observations that we can evaluate and respond to. That we suppose that the process allows us to consider externalities for what they are internally, in and of themselves, separate from our needs and interests, unaffected by our cognitive limitations, is an illusion created by an accident of evolution that we call the *purblind defect*. The purblind defect is what we call our inability to see inside our own mind, to see its various layers and components. This perceptual blindness also results both in our inability to see our own limits, and in our proclivity to blur the boundary between our internal self and external reality.

Think about it for a minute: what are we? We are sentient, volitionally mobile creatures. The fact of being able to move at will, to move how we *decide* to move, means that we embody a process that finds movement solutions to any and all survival problems. That means that we evaluate our sensory input in a stepwise process that eventually reduces the infinite complexity of reality down to a simple action command that tells our body how to move towards opportunity, away from threat, or to ignore the unimportant.

Our minds (figure 2.2) are not some ethereal, abstract wonder mechanism, they are organs made of tissues made of cells, polymers, monomers and simpler molecules that are ultimately

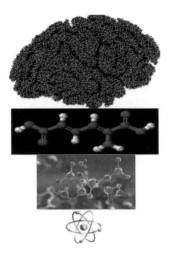

Figure 2.2: Brain is made up of a finite number of elements

made of atoms. Reasoning, ultimately, is a physical event on physical structures, not some kind of mysterious mental event that transcends physics, but is a normal process subject to hard physical constraints.

Normal stupidity is, therefore, a term of art that actually describes a fundamental intellectual function that successively disregards, or discards, the vast majority of data available in a set of perceptions in order to distill it down into the minimum number of bits necessary to support an actionable evaluation. Normal stupidity is the mental bent that discounts external reality down to the level where it directly impacts our mortality interests. Normal stupidity is the structural bias that favors our mortality interests over the irrelevant, myriad details of external reality. Seriously, how else would you design a perceptual/cognitive process whose sole purpose is to specify survival-relevant movement? Normal stupidity is *good*.

It is important to stop and appreciate that being normal stupidity is not a flaw, rather, it is the only way that unbounded input can be mapped into an intensely constrained data structure. Trees grow as much as their genes and circumstances permit, and at no point is their growth stopped because they have run out of memory or processing power, but our cognitive *model* of a tree is severely constrained both in complexity and size by the limits of our mind's processing speed, data structures, storage space, and learning capacities.

Normal stupidity is a structural phenomenon that is defined by the relation between organic cognitive structures and external, physical reality. Cognitive structures have a limited capacity to store data, while phenomenological reality is characterized by a perspective-dependent fractal dimension that makes it effectively infinite in detail. Since normal stupidity is an inherent limitation of the equipment we use to perceive and think, it is not something we can grow out of, transcend, or overcome.

Merely realizing that our cognition is fundamentally stupid by design does not, by itself, make us smarter, but realizing that our vision is blurry does not automatically give us greater visual acuity, either. What these realizations do give us is the opportunity to begin to compensate for, to work around, or to supplement our deficiencies in any number of ways that we can imagine, such as lenses, braces, or concepts.

For example, why would our primordial mind, $L0$ — an engine whose sole job is to process sensory input into approach/

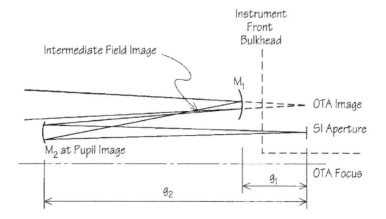

Figure 4. Schematic optical design for the COSTAR corrective optics, M_1 and M_2.

Figure 2.3: Hubble telescope fixed by adding, not regrinding.

retreat/ignore commands — the one which we share with squirrels and bugs, ever develop the ability to perceive or understand newer levels of the mind that would only develop millions of years later? It makes no sense, of course, for that ability ever to have evolved, and it never did. As a consequence, we have no mental faculty that allows our lower mental levels to see the newer ones, even though they exist, but our latest layers can, with training, learn to conceptualize and recognize the lower level functions for what they are.

While we cannot eliminate, or even modify, the limitations of the various layers of our mind, we can, if we are willing to put forth the effort, learn how to compensate for these limitations, just as we use corrective lenses to fix our vision, or how scientists were able to fix the Hubble telescope by *adding* additional optical elements in order to compensate for its badly ground main mirror, rather than trying to fix the mirror itself while in orbit.

While we cannot innately sense the difference between those parts of our mind that developed earlier from those that developed later, we are not entirely without discrimination. Of course, we can differentiate between passion and calculation, but since we often attach feeling to conclusions we have reasoned out, even that line is often blurred. For example, we invariably think that our political and personal opinions are "right", even though this is a perfectly indefensible notion, but we *feel* that our ideas are right, so they must be, right?

No, instead of seeing our mind as the layered conglomeration of independent levels of functionality that developed one at a time over eons, we see it as a relatively smooth, continuum of consciousness, like an open field:

Figure 2.4: The mind cannot see its own boundaries...

But, again, this is ludicrous and indefensible, and this failure to see boundaries, to see limits, is just the purblind defect at work, one symptom of which is that we cannot reliably distinguish between emotion and reasoning, or between reasoning and reality. There are limits in our mind that we must learn to understand and appreciate because, rather than being like the open field in figure 2.4, our mind is much closer to the fenced fields in figure 2.5.

Figure 2.5: Boundaries do exist within our mind.

The significance of finally being able to see our internal fences is that it makes it much easier to navigate around, or jump over, them when we want to.

Figure 2.6: Visible fences are easier to jump

The parameters of normal stupidity are defined both by the structure of our brain elements as well as by how well, by one measure or another, we use those structures. There are limits to what we can think with each separately evolved part of our mind. Learning what these limits are, and how to switch from one part of the mind to another to achieve a specific purpose, are skills that will make everyone, all *normally* stupid people, much more intelligent and intellectually effective, even though the structural basis of normal stupidity, itself, can never be overcome.

Actually, what we are calling the structural basis of normal stupidity is really a set of ingenious, miraculous solutions to the evolved organic cognition problem (how do molecules become living organs that generate self-awareness?). Our minds are the single greatest miracle in our universe because it is their combined function, their normal stupidity that, when linked with message networks, actually contrive to create an entirely new reality, *semantic reality*, that sits on top of, but separate from, physical reality, $\mathbb{R}$. It even turns out that semantic reality,[1] an abstract reality created by our limited cognitive ability, is actually potentially larger (has a greater magnitude) and more complex that the simple physical universe.

Our minds are normally stupid because our intelligence is constrained by hardware and process limitations, but we have developed a number of ways to compensate for this over the years that are, in many cases, remarkably effective. Our lim-

---

[1] See *Ultrareasoning.*

itations are like fences that we have to learn to recognize and work with, not try to discredit and renounce the way intellectuals have repeatedly insisted we do.

Super stupidity, on the other hand, is the domain of the educated elite, a rarefied region of self-indulgent, archly deliberate stupidity that, unlike normal stupidity, is neither structural, natural, nor necessary. Rather, it is the product of the deliberate application of arrogance and education to the systematic denial of our natural myopia. Hubris, as the ancient stories warned us, is the reef on which grandiose claims of extreme competence are dashed, and on which the feeble attempts by higher educational institutions to solve complex and important problems run aground and sink.

Chapter 3

Core Constraints

Higher level organic beings experience thoughts, feelings, and self-awareness on inherited brain structures that arose from the interaction of the forces of physical reality, organic nature, and evolution. This trio of brute, unguided, generative forces necessarily imposes constraints on the nature of every class of cognitive capacity that emerges from the mix. These constraints define the level of normal stupidity that is found in every cognitive entity on earth, and will also be found in every cognitive entity we will ever find anywhere in our physical universe.

Over time, an organic cognitive complexity ladder arose from the scatter shot workings of the evolutionary trial and error process, with more complex cognitive structures gradually developing on top of earlier, more primitive ones. At each rung of this complexity ladder, the progress of structural evolution placed hard constraints on the cognitive abilities available at that level.

Our mind's core constraints both limit and focus our cognitive abilities in significant ways, regardless of whether or not we recognize, understand, or agree with them. They fall into three different categories: those defined by external reality, those defined by internal reality, and those defined by the very nature of the evolutionary process. We will examine how each of these forces constrain cognitive function by influencing how it develops, how it works, and what it can achieve. Only by understanding the forces behind the curtain can we begin to appreciate why we think the way we do, and how that has historically made our reasoning so frustratingly impotent in the effort to solve the more difficult human and social problems.

Realities

If you discuss reality and the nature of life with habitués of an opium den, you are likely to hear things that aren't entirely consistent with physical reality outside of the den, but, disturbingly, these hallucinatory ramblings will be entirely consistent with the mewlings of humanities graduates. Listening to intellectuals trying to discuss reality is like listening to children trying to discuss cosmology: you're unlikely to hear anything incisive or even vaguely useful, and the longer you listen, the dumber you'll get.

Intellectuals used to get a lot of mileage out of pondering paradoxes until, early in the twentieth century, it was shown that most of them come from simple violations of set theory.

So, in order to maintain their franchise of pondering the imponderable, in the later part of the last century they switched from wrestling with paradoxes to questioning the vagaries of reality itself. "What is reality, what is real?" "Is there any such thing as objective reality, or objective truth?" "If reality is just a concept, and not real itself, then what about truth? How can it be real? Isn't truth subjective, and really just whatever we decide it is?"

Well, much to the surprise and disappointment of intellectuals, it turns out that reality is a simple, fundamental concept that can easily be defined formally, and even more easily explained informally in just four words. The reason academics and intellectuals have been so stymied for so long by such a simple concept is both psychological ("I agonize, I ruminate, therefore I am important!"), and intellectual. The intellectual problem is a direct consequence of them not being able to define reality in the abstract, because the inability to crisply define the membership rules of a set leads not only to poor reasoning on the set itself, but also inevitably cripples reasoning on everything else that now might, or might not, be part of, or related to, that set.

This obtuseness on the part of intellectuals is caused primarily by their lack of understanding about how the mind works, about how evolution applies to present day mental function, and about how the difference between studying the known versus exploring the unknown has profound implications on the course of one's education. What this smug blindness has caused them to completely miss is that there is actually no reason whatsoever to begin the examination of reality with the assumption that there is only one reality to discover. Making such an assumption in advance of clearly defining what a reality is, is both foolish and lazy.

So, let us first define what *a* reality is, and then we can go on and define the realities that are actually germane to us.

> **Reality**: an isolated set of elements and the means by which the elements interact.

The key words in this definition are:

- **isolated**: a reality is not affected by events outside of itself;
- **elements**: roughly, the things in the reality;
- **interact**: the means by which the elements affect each other.

In other words, the elements in a reality are affected by the forces and elements inside the reality and nothing else.

This definition is clear and simple, but from the perspective of cognition, it is incomplete, because it doesn't address how we *know* whether some particular x actually exists in an external reality as opposed to just existing inside of our head. For us to ascertain that any idea, i, which we have inside our head, corresponds reasonably well with some actuality, a, in some reality, we must be able to:

- observe it,
- measure it, and
- formally describe it, so that

- we can reproduce the observation within tolerance.

That is, the only way we know how to prove that something actually exists outside of our mind is to use the scientific method.[1]

Thus, we have two different issues here: first, the simple definition of a reality, and second, the process by which a cognitive entity can determine whether, and to what degree, a mental event corresponds to a phenomenon in a given reality.

One of the limitations of organic cognition is that, while events that happen *within* the cognitive apparatus are themselves real in chemical or electrical terms, whether or not the semantic content of those ideas accurately maps to any phenomena *outside* of the mind is undefined unless and until reproducible tests verify that the mapping is accurate to a certain degree.[2]

So, given that, in the abstract, a reality is an isolated set of elements and interaction modalities, how do we define the specific realities in which we live and reason? Let us start with the most obvious one, physical reality, the reality that science succeeds so well in studying, and then we will proceed to examine the much more complicated one, semantic reality.

---

[1] In the course of normal life, it is rare to have the opportunity to prove every observation or thought, so in practice, we rely on validating our observations through conversation and against experience. This works reasonably well for common occurrences — albeit with a large, unspecified margin of error — because different types of validation are done by different parts of our mind, some of which are pretty reliable.

[2] By default, the presumption has to be that ideas do not map to externalities in any predictable or precise fashion, because the overwhelming majority of our ideas verifiably do not.

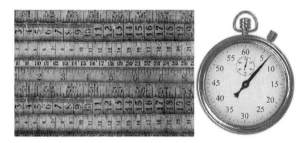

Figure 3.1: Physical reality is the set of all measurables

Physical Reality, $\mathbb{R}$

We can define physical reality, $\mathbb{R}$, the reality in which our bodies live and die, as:

$$\mathbb{R} = (\mathbf{E}, \mathbf{F}) \tag{3.1}$$

That is, physical reality, $\mathbb{R}$, is the product of a set of elements, $\mathbf{E}$, and a set of forces, $\mathbf{F}$, interacting in spacetime as described reasonably well in the Standard Model. In four words, a more pedestrian, but fully serviceable definition of physical reality is this: reality is the "set of all measurables." This simple definition works because everything in physical reality can be reproducibly measured, since everything in physical reality has either positionality or effect. This means that the only way we know for sure that a reported phenomenon is real, or that a concept actually describes an external reality, is because predicted aspects of it can be reproducibly measured.

One of the key characteristics of physical reality, $\mathbb{R}$, our universe, that we have learned over time, is that it is a flat space (figure 3.2) in the sense that no location is special, that there

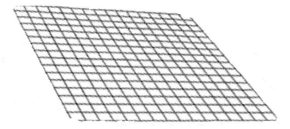

Figure 3.2: All perspectives are equal in flat space.

is no center point in our universe, that no special place has a privileged perspective which is truer or better than any other perspective. This means that we don't have to include a location parameter in our calculations to correctly describe events with otherwise identical parameters, because nothing special or different will happen at any location that wouldn't happen at any other. (While black holes seem to suggest an exception to this claim, remember, it is the black hole that has special properties, not the coordinates in space where it is located.)

Thanks to the scientific method, we can readily determine whether a reported phenomenon is real, or just an idea in someone's head. Certainly, (except in the minds of gullible idiots) once these fundamental concepts are clearly defined, no amount of jejune philosophizing can challenge the reality of reality, since the method of defining reality is invariant across different competent minds.

Limits of $\mathbb{R}$

The confusion people experience trying to understand reality is generally caused by their failure to clearly define it, since this failure will inevitably lead them into self-indulgent bouts of silly reasoning. Postmodern intellectuals, for example, muse about such things as trying to prove that, since things not in reality are not in reality (yes, it really is exactly that stupid), then therefore, reality must be just a subjective construct, etc. All of this silliness can be avoided simply by sticking to the measurement test: if it can't be reproducibly measured, then we cannot know whether it actually exists in physical reality outside of our minds.

Let us consider string theory as a test case for how we should handle unmeasurable ideas. String theory is a rigorous scientific theory heavily laden with math that postulates that fundamental entities called strings exist in $\mathbb{R}$. But the theory has a fundamental problem: we cannot detect or measure strings or their effects, so we are left to ponder, do strings actually exist? With the aid of the measurement rule, even non-physicists can answer this question: until we can measure strings or their effect, we cannot know whether or not they exist in physical reality. So, until they can be measured, until we can place them in the set of measurables, all we can say is that strings are part of an untested theory, that they are just an idea.

But if we are saying that anything not shown to exist in $\mathbb{R}$ is "just an idea," then this posits the startling conclusion that *ideas themselves do not exist in physical reality*, $\mathbb{R}$. Why not?

Because, since they cannot be measured in terms of $\mathbb{R}$, they are not a part of the set of measurables. But, you protest, we can measure electrical signals in the brain associated with ideas, so ideas must exist in reality. No, all this means is that the brain and the electrical signals exist in physical reality, but, even after the day comes when we will be able to identify the specific memory storage locations for specific ideas, it will remain the case that the *meaning* of ideas does not exist in physical reality. Meaning cannot exist in physical reality because meaning is constructed from language, and while the sounds of spoken words, and the sight of gestures and written words do exist in $\mathbb{R}$, what they *mean* is an understanding that we arrive at through communication and consensus, and these only exist on the plane in which our ephemeral relationships occur.

"But," you object, "we all can agree that ideas exist, so if they don't exist in reality, where do they exist?" By the time you finish asking that question, you should have already guessed the answer: they exist in a *separate* reality, one that we, rather appropriately, call *semantic reality*, $\mathbb{SR}$, the reality that arises as an emergent property from the interaction of conscious minds that were themselves produced by physical reality and evolution. In fact, it is only in $\mathbb{SR}$ (and cognitive space, $\mathbb{CS}$, see below) that meaning and value exist, not in $\mathbb{R}$. Thus, when intellectuals and academics bitterly aver, with all of their world-weary wisdom, that reality, $\mathbb{R}$, has no objective value, no meaning, they are simply stating a trivially true, and, ironically, meaningless fact.

It cannot be overemphasized how damaging it has been for intellectuals to stupidly mix ideas in with rocks and animals as first class elements of reality, $\mathbb{R}$, and then for them to search for *meaning* in the dust at our feet or the wind in our face, as if there were no difference between an idea and a physical thing. It may be understandable that regular people who are busy living their lives conflate a perception with the thing, an idea with a reality, since this is how the purblind defect causes us to see it, but for intellectuals, whose job it is to figure such things out, to make this elementary mistake, millennia after millennia, is simply unforgivable.

Semantic Reality, $\mathbb{SR}$, Part I

Semantic reality[3], $\mathbb{SR}$, the second reality we will examine, is much more complex than $\mathbb{R}$, so explaining it will take a little time and some work on the reader's part to grok, but it's really not that hard once you separate the *idea* of a thing from the *thing* itself.

When higher level cognitive entities, such as humans, connect together through communication links, they generate a new type of reality that is separate from $\mathbb{R}$, albeit created on top of it. Social interaction realized on a network of message links doesn't just make groups and hierarchies possible, it actually creates a new type of reality which supports levels of complexity that make the structure of physical reality look like child's

---

[3]Semantic reality and related concepts are explored extensively in *Ultrareasoning*. In the current volume, we will explain the highlights in just enough detail for the reader to get the big picture.

play.

While it may sound surprising to say that the reality created by semantic interactions between people is more complex than the reality of the entire cosmos, it is demonstrably true, since physical reality is essentially just a formal language (albeit, one that we don't fully understand yet), and as such, the mysteries of the universe will gradually resolve into understandings the closer we get to mastering its language. The same, however, cannot be said for $\mathbb{SR}$, for there is no upper bound to the complexity of the structures that ideas and interactions can create. Essentially, $\mathbb{SR}$ is to $\mathbb{R}$ as uncountable infinity is to countable infinity.

$\mathbb{SR}$ is inherently more complex than $\mathbb{R}$ because, not only is it a verifiably higher dimensional space, the actual number of dimensions in $\mathbb{SR}$ is, in fact, unbounded, limited only by the imagination, intellect, and requirements of the $\mathbb{CS}$'s involved. In our current discussion, we are only addressing two such dimensions of $\mathbb{SR}$ that don't exist in $\mathbb{R}$: value and meaning. The reason we know that neither value nor meaning can ever be found in $\mathbb{R}$ is because: 1) value curves space, and therefore can never exist in the flat space of $\mathbb{R}$; and 2) meaning depends on value, and intergenerational meaning only exists in semantic realities capable of propagating culture.

Exactly what it means to say that a space has a particular geometry (flat, curved, compound), and what a semantic reality is, will become clear presently, just as soon as two more pretty straightforward concepts are explained: curved space (a distortion field), and compound curved space.

Cognitive Space ($\mathbb{CS}$) = Curved Space

In contrast to a flat space, a distortion field (figure 3.3) is a
curved space where perspective changes with position. Where
lines in a flat space run straight and true, as in figure 3.2, in
a distortion field all lines within the sensory horizon converge
in a point in the bottom of the distortion well, known as the
conscious moment of our mortality. This kind of curved space
models the fact that natural selection requires that the cognitive circuitry of volitionally mobile creatures be built around
a preference for the good, an abhorrence of the bad, and an
indifference to the unimportant, and that these three terms be
defined in terms of our own mortality interest.

The exact profile of the distortion field is determined by
a built-in, parameterized function that relies on constitutional
and experiential values that vary by individual, such as aggression, agreeableness, and vitality, as well as attitudes towards
other beings, life, and experience that develop over the course
of a lifetime.

Figure 3.3: Our mortality distorts reality
with value

Evaluation begins to happen as soon as something noteworthy grabs our attention. For example, a rock flying through the air does not have any inherent value or meaning, but it instantly acquires a value dimension when it intrudes into our perceived interest space simply because we choose to assign it a value. On seeing the rock, we rapidly evaluate its trajectory and calculate the likelihood that it will get close to, or even hit, us. This evaluation of risk/opportunity/unimportance results in the phenomenon being assigned a value in our interest frame of reference. The moving rock, itself, becomes — to us — a threat, a boon, unimportant, or a combination of the three.

We assign higher negative or positive values to things that more directly impact our perceived self/mortality-interest, effectively positioning them appropriately in our value distortion field. Truer, higher values converge to the maximum value at the deepest point in the well, the point of highest distortion which represents the maximum concern we can feel about our life, so more important things are situated closest to our core values.

The deeper we get into our interest well, the more important our evaluation of the thing becomes relative to the significance of the thing itself as the ratio $\frac{feelings}{facts}$ increases. Hence the concept of a distortion field: the less personally invested we are in something, the closer it is to flatter space, and the easier it is to see it as it is, while the more invested we are in something, the deeper it is positioned in the value distortion well, and the more our perceptions are correspondingly colored by our needs and prejudices as our concern for our feelings overwhelms our dispassionate interest in the facts. In this way, the higher value we assign to something, the more quickly the complexity of the external reality gets resolved down into the simplistic, self-interest-based evaluation of good, bad, or indifferent.

Phenomena that we connect to our vital mortality interests — to whatever degree — thus acquire a new dimension that objects in $\mathbb{R}$ simply do not have, a dimension that only exists in our mind, in our cognitive space ($\mathbb{CS}$): *value*. This value dimension is created, and only exists, in our mind, yet due to the purblind defect, it looks to us like it is part of the phenomenon, part of the world, itself. Take gold, for example, we think that it is actually valuable, when in reality it has no more intrinsic value than granite or even dust. Yet, when we have a use for something, be it for luxury or industry, it is given a measure of value by us. The value dimension relates external phenomena to our mortality interests, to *us*, and the idea we form of a material object which has no inherent (or actual) value in $\mathbb{R}$, now has a very personal value in $\mathbb{CS}$.

The fact that value is both intrinsic to the curved cognitive space of the mind (it is what curves it), and extrinsic to the flat space of reality, $\mathbb{R}$, and that it is assigned to phenomena by us rather than inhering in the externality, constitutes a fundamental limit of cognition that we have never before been able to properly acknowledge. Even now, we will only be able to understand this limit if we learn how to distinguish between the *idea* and the *thing* itself.

Reference (ideas in $\mathbb{CS}$) and referent (things in $\mathbb{R}$) are not,

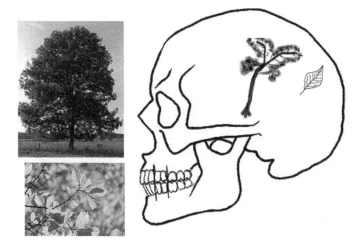

Figure 3.4: Reality vs. mental images

and never can be, the same, or even equal. The data structures are fundamentally different because the referent lacks the most significant dimension of the reference idea, the value component. Even more importantly, the referent has an unbounded virtual data structure that comprises all of its physical details, while the reference idea is a contained in a tiny little mental structure that has perhaps only a few dozen actual data points in addition to the added value element.

The idea can thus never be more than a simplified internal representation of a complex external entity, and should never be confused as being its equal or substitute, yet, as long as we think we see reality for what it is, this is exactly what we are doing.

Interpreting the cognitive mind as a curved geometric space not only conforms with the observable fact that reality looks different to different observers with different values and experiences, it also allows us to use familiar mathematics to explore it, and endows the metaphor with extraordinary power. This approach allows us to model attraction and repulsion, not only between individuals and things, but also between groups of individuals situated in semantic realities. It also allows us to probe deeply into the mathematics of hierarchies, and will support testing to compare the cohesive power of different status dimensions, such as knowledge, skill, kinship, or fealty. For the first time, we will now be able to subject what were previously vague, verbal notions of the strength of the ties engendered by social, religious, national, and military organizations to rigorous mathematical analysis and reproducible tests of executable models.

Also, note how, at a stroke, with no additional effort, this approach explains why different people see the same phenomenon so differently, since it models how all observers distort their perceptions according to their own particular interests at the moment. This also explains our frustration when our friends and loved ones don't have the same response as we do to something we feel very strongly about: the variant responses rudely prove the existence of different perspectives, and this emphatically rebukes our delusion that the axis of our own personal distortion field is actually THE true axis of reality.

Compound Curved Space

Cognitive space distortion fields exist in cognitive beings that exist in a physical reality. Thus, $\mathbb{CS}$ nodes are created by, depend on, interact with, and live and die in $\mathbb{R}$, but their *experience* of $\mathbb{R}$ is defined by the distortion field in their cognitive apparatus, not by $\mathbb{R}$ itself.

Compound space is a curved space (figure 3.5) defined entirely by the distortion of the value fields in the messages transmitted from ξ node to ξ node. There are flatter regions in compound space that do not follow the distortion curves of any particular participating ξ node, but while the curves do appear to flatten, they are actually the product of the curves of the neighboring distortion fields.[4]

Semantic Reality Part II

With the concept of a compound curved space in hand, we can now address the formal definition of semantic reality:

> **Semantic Reality**: a graph[5] of externalized cognitive space nodes, ξ, connected by message links, $\mathcal{M}$.

---

[4] **Advanced:** One of the difficulties of $\mathbb{SR}$ is the inherent instability of the ξ elements: they are subject to constant change as the underlying $\mathbb{CS}$ processes messages. Thus, studying $\mathbb{SR}$ from the flat, objective space limits our knowledge to however we measure ξ, and we have to infer the curvature of the space from evidence of attraction, repulsion, and distortion in messages and actions. This problem can be mitigated by using a quantitative model for $\mathbb{CS}$ (see *Xiom*).

[5] **Advanced:** The term *graph* is being used in the technical sense of a set of vertices and a binary relation between vertices, adjacency. A graph G is a pair (V,E), where V is a set of vertices, and E is a set of edges between the vertices such that $E \subseteq \{(u,v) : u, v \in V\}$.

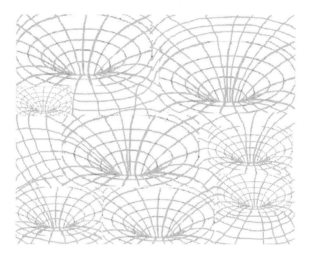

Figure 3.5: Compound space

Formally,

$$\mathbb{SR} = (\{\xi\}, \{\mathcal{M}\}) \qquad (3.2)$$

Since cognitive space, $\mathbb{CS}$, is our personal, internal cognitive experience of external and internal events, it cannot be the external node in the $\mathbb{SR}$ graph, so we use ξ to represent the subset of $\mathbb{CS}$ that we externalize through word and deed. $\mathcal{M}$ represents the message links that the ξ nodes create between themselves to form a communication and action group, links that can represent any communicative interaction, such as perceptible words, sounds, signals, facial expressions, gestures, and/or actions.

The geometry of $\mathbb{SR}$ is a compound curved space[6], in which

---

[6] **Advanced:** Technically speaking, it should be possible to define a flat semantic reality as one in which all messages are restricted to a formal language. The fantasy pushed by scientists is that this is what scientific discourse always is, but, alas, in reality, since scientists do not yet understand that value elements curve the space they are in, such a thing as a

ξ nodes connect to ξ nodes across message links.[7] The density of the graph varies with the strength of the message links, and reaches a maximum at the center of the group, where the connections to all participating ξ nodes combine to maximally deform the shared connection space. A hierarchical organization chart would be represented in this geometric model with each level of the hierarchy occupying concentric rings around the top of the hierarchy at the center of the system.

The space in $\mathbb{SR}$ between ξ nodes is only relatively, not actually, flat (figure 3.5), because the adjacency relation that defines the graph is the curved value relation (the more value in the messages, the more curved the space, but the value is assigned by the recipient and only suggested by the sender). Since messages and actions in a semantic reality are generated by cognitive spaces, *everything* in semantic reality has a value dimension that curves the space they are in.

This geometric picture of social structures models social groupings using an astronomical metaphor, so systems such as galaxies, solar systems, and planet-moons can represent different types of groups, depending on their magnitude and density. Thus, tightly knit, powerful groups combine the space-bending power of their members' interactions to bend space on a much larger scale in order to influence the distribution of resources

---

flat semantic space really only exists for moments at a time, until it is inevitably destroyed when its members inject interpretation, which entails value. The only way to maintain a flat semantic reality over time would be in a cleanroom-type environment, which had mechanisms both to prevent and regularly clean up value infestations.

[7]**Advanced:** The ξ nodes are represented as distortion fields in the diagrams because the interpretation and expression of the messages occurs below the ξ node in the underlying $\mathbb{CS}$.

coming both from outside and inside the group, as well as rele-gating exposure to risk to the outer ranks. Not surprisingly, this manages risks and opportunities in a manner more beneficial to the group hierarchy than to its common members. Imagine a rubber sheet with a heavy weight in the middle; naturally, any liquid (representing resources or power) poured on the sheet at any point would tend to collect in the center after dampening intervening points, while risk from external attack is naturally first encountered by those furthest from the center.

This geometric/force model allows us to model group dy-namics separate from the advertised group ideology or theol-ogy. This allows us to separate ideas and claims from practice, so that we can easily understand, for example, that a group that insists on segregating its members from non-members does so only to create a stronger group, not at the behest of divine guidance (see *Xiom*). This allows us to apply Occam's razor to the analysis of ideological and religious group behavior be-cause, once we can account for creed rules and practices as being related to standard $\mathbb{CS}$ or $\mathbb{SR}$ dynamics, then there is neither need nor justification for looking to a higher authority to be the source of that rule. Strong leaders make rules to make strong groups, period, and this has nothing to do with divine inspi-ration or ideology. After all, none of us would find a prophet who claimed that God told him to eat, drink and sleep to be credible, nor his god very impressive, since there is not a person alive who cannot figure these things out for himself.

The most difficult part of living in a semantic reality is

caused by the fact that the message processing functionality exists in $\mathbb{CS}$, not $\mathbb{SR}$. Messages are transmitted through the physical medium of $\mathbb{R}$ by observable ξ members, but the value context of the message remains in the $\mathbb{CS}$ underlying the ξ sender, and is not transmitted. Likewise, the interpretation of the message is done in the recipient's $\mathbb{CS}$, and does not exist at, and is not easily controllable from, the $\mathbb{SR}$ or the sender $\mathbb{CS}$ level. While this duality may seem to contradict the previously stated definition of reality, I suggest that it is more like the 'particle or wave' problem found in physics: the model looks different from different perspectives. From the outside, we cannot penetrate the depths of the $\mathbb{CS}$ because its values are native and cannot be exported, so we have to use the externalized ξ in our calculations. However, we can use parameterized $\mathbb{CS}$s in our models and simulations, so it might help to think of this as being similar to the problem of studying the atom: chemistry describes the interaction between elements based solely on the electrons in their outer shells, while physics describes the internals of the atom.

One subtlety that may be difficult to understand is the claim that $\mathbb{SR}$ is independent of $\mathbb{R}$, even though it exists on it, and survives only so long as conditions in $\mathbb{R}$ allow. The key here is *reproducibility*: there is no event in $\mathbb{R}$ that *forces* or *causes* a `comprehension event` to occur in an $\mathbb{SR}$'s underlying $\mathbb{CS}$s within any meaningful error bound. It is precisely the stupidity inherent in cognition that dictates this must be so: a cognitive entity is only aware of external events to the extent that its own senses and cognitive processes produce a representation that is deemed *by it* to be relevant to its survival interests. In other words, cognitive entities are actually built only to see the world for what they can appreciate it means to them, and this is what separates $\mathbb{SR}$ from $\mathbb{R}$.

Another subtlety in the semantic reality concept relates to subgroups within groups, and unrelated groups. The question is, how many semantic realities are there? The simple answer has to do with the concept of isolation. Isolated groups function as separate semantic realities until their isolation is breeched by an encounter with the outside world. Anthropologists have documented a number of virtually isolated societies over the years, and for all intents and purposes, they existed in their own $\mathbb{SR}$s.

The proper answer seems to be that, since all value-based semantic realities can communicate and connect together, then they are really all the same species of semantic reality, just different variants. Take, for example, isolated social groups that connect to a limited number of other work, financial, and commerce groups: even in large cities, these can create isolated populations that have minimal interaction with the outside world. Even in our normal lives, we tend to live in an interaction bubble that can be thought of as a union of separate sub-realities, connected to us only by our interaction with them. This kind of semi-isolated reality conforms well to commonly observed phenomena, such as the split in outlook between different population groups: urban and rural, affluent and poor, various ethnicities, age groups, and so on.

It would seem that the explicit aim of self-isolating communities is precisely to live in an isolated semantic reality of their own making where they define, and live in, their own scriptural or traditional reality. Except for the extraordinary incursion of other $\mathbb{SR}$'s into their world, it would seem reasonable to analyze these as separate realities, although technically, they are not truly isolated.

It is important to appreciate the peculiar way that participants in a semantic reality perceive each other: they are seen not as a combination of their external and internal parts, but as the product of their externalized behavior and messages plus the *observer's* internal reality; the actor produces actions and messages, but their meaning is supplied by the observer interpreting them through his distortion field, not by the actor.

This problem arises because the purblind defect makes each participant mostly erase the distinction between their own exposed ξ and their internal $\mathbb{CS}$, so they mistakenly think that others see them as they see themselves, and that they see others as they really are. That is, we are unaware of the powerful, distorting role that everyone's $\mathbb{CS}$ plays in framing our perceptions of reality. In other words, I ($\mathbb{CS}_1, \xi_1$) tend to see *you* ($\mathbb{CS}_2, \xi_2$) as ($\mathbb{CS}_1, \xi_2$), and you tend to see me as ($\mathbb{CS}_2, \xi_1$). That is, we each see the other as a combination of *our* own internal thoughts and feelings and *their* words and actions. As might be expected, this causes a considerable amount of communication errors and misunderstandings.

Value and Meaning

Value is the name we give to the [a,p,n] coordinates in the
$\mathbb{CS}$ distortion field. The higher the coordinates, the greater
the value.[8] Value is a composite quantity calculated from the
level we assign to the three basic emotional response dimensions — negative (**a**nti-self), positive (**p**ro-self), and indifferent/
alienated (**n**on-self) — that we use to evaluate the significance
of an experience.

While value is the basis for meaning, it is different in that
it comes from the primitive interest evaluation of input, which
is an automatic process, while meaning is synthesized, more or
less deliberately, by our language-level intellect from a field of
internal and external evaluations.

Our $\mathbb{CS}$, our mind, has a native ability to assign value to anything from ideas to things to experiences. At the lowest mental levels — those which we share with the simplest creatures
— assigning value just amounts to assessing how well something matches our genotypical threat or opportunity archetypes.
Defining meaning, however, is a language and culture-dependent
judgment that occurs at a much higher cognitive level than value
assignment, and it projects value into the future, rather than
merely assessing it in the present.

All language activities originate in, and involve, $\mathbb{SR}$: we
learn our language from the semantic reality we share with our
families and community, and we gain an orientation to the pur-

---

[8]See *The Structure of Truth* for a detailed and advanced examination
of the way value arises from such a simple three dimensional structure as
the evacule (the [a,p,n] array).

pose of life (which we can accept, modify, or reject) from the various semantic realities in which we participate.[9] Thus, while we can *feel* value inside ourselves, inside our own $\mathbb{CS}$, we *conceive* of the meaning of life in a linguistic and conceptual framework that originates on the $\mathbb{SR}$ level. This is why it is elementary to observe that value is a $\mathbb{CS}$ phenomenon, while meaning is an $\mathbb{SR}$ phenomenon, which is why it is utterly ridiculous to search for, or expect to find, either of them in $\mathbb{R}$. Thus, it is just egregiously stupid and irresponsible for intellectuals to try to draw conclusions about reality and life from their failure to find value and meaning in $\mathbb{R}$.

Internal Reality

The strict definition of reality is that it is an isolated set of elements and forces in the set of all realities, but this new, stricter specification does not erase our traditional uses of the word. If we qualify the conventional use of the term with *external*, then we can say that *external reality* is the set of all things that can be independently verified, in some way and to some level, as existing outside of ourselves, outside of our internal minds.

This leaves us with our internal thoughts, feelings, and ex-

---

[9] **Advanced:** The stopping case for the inductive proof that higher thought is $\mathbb{SR}$-based would be the first person who communicates — by sound or gesture — an insight to his clan members. The next step would either be another new idea, or more likely, a modification of the earlier one, and in this way, externalized insights originating in the $\mathbb{CS}$ would begin to define a cultural library of knowledge. After the first few purely experience-based insights, the accumulating knowledge would be passed on to the new generation, so their new insights would generally build on this knowledge system or on new experiences.

periences that exist in $\mathbb{CS}$, cognitive space, a pseudo-reality that exists inside the consciousness created in our brain, thus preserving conventional usage alongside the formal definition. We can add a symmetry to our discussion of how internal events and sensations relate to verifiable phenomena in the shared spaces between us, by introducing the term *internal reality* as a synonym for $\mathbb{CS}$ to stand in opposition to external reality. Internal reality *seems* like a reality to us since *we* can verify to ourselves that we think what we think, feel what we feel, and experience the events in our life. However, the term internal reality also correctly orients us to the fact that internal reality is a personal world that is not subject to external verification by others, so, technically, it is not, and cannot be, a true reality.

Reality is what can be independently observed and verified to exist *between* cognitive spaces, whereas perception, evaluation, and interpretation place a concept *within* a $\mathbb{CS}$. If you think about this definition for a minute, it may occur to you that events in an external reality have observable consequences, while events in internal reality do not. Ideas in our head may stimulate or lead to a chain of thoughts, but these thoughts are just linked ideas, maybe even predictions, but they are not consequences. Events in internal reality do not perform any work. Aside from connections between ideas, nothing is moved or changed merely by the force of an idea because the thought itself is impotent, unless we choose to *act* on it (i.e., express it in the Abstract Action Language, AAL, and send that to the body to implement as action or speech).

Cognitive spaces are like black holes that swallow experiences as they are evaluated, never to release them into flat space again. We can tell each other that we feel certain feelings, think certain thoughts, have certain needs, but we can neither measure nor verify these subjective, internal assessments (my understanding of what you said does *not* match what you feel) because only observable phenomena in $\mathbb{R}$ can be verified, and value cannot actually be transmitted from person to person, since it is part of a value web peculiar to each individual. While the physical component of messages and actions can be verified, unless the semantic content is expressed in a formal or semi-formal language, it cannot be. Even if we produce a painting or a story and claim that this portrays our inner feelings, all the observer can do is verify the existence of the objects in $\mathbb{R}$, but they have no way of verifying how the elements of the pieces map to our personal web of needs, feelings, and experiences.

So, the physical world, $\mathbb{R}$, and the world of communication and meaning, $\mathbb{SR}$, are distinct, verifiable realities, but internal reality, $\mathbb{CS}$, is just a circus whose own performers are its only audience.

It is difficult to overstate just how isolated our internal reality is from both $\mathbb{R}$ and $\mathbb{SR}$. Figure 3.6 represents that, while our sensorium apparently processes a large number of inputs, x, we can only prove that someone else's cognitive apparatus actually processed something when we can perceive a physical event initiated by their action module.

The real difficulty, though, arises when we try to prove cor-

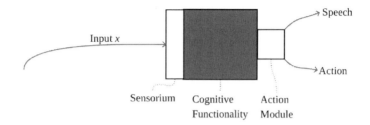

Figure 3.6: Some inputs are followed by actions

relation, because, even though actions initiated by the action module seem to demonstrate the functionality of the entire perceptual/cognitive/action system, yet from the outside, we actually have no way of associating a specific action with a specific input. We can assess an organism's state of health by testing to see if the autonomic nervous system is producing the normal reflexes to specific input, but this is worlds away from determining that the perception and evaluation of a specific event produced the entirety of a response that follows after some indefinite delay.

The basic problem of measuring the correlation between an idea we have inside our head and a phenomenon in $\mathbb{R}$ is well-handled by the scientific method, but measuring the correlation between an internal idea and some event or node in $\mathbb{SR}$ is a different problem. Before we recognized $\mathbb{SR}$ as a separate, first class reality, formally proving the correlation was simply impracticable, but now that we have the necessary foundation at hand, this is something we should not only be able to do, but should be able to automate. However, the math and testbench will first have to be invented, and this will be no small task, since verification in $\mathbb{SR}$ seems like it will be conceptually more difficult than most testing against $\mathbb{R}$ is.

Evolutionary Reality

It was not until the sixth edition of *Origin Of The Species* that Darwin introduced the erroneous notion — which incidentally came from a suggestion from one of his readers — of evolution being about the "survival of the fittest." Erroneous, because the process of natural selection is strictly and solely concerned with the survival of the *fit*, not the fittest.[10] The underlying principle is that any species suited well enough to its ecological niche to reproduce in sufficiently large numbers to survive, will survive. Lacking a judge to declare one competitor the fittest, it can be no other way, so *good enough*, not *best*, is, and has to be, the standard for evolutionary success.

Why is this important? Because evolution is an inefficient, extravagantly expensive process, not a replacement for an all-knowing god. Since we only see the successes, we invariably fail to appreciate just how many mutations are complete failures. It can truly be said of evolution that from a sea of failures come a few islands of success, and that success comes directly from building on a previously proven base. So, for the purposes of the current discussion, we will focus on the fact that most evolutionary changes fall into the category of modification or

---

[10]Sexual selection can be said to involve survival of the fittest, but this depends on really weird, changeable definitions of 'fittest' in very small population subsets.

extension, rather than *de novo* creation.

This concept of maximal preservation and reuse in the evolutionary process greatly simplified the *asomatous psyche* simulation,[11] presumably in the same way that it simplified the evolution of organisms. For example, the concept of the action module and the abstract action language as implemented in the simulation is based on this insight: in real life, the action module barely had to change over the eons, since the same command (e.g., *flee fast*), derived from the same evaluation of sensory input, could be implemented differently in each new body type that arose, from swimmers to crawlers, runners, and flyers. Thus, as new species evolved with new capabilities, very little of the original approach/retreat/ignore mechanism had to be modified because the command would naturally mean something different to birds than it did to rodents, and it was this simple, stable design that was followed in the simulation.

This is why we often see more primitive versions of our own capabilities in creatures that arrived in their current form long before we did. Lungs were preceded by air sacs which were preceded by gills, but air sacs elaborated structures present in gilled fish, and lungs elaborated air sacks.

There is no reason for us to expect that our higher cognitive functions would have violated this principle: language and abstract reasoning was preceded by pattern recognition, creation, and processing, which was preceded by memory, which was pre-

---

[11] The author has built multiple versions of a simulator that tests the various models being discussed. The code for the current version is on a public site, but is not currently accessible.

ceded by choice. While this type of reasoning by analogy only gives us possibilities to consider, and does not force a particular model on us, nevertheless, in this case, it is validated by simulations we can build based on it that produce results in line with our expectations and experience.

Evolution generally preserves earlier developments, and this places hard limits on the nature of both the cognitive process, and the results produced by it. To put it simply: the part of our mind that we share with squirrels still does in us what it does in squirrels; the ability to learn from experience exhibited by many animals still works for us as it does for them; and our ability to problem solve through pattern processing merely elaborates what is found in many animals and higher intellect birds. Our brain contains extensions and elaborations, of course, that support language and abstract reasoning, such as more storage for larger data structures, as well as a more sophisticated abstraction query mechanism, but it is neither possible nor desirable to try to separate the layered nature of our mind from that found in all of our evolutionary relatives.

In order to appreciate the significance of this reality, though, we do have to switch from using the customary mudball model of the mind (where we simply think that the 'mind', as a unit, does all the thinking, and emotions somehow do all the feeling) to using an articulated, layered, executable model of the mind.

For the purposes of this discussion, we will use the articulated, layered, executable model of the mind that was developed for the *asomatous psyche* simulation. An articulated

model must be finely structured, have layers, and must be programmable. The model we are discussing meets all of these
criteria, and the expectation is that interested scholars will
eventually begin to build their own simulations using their own
specialized versions of, or replacements for, this model.

One of the decisions we have to make when we construct
such a model is how many layers do we need? Simply put, the
number of layers you require in your model will be determined
by the type of tests you want to run, and the type of questions
you want to explore and answer. For our current discussion,
four basic evolutionary levels of cognition will amply suit our
needs (but only the three most commonly used will be discussed
very much).

The names and function of the four layers in our model are:

- L0: makes the decision to approach, retreat, or ignore;
- L1: evaluates and remembers experience, and is able to
  act on those lessons;
- L2: sees and creates patterns, uses language, forms ab-
  stract thoughts, creates and follows plans;
- L3: executes free queries.

Each level can use the functionality of the lower levels, and may
implement higher level versions or extensions of lower functions
to match its own higher level data structure. Also, while higher
levels are aware of lower levels, lower levels cannot know that
the higher levels exist.

Another way to look at these different levels of cognition is
that each of them endows us with successively more complex

capacities, such as the ability to:

- L0: respond to the present,
- L1: learn from the past,
- L2: anticipate the future,
- L3: explore/discover the unknown,

Each of the data structures necessary to execute these functions requires more space than is available on the level below. The lowest level, L0, for example, is simple enough to fit into a mosquito's cognitive structure, which has about 100,000 neurons. Rodents seem to have some ability to learn from experience, and since a mouse has about 750 times more neurons than a mosquito (75,000,000), they have ample room for a little memory and rudimentary analytical functions. Humans have the ability to create, manipulate, store, and recall quite complex patterns, as well as having the ability for abstract thought, and with a brain that has 1,300 times more neurons than a mouse (100,000,000,000), we have enough room to store larger, more complex cognitive structures.

The data model structure sizes (not memory sizes) used in the *asomatous psyche* application for the basic mental construct that is used by each level, are shown in table 3.1. (How many of these can be stored in the brain is species-specific.) The level zero structure is the smallest, but can be made even smaller and squeezed into 2 bits when necessary.[12] Level one elements require some space, but not much, since memory varies as the

---

[12] **Advanced:** It can be forced into 2 bits by virtualizing the third dimension, since unimportant things can just be ignored without having to even temporarily store any data.

Level	Example	Data Structure Size
L0	mosquito	2-9 bits
L1	mouse	1,000 bits
L2	human	1,000,000 bits

Table 3.1: Data structure size by level

space available, so tiny level one brains are limited to learning only a few lessons, while larger ones can remember a lot. Similarly, creatures with a rudimentary level two capability can plan a little, while those with a greater cranial capacity, such as elephants, can apparently remember a lot of different paths and plans.

Different species are capable of creating, and possibly storing, different numbers of each type of object, but there also appears to be a significant amount of variability at the individual level, too.[13]

It is important to understand that one of the things that hasn't changed in the evolution of the mind is that the lower levels are always on, they are always working, and they execute before upper levels ever get a chance to process input. Also, the lowest level, L0, is the decision and action level, so, regardless of how complex our reasoning may be, before we can actually *do* anything with our complex ideas, we first have to convert them down into a form that maps into an evaluated action command that can be understood by the primordial action module.

---

[13] **Advanced:** The size of the L2 level data structure is virtual rather than hard, both because the pattern object chains without bound (complex ideas can be huge), but by itself, is very small (simple ideas are small), and because it is achieved mainly by linking preexisting individual ideas, instead of by copying them.

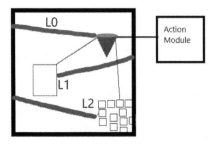

Figure 3.7: Primitive layers process input first

The illustration of this mental model shown in figure 3.7 is intended to suggest a Rube Goldberg-type machine where an input 'ball' enters at the top left, is processed by L0, then drops to the L1 level to be processed there, before it finally becomes available to the higher L2 level functions. Each of the more complex levels can initiate an action by downcasting their data structure into an L0 action object before sending it to the action module, even though L0 may already have moved the body, according to its own lights, before their commands can be acted upon.

It is important to understand the responsibilities and limits of each level, because this will directly influence how we understand our ideas. For example, since crustacean level reasoning is not always the best guide to follow in modern social interactions, then, if we can identify an idea as an L0 impulse, rather than a logical, rational L2 idea, we might want to take another look at it before we act, or at least consider tempering our enthusiasm for it a little.

L0

At its simplest, the L0 evaluation directly corresponds to the decision to approach, retreat, or ignore something we see. It is hard to see how volitional mobility would be an evolutionary advantage if those movements were not chosen based on an assessment of the situation from the perspective of the organism's self-interest (which would ultimately be validated or refuted by natural selection). This ability to make self-interested choices seems like it would have had to precede the ability to move in order for mobility to provide an immediate advantage.

This primordial ability to make choices based on self-interest is shared by most animals, and it is the basis, not only for our physical seek or avoid behavior, but it also underlies our most firmly held moral notions, such as: good/evil/innocuous, right/wrong/unimportant, true/false/unimportant, good/bad/ neutral, do/don't do/ignore. To put it bluntly, the primordial mechanism that triggers our physical responses is the same engine that formulates our moral and emotional judgments and provides their power and meaning.

Since actions can only be initiated by evaluations reduced to this simple tripolar form (indecision results when the dimensions are roughly equal), then L0 cannot be dismissed as an archaic impulse, nor can it be replaced by higher functionality. This means that we have to understand that L2 opinions can never actually be either L0 right or wrong, because the feeling that they are is just an L0 value we assign them by deciding either to accept and follow, or to reject them. No matter how complicated the idea or plan is, it has to be downcast into the simple L0 data structure before it can trigger a decision to go this way, that way, or an unrelated way; to act, not act, or defer; to agree, disagree, or be silent.

Agreement, disagreement, or any binary response, merely means that we are, or are not, willing to follow the speaker's suggested path, or join their group, it doesn't actually mean that we know or understand the speaker's actual thoughts, so it only belongs in recruitment meetings, not intellectual discussions.

The concept of absolute truth is based in L0 values, and this is the basis of religious faith. Although religion has fallen from favor among the educated elite, this is a mistake caused by their inability to differentiate erudition from education, not on any actual understanding of knowledge or reality. One of the reasons that primitive beliefs have worked as well as they have over the millennia to guide us through troubles, despite their fundamentally arational nature, is that they are validated against archetypal images in our genotype instead against our personal opinions. To the extent that conditions hold stable, we can expect that our ancestors' notions of right and wrong should also work reasonably well for us (of course, that conditions are constantly changing is a nasty little complication).

L1

Memory, and the ability to learn from experience, are the core functions that distinguish the L1 evolutionary level of mental

Figure 3.8: L0 decides to approach, retreat, or ignore

Figure 3.9: L1 - Experience

Figure 3.10: L1 looks to past lessons to guide current actions

development from L0. Evolving the ability to learn from experience required the development of very little new functionality: 1) the ability to remember and evaluate a collection of perceptions, which we call a *situation*, and 2) the ability to evaluate the δ (delta), the difference, between a pre-action and postaction situation in terms of threat and benefit. Evaluating the difference between two conditions is an ancient skill that most intelligent animals possess.

L1 provides the basis for traditional cultures and belief systems. While the educated elite dismiss such an approach to life

as backward and ignorant, nevertheless, relying on the sound-
ness of learned lessons is often a very reliable guide to successfully coping with the challenges of life. L1-based societies use
the past as a guide to understanding both the present and the
future. By combining belief, tradition, and experience, traditional societies tend to favor fealty to the authority of the leader
and the power structure. Since the ability to punish miscreants
is vested in the top of the hierarchy, experience suggests to the
average L1 citizen that going along with the customs and mores
of their society is the prudent thing to do.

L2

The capacity to use language is built on the ability to recognize,
create, and link patterns, and together these abilities provide
the basis for abstract, high-level thought. These different functions all evolved on top of previously developed abilities over
the course of ages. They are combined into just one conceptual
level, L2, in our model merely because it suits the needs of our
current experiments and tests. Other modelers will undoubtedly reorganize this one level into several to suit their needs.

L2 patterns are single input, multiple contingent output objects[14] that give us the ability to create complex plans that deal
with contingencies by providing a choice of different next steps
based on the result of the last action. Of course, we have to
program ('learn') all of this into our minds, and poor students

---

[14]See Appendix D.

Figure 3.11: L2 - Patterns

Figure 3.12: L2 patterns connect to patterns by their own rules without limit

tend to create single path plans that fail under adversity, but the L2 pattern object supports associating a high number of choices based on how well the current situation matches the plan.

Language is also encoded in pattern objects, so that, depending on current circumstances, for example, the word *plan* can become plan**s**, plan**ned**, plan**ning**, etc. In school, we are graded down and corrected for failing to program all of the expected options into our minds when we are being taught a word, language, math, or general pattern construct.

Methods, procedures, and plans, whether taught in school or in practice, are patterns. Patterns can link to patterns without limit. Pattern languages have their own grammar, their own set of rules that validate proper form, whether it is a verbal language such as Latin or French, or a technical language such as those used in chemistry, physics, or an engineering discipline. In primary school we learned the pattern language of printing after we learned the patterns of the alphabet letters. Anything in the form of: in case w, do this, unless x, y, or z, in which case do this, that, or the other thing; is implemented with an L2 pattern.

The true power of L2 patterns is that it allows us to predict the future because it associates a number of possible next cases with a single current case. This allows us to anticipate what is around the corner or over the hill, so we can begin to react *before* we are attacked.

The downside, of course, of being able to anticipate the future is that, at most, only one of the possibilities encoded into a pattern can actually happen in a given situation, but our mind is nevertheless presented with them all. When the predicted futures are strongly positive or negative, they tend to arouse persistent agitation (in the form of anxiety or excitement) in us because excited patterns stay alive for a considerable time in our recently-accessed-pattern cache. This means that accidentally energized ideas often hang over us like an anxiety producing cloud of doom or hope, even after they are no longer relevant.

Everyday, we see evidence of this habit of considering ranges of possible outcomes when our news outlets spend maybe half their time reporting, not on events that have already happened, but on events that, by some stretch of their imagination, might happen in the future. They do this to engage the audience's innate ability to obsess about possible future events, in order to intensify the viewer's connection to the news source.

L2 also supports collections of patterns organized around a central pattern. These collections make ideologies, religions, and philosophies possible by defining their own pattern language with their own grammar to prescribe and proscribe sanctioned or prohibited thoughts and behaviors.

An example of a pattern language grammar is what is commonly called *logic* (as opposed to symbolic logic). The problem with pattern language grammar or logic is that it is both informal and optional, which means that it tends to be indifferently applied to suit a vested interest, so it is generally not actually strong enough to be sufficiently externalizable to support reproducible results.

The most profound limitation of L2 processing — beyond the fact that most of its predictions are necessarily wrong — is that L2 is the first cognitive level that deals exclusively in abstract ideas. Where L0 and L1 are strictly concerned with making sense of sensory input, L2 deals solely with organizing and connecting abstractions of experience into narratives that flow from a to b to c. This enables us to see patterns, to make plans, to anticipate eventualities, and to understand themes.

But, the problem with L2 abstractions is that there is no direct physical connection or traceable lineage between any abstract idea in L2 and any real event or thing in $\mathbb{R}$, and this means that there is no automatic or natural error correction of any kind. Ideas in L2 can be as stupid as you want, because they will seem to be true as long as you choose to hook them up to a high value and an important meaning. *You* make your L2 ideas true, not nature, not reality, not truth, not even experience. You decide your ideas' truth, for whatever realistic or silly reason, by whatever logical or ridiculous process you choose.

Nothing stops you from chasing horrible, unrealistic L2 ideas even to the point where your malign, idiotic ideology causes the death of millions. There is nothing in your cognitive apparatus that makes you connect the dots and take responsibility for the disaster you cause, nothing that makes you see the connection between idea and reality, or to accept the responsibility for your actions. The instant we decide our internal ideas are more important than $\mathbb{R}$, or other people in $\mathbb{SR}$, is the moment we cross the border separating normal stupidity from super stupidity to become agents of evil and destruction.

Conclusion

As previously explained, the effect of the purblind defect is to obscure our internal boundaries such that we can neither perceive the various layers and sections of our mind, nor clearly see the mind's limits. This is why we have such a problem differentiating ideas that only exist in our mind from those that actually have some reasonable relation to phenomena in external reality.

However, the effect of our blindness is actually much worse and more far-reaching than that, because we can't even see the boundary between our specific and our extended self. The `specific self`, as you would expect, is defined by the boundaries of our physical body, while the `extended self` reaches far beyond that to include both our interests and the people with whom we have bonded, including family, friends, and community. This means that our strongest feelings and protective/providing impulses can be instantly triggered by people or things that are really quite peripheral to our actual self-interest. Add to this the fact that everyday, day in and day out, our L2 intellect alerts us to dozens of possible opportunities or dangers that might affect us or people and things in our extended self, and it becomes easier to see that many personal and societal issues that arise from self-interested, often impulsive, acts initially erupt from fundamental mechanisms in our cognitive equipment, long before we even have a chance to decide what we, as individuals, want to do.

Living simultaneously in a physical and an idea reality, both of which we experience through a mind which is trapped in an internal reality that has an undefined relation to either of the external realities, creates a whole host of problems that makes successfully navigating reality difficult and error-prone.

However, knowing about this issue, and knowing that the bridge connecting the internal and external worlds is made of verifiable tests, does point a way forward, however difficult it may seem. By learning to understand the impact evolution has on our thought process, we can find the way to the insight that *which* level of the mind knows something absolutely determines how well we can know it:

L0: the purpose of *certainty* is to prepare an idea to become an actionable decision;

L1: the purpose of *tradition* is to offer us the safety (to the extent that circumstances haven't changed) of the tried and true;

L2: the purpose of *logic, plans,* and *procedures* is to guide us on the path of known solutions to known problems.

The fact is that each of these ways of knowing is strong for its purpose, but more or less useless for anything else. Learning even just that much can have a very powerful effect on the quality of our reasoning.

Chapter 4

Limits

We cannot learn how to think effectively and responsibly until we understand and respect the inherent limits imposed on the reasoning process by the physical, organic, and evolutionary realities.

Figure 4.1: Ignoring limits is perilous

The fundamental nature, structures and processes of cognition put limits on perceptual/reasoning abilities — not just in humans, but in all volitionally mobile creatures — that cannot be ignored. These limits don't necessarily obstruct our potential, but they do demarcate where our problems cannot be attacked. This doesn't mean that we have to accept them as inescapable roadblocks, but we do have to recognize them in order to work around them. We can usually pick our own destination, but we cannot always insist on a particular path to it.

Think of these limits as axioms, laws, or provable assertions, whatever you please, but you cannot seriously discuss reasoning or any substantial social or philosophical question without first taking them into account.

Limit 1. Physical Reality, $\mathbb{R}$, is Real

Physical reality is defined as:

$$\mathbb{R} = \{\mathbf{E}, \mathbf{F}\} : \mathbf{E}, \mathbf{F} \in \mathbf{M} \qquad (4.1)$$

where both the elements, $\mathbf{E}$, and the forces, $\mathbf{F}$:

1. are members of the set of all measurables, $\mathbf{M}$, and
2. are not affected by external phenomena.

Everyone knows that reality is real, *except* intellectuals and academics who seem to have a great deal of difficulty understanding reality, as well as everything that depends on it. Notwithstanding their confusion, there is no serious philosophical

Figure 4.2: Reality is real

Figure 4.3: Feel free to dispute it

question about the reality of physical reality. Yes, we still have questions about the elements and forces in ℝ, but science is doing just fine working that out. And yes, there are an unlimited number of questions about whether some idea we have corresponds to an element in reality, but reproducible tests and advances in theory will generally answer all of them in time. ℝ becomes a lot less confusing once you grok that it doesn't include ideas, feelings, value, and meaning. It only includes measurable things and forces. As long as you never forget this, you can begin to move forward to explore reality with confidence.

Limit 2. Semantic Reality, $\mathbb{SR}$, is Real

$\mathbb{SR}$, semantic reality[1] is defined as:

$$\mathbb{SR} = (\{\xi\}, \{\mathcal{M}\}) \tag{4.2}$$

where $\{\xi\}$ is a set of externalized cognitive spaces, and $\{\mathcal{M}\}$ is a set of message links between the vertices such that $\forall \, \xi_i \in \{\xi\}$ the message connection set between it and at least one other ξ_j is not null.

Since ξs are formally, albeit fluidly, defined, they are shown in figure 4.4 as flat (black) vertices, while the entire rest of the graph is curved to a varying extent by the asymmetrical message value connections (sender and receiver assign their own values to each message, so space curves more at the higher value end). The ξ nodes are shown as opaque black shapes to suggest the invisibility of the underlying cognitive space.[2]

$\mathbb{SR}$ is wickedly real. Any lingering doubts you have about the substantiality of semantic reality will be immediately resolved

---

[1] See *Ultrareasoning*, chapter 31.

[2] **Advanced:** Is $\mathbb{SR}$ actually independent of $\mathbb{CS}$? While it may not seem so, it is, because only the actions and messages sent by the visible ξ exist in semantic reality. We are supposing that the private agonies in the $\mathbb{CS}$ drive those messages, but from the point of view of $\mathbb{SR}$, that is an unsupported supposition, because we can just as easily assume that messages are only triggered by other messages, and that there is no underlying $\mathbb{CS}$. The simulation does not require $\mathbb{CS}$s.

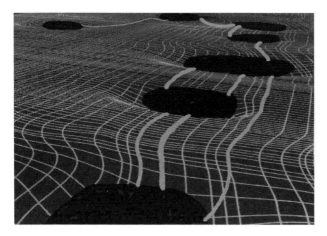

Figure 4.4: Semantic reality is asymmetrically curved
by message value

for you if publicly violate some of its more important norms
and rules to harm those closer to the center of power than you.
If your offense is serious enough, you will likely immediately
experience the extent to which actions and errors in an abstract
reality can rain down harsh consequences in a physical one. $\mathbb{SR}$
is abstract in the sense that it is defined and held together by
message links, but the actions of each ξ node very definitely
happen in $\mathbb{R}$.

Links in $\mathbb{SR}$ connect ξ node to ξ node through $\mathbb{R}$ as observable, measurable, reproducible phenomena: voices can be
heard, words read, gestures are visible, actions observably move
objects in space, etc. However, even though the elements of $\mathbb{SR}$
may arise from $\mathbb{CS}$, most things that exist in $\mathbb{CS}$, like our random thoughts and feelings, just stay there, forever, and are not
a part of $\mathbb{SR}$. Only when an internal idea matures to the point

that it motivates action in word or deed observable in $\mathbb{R}$ does its semantic content become available in $\mathbb{SR}$.

Organization (voluntary or conscripted hierarchical coordination of independent actors) **only** exists in $\mathbb{SR}$, and neither families, clans, groups, religions, political parties, corporations, armies, nations nor alliances are possible without it, and without them, civilization, as we know it, would not exist. Society and civilization can only exist in structures that are created, and exist, only in $\mathbb{SR}$.

How can something that exists only on a semantic plane, with no physical component have a substantial, even crucial effect on our physical reality? The simplest answer is illustrated by one special type of transmissible message: the *license to violence* message, which authorizes the receiver to organize and use sufficient force to compel recalcitrant ξ nodes to comply with the hierarchy's dictates. These messages, once decoded by a willing recipient, can be implemented to great effect in $\mathbb{R}$, which, by **Limit 1**, we already know is real.

ξ nodes coordinate and cooperate specifically to achieve visible results in $\mathbb{R}$: buildings are real; crops are planted, harvested, and sold; armies can force all manner of changes in physical reality; but the threads that tie the participants together exist only in $\mathbb{SR}$, not $\mathbb{R}$. Written orders *mean* nothing if not understood and acted upon by $\mathbb{CS}$s. Although the elements (participants' externalized self, ξ) and forces (semantic messages, $\mathcal{M}$) in $\mathbb{SR}$ do not exist in $\mathbb{R}$ (every ξ is actually defined both by the underlying $\mathbb{CS}$ and by other ξs that interact with, and judge it), they are just as real as any object or force in $\mathbb{R}$, just real in a different way, on a different plane. While the $\mathbb{CS}$ vessel (our body) and the physical form of the messages both exist in $\mathbb{R}$, identification of ξ attributes, and assignment of meaning to messages only happen inside of $\mathbb{CS}$s — not in either $\mathbb{R}$ or $\mathbb{SR}$.

Emotionally charged (affective) messages explicitly reference emotional superlatives in an attempt to trigger certain emotional responses in receptive listeners. Such messages effectively bend the space they are in, but it is important to understand that the amount of distortion is a product not of the speaker's intent or the message content alone, but necessarily involves the product of the sender's relative status in the hierarchy times the evaluation placed on the affective portion of the message by the recipient.

The main function of rhetoric is to use affective language to manipulate the audience's emotional state to match the way the speaker wants the enveloped message to be evaluated. When the attempt is successful, then, when the crux of the message is finally presented, the audience will tend simply to attach it to their currently aroused emotional state, rather than taking the time to independently evaluate the message for themselves. They thus effectively voluntarily agree to absorb what they take to be the speaker's evaluation as the meaning they now assign to the idea in their own mind.

Messages transmitted in the physical medium of $\mathbb{R}$ have to be taken down into the ξ's $\mathbb{CS}$ workings to be interpreted, and then whether or not a response is produced is dependent entirely on the calculations performed by the individual $\mathbb{CS}$. That is, an action in $\mathbb{R}$ can impact an object in $\mathbb{R}$, such as a body, but it cannot *force* a response from an underlying $\mathbb{CS}$, regardless of whether or not the message was actually received by it.

$\mathbb{SR}$ is infinitely more complex than $\mathbb{R}$, and yet, while we would never build a bridge, or construct a building without following plans that incorporate engineering principles based on known physics, geology, chemistry, and metallurgy, etc., yet unbelievably, we happily plan our lives, create organizations and states, and design and implement policies in $\mathbb{SR}$ without so much as a passing nod to the sciences that are necessary to understand and describe $\mathbb{SR}$'s laws and complexities.

We may be frustrated by the workings of large social, economic, or political organizations, but this is because their nature is fundamentally more complex and harder to understand than quantum mechanics. While it is true that very few of us ever took even the elementary courses required to begin to study physics, even fewer of us have had the opportunity to begin taking the many courses we would need in order to learn how to perform $\mathbb{SR}$ calculations.

$\mathbb{SR}$ is complex and little understood, yet it entirely defines the world of thoughts swirling about in our heads at this very moment. Since we have lived in groups and societies every day of our lives, it should not be a surprise that $\mathbb{SR}$ is very real, but really grokking that it is separate from $\mathbb{R}$, more complex than $\mathbb{R}$, and can be studied with formal, quantitative models, will take a little effort on the reader's part.

Limit 3. Mortality is Real

Mortality is a provable fact in $\mathbb{R}$; its value can be realized in $\mathbb{CS}$; its meaning can be articulated in $\mathbb{SR}$. Everything we think, feel, and do is framed by the fact of our mortality.

Mortality defines the context of value and meaning. Disrespecting the valid mortality concerns of an individual is often a crime, but disrespecting the valid mortality concerns of the individual as a class — or of humanity as a whole — in the name of some fatuous ideology or philosophy is a favorite pathological fetish of the super stupid academic elite.

Limit 4. Cognitive Space Is Personal

Cognition creates evaluable models inside our brain to represent internal and external events that were experienced through our various senses, or generated by our mental apparatus itself. These internal representations constitute internal knowledge which exists in our internal reality or cognitive space, $\mathbb{CS}$.

Internal reality is only a pseudo-reality, a felt, rather than actual, reality, that we conflate with the greater reality outside of our minds because we lack the faculty (due to the purblind defect) to perceive the boundary between internal and external reality. Even though we are sure that we *know* that our minds fully experience an all-encompassing reality that includes both ideas and things, nevertheless, regardless of our heartfelt conviction, this most fundamental, deeply known truth of ours is wholly false. Hmmm.

While it is true that we chop down trees in external reality, it is also true that we plan the path of their fall in internal reality. But, because the two realities are separate and not at all guaranteed to match, sometimes the tree falls onto the house, rather than next to it. The elements of external reality are observable and measurable, but the elements of internal reality are value ideas that cannot be reproducibly measured. This makes internal reality and external reality disjoint sets: while there may be some correlation between a given idea, i_i, and its referent, r_i, in $\mathbb{R}$, internal and external reality not only are not equal, they don't even overlap.

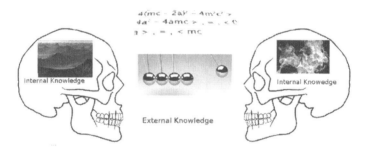

Figure 4.5: Internal vs. external knowledge

Internal ideas, feelings and evaluations of perceptions and experiences do not equal external phenomena. It seems that everyone of any intelligence will dismissively grant the truth of this limit, but then, within that very minute, most will also loudly insist that their idea of reality is rational, correct, and complete. Educated people, especially, are certain that the chain of knowledge and reasoning they've put together in their mind accurately describes reality.

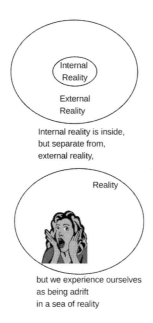

Internal reality is inside,
but separate from,
external reality,

but we experience ourselves
as being adrift
in a sea of reality

Figure 4.6: Lost in reality

Notwithstanding the vanity of intellectuals, the simple fact is that all of our knowledge, from whatever source or by whatever method it was gained, is personal, and the relation between it and external reality is undefined, uncertain, and has a potentially huge margin of error, except in those rare cases where it has been adequately tested and verified.

Corollary: We Think Inside Our Head

We think inside our own personal cognitive space:

- Thinking happens inside our heads, not out in the world.
- Ideas exist inside our brain, not outside.
- The value field in the idea data structure creates a dis-

Figure 4.7: Idea vs. Reality

tortion curve that pulls the idea away from the reality it
supposedly represents.

- The limited size of the idea data structure, compared to
  the unbounded amount of detail extant in reality, means
  that ideas can never be more than simplified models of
  complex realities; our idea of a tree is *not* the same as the
  real tree.

- The relation between internal knowledge and external reality can only be defined by reproducible tests.

Our ideas exist inside our head, they are a sketch we create
in an attempt to orient ourselves to experience. The purpose
of an idea is *not* to describe reality, but to maintain our orientation to reality, to maintain our ability to make decisions we
have confidence in. This does not mean that the decisions are
right, or that they will objectively protect us or our interests,

Figure 4.8: The internal detached world.

it just means that in order for decisions to be made, we have to asymmetrically evaluate our experience and ideas so that we can prep an idea to become a decision that can be translated into an action.

Ideas exist in cognitive space with no defined relation to anything in $\mathbb{R}$ or $\mathbb{SR}$ until we establish that correspondence through formal or informal tests. As pictured in figure 4.8, our higher intellect is a funny place where knowledge, order, logic, and nightmare are all neighbors that express their images and ideas in their own idiom with a native logic that seems to make sense from their point of view, but not necessarily from any other.

We think inside of our head, and some of our ideas correspond pretty well with reality, but a lot of them do not. When

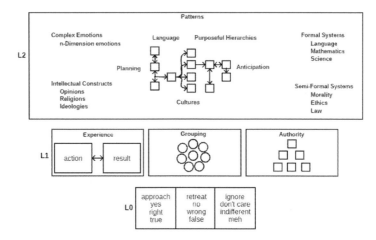

Figure 4.9: Evolutionary model of the mind

we use common sense to validate our opinions, what we are really doing is informally checking them against experience, and this works reasonably well some of the time. However, when we try to use higher level thought in the form of logic or reason to validate our opinions, we are trying to validate internal knowledge with internal knowledge. Since internal knowledge has no known relation to reality, it cannot be reliably used to validate itself.

Limit 5. The Mind Evolved in Layers

Evolution happens over time, and the tree of life branches as new structures and abilities differentiate species. Our minds evolved over time, and the result of that process is a series of layers that stack ability on ability, like a geological formation with visible layers of rock on top of earlier layers.

Since we are unable to directly observe the inner workings of our mind, the only way we can study it is to create a model of it which we must iteratively test and tweak before it can be considered viable to any significant degree. This means that, in order to understand how we think, feel, and act, we first have to abandon the mudball model of the mind in favor of an articulated model in which functions are layered by degree of primitiveness to sophistication. Next, we have to make sure the model works under the constraint that earlier layers cannot know about, or communicate with, later layers.

The specific layers we choose for our model will be determined by our experimental needs, rather than by an objective correlation with reality, because we learn about the unknown by creating a succession of heuristic models of it that help us get to the next step, not by trying to come up with the final answer on the first try.

The functional layered levels we are using in the model we are discussing here are L0, L1, L2, and L3. The functions associated with each level are:

- L0: evaluate x into the [approach, retreat, ignore] structure
- L1: learn from experience
- L2: pattern creation and manipulation, language, abstract thought
- L3: formulate and execute free queries

The functionality of these layers correlates with our ability to:

- L0: respond to the present
- L1: learn from the past
- L2: anticipate the future
- L3: explore/discover the unknown

We are able to do these things because we can:

- L0: evaluate input, make self-interested decisions
- L1: retain, evaluate, and compare memories
- L2: patternize experience, and create and manipulate patterns and plans
- L3: construct fractal query trees and analyze patterns with a foreign grammar

Note how, in the layered model, conviction (L0), experience (L1), and logic (L2) execute on different data structures on different levels of our evolved mind. It is only the purblind defect that makes us think that they all exist on the same plane.

Corollary 1: Layers Limit Thought

Different types of thought execute on different data structures in different layers of the mind that evolved in widely separated historical eras. The earliest layers use simpler data structures to accomplish simpler goals, while the later layers use more complex structures to produce more sophisticated results. Thus, the reason that layers limit thought is because earlier, simpler layers use smaller, simpler data structures that simply cannot hold or process larger, more complex ideas.

The L0 intellect doesn't have the space to hold complex thoughts, but that's fine, that's not what it was built for, it was

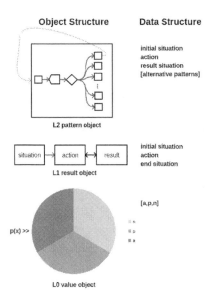

Object Structure　　　　**Data Structure**

L2 pattern object

initial situation
action
result situation
[alternative patterns]

L1 result object

initial situation
action
end situation

L0 value object

[a,p,n]

Figure 4.10: Different levels of the mind use different
data objects

built to evaluate input and make movement decisions quickly,
and it's very good at that. However, there is a surprising, hidden corollary to the limit of the small data structure: only the
small data structure can express the binary nature of certainty:
either you are certain, or you are not. This means that by the
time you are certain of something, you have already downcast,
or reduced, your complicated thought to fit into a 6-bit value
judgment object that becomes a *truth handle* that supplants the
idea's semantic content role as its defining characteristic.

Certainty is black and white, and if there are too many
shades of gray in your thought, you are not ready to make a
decision, because you are still thinking in L2, not L1 or L0,
terms.

The cognition limits place hard boundaries on thought: L0 cannot think above the self-interest binary[3] of good/bad, right/ wrong, true/false, yes/no, etc.; L1 cannot think above how closely the current situation compares to a familiar one; L2 cannot think in terms that have a resolution finer than the width of a pattern object. This means that: L0 cannot learn from experience; L1 cannot learn sophisticated patterns; and L2 cannot deliberately explore the unknown (hence the serendipity of insight and flashes of genius).

Corollary 2: Intelligence Is Layer Specific

The core ability being measured by IQ tests is L2 pattern processing, the skill used in language, math, and other academic fields. While pattern processing and acquisition is important, it is not the only dimension of intelligence. Since the intellect is layered, it should come as no surprise that intelligence is also layered, and each is important in its own way.

L0

The primordial intellect, L0, enables us to perceive, recognize, evaluate, and decide to approach, retreat, or ignore phenomena. Speed, decisiveness, and an ability to choose based on a demonstrably valid interpretation of one's fundamental self-interest are the hallmarks of L0 intelligence.

---

[3]The nil, non-self, evaluation is implicit in these discussions. It becomes more important when we examine emotions (see *The Structure of Truth*), instead of simple motion choices.

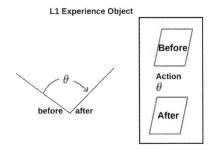

Figure 4.11: L1 result/experience object

L1

The key L1 skill is the ability to compare a new situation to known situations and to quickly select the appropriate proven response. Memory and aggregate evaluation of multiple element scenarios are the new levels of functionality that make L1 possible. The new data object created by the L1 mutations is the result object (figure 4.11), which supports associating complex situations with an action and the situation that results from the action. The result object thus supports the ability to learn from experience so that we can get better at surviving as we mature. Valid measures of L1 intelligence include: experience imprinting and recall (memory), fuzzy comparison, decisiveness of judgment, and the ability to improve results in $\mathbb{R}$ over time.

Since L1 is built to use the past as a guide, it makes sense that the L1-dominant intellect tends to exhibit a certain reverence, or respect, for functions that leverage the benefit of the past, such as authority, tradition, and experience.

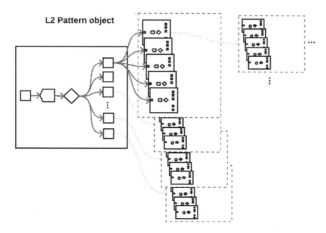

Figure 4.12: L2 pattern object supports contingency branching and chaining

L2

The L2 pattern object (figure 4.12) elaborates the L1 result object by associating a range of options with the result of an action, instead of just the one result in the L1 object. The pattern object supports complex plans that include alternative paths depending on the result of the previous action by using pattern objects as the next step in the plan. This means that pattern objects can be linked together in unbounded chains of arbitrary length. Chained contingency patterns in L2 give us the ability to anticipate the future by showing us many different possible futures that might flow from current conditions and actions.

L2 intelligence begins with the pattern recognition, manipulation, and extension skills that are evaluated by IQ tests, but it goes beyond that. The downside of L2 is that its design always results in our mind being excited or threatened with many more visions of the future than will ever happen, so the ability to quell errantly aroused ideas is also a very important L2 intelligence skill. However, the most important, and least understood, L2 intelligence skill is the appreciation of the need for, and the ability to execute, validation of L2 ideas against independent quality measures, instead of just checking them for consistency with their own grammar. The fact that unproven, self-validating grammars have no defined relation to any external reality makes the proclivity and ability to validate L2 ideas against reality the under-appreciated character skill that definitively separates useful people from academic idiots.

Limit 6. Error Exceeds Content

Since what we actually, verifiably, know is restricted to the tiny subset of successfully tested data points from the facts we deliberately added, one by one, to ideas in our head, the following can be taken as a law:

$$|m_i - r_i| >> |m_i| \qquad (4.3)$$

That is, the magnitude of the difference between an internal model, m_i, and its reality referent, r_i, is *much* greater that the amount of content in the model, $|m_i|$.

This disparity between how much there is to know, and how little of that we actually do know, explains why the results of our efforts to make policy changes often cause more problems than they solve: we never see most of the puzzle, we just see our own little part. So, little changes we make in one place often affect areas we didn't realize were connected, in ways we never anticipated. This is the basis of the well-known law of unintended consequences.

Our models are mental constructs that simplify perceptions of phenomena in order to support our ability to choose an action. Even in physics, while gravity calculations work fine when we assume that all the mass in a body is concentrated in a point mass at the center of the body, this simplified model is not adequate for other purposes, such as explaining why a planet wobbles on its axis.

Simplified models are often adequate because they are what our minds use to evaluate reality and guide actions. A lot of our models are perfectly adequate for our purposes because any reduction of any amount of data is acceptable as long the end product supports an evaluation that translates into action that produces results with a positive viability quotient. But we shouldn't mistake adequacy for completeness or correctness.

Chapter 5

Coping Tools

Traditional Coping

Humanity has coped, more or less well, with normal stupidity simply by developing societies based on codified experience. Traditional societies based on the accumulated lessons of experience pass wisdom on to the next generation through socialization. The upside of this is that such societies tend to work well in relatively static conditions, while the downside is that they tend to fall behind, or fail, in dynamic conditions, because they generally neglect or shun the exploration of the unknown in favor of staying within the pale of the known.

Traditional societies that rely primarily on belief and experience are leveraging the functions of L0 and L1. The L0 archetypes tell us, for example, that loud noises and rapidly approaching large shapes are dangerous, but there is only so much reactive behavioral instruction that can be passed on genetically. The L1 memory and comparison functions enable us to get beyond that limit by giving us the ability to adjust our own behavior based on our own evaluation of real, personal experience. Once we add rudimentary L2 communicative skills to that base, we are able to learn from other people's experience as well as our own, and over time, to create a social fabric that can store wisdom which, if passed along and used, can save our society a lot of unnecessary failure and pain.

The Ten Commandments and the Seven Virtues are two of many different codifications of these traditional L0 beliefs and L1 lessons. They are time-tested ideals and behavioral constraints that have been developed and propagated by traditional societies in Western culture to act as a constant guide for current and succeeding generations. Codified ideals and laws of behavior should be seen as tools that were developed and used by traditional societies to help them cope with, and work around, the cognitive defects of normal stupidity that impair our perception, understanding and behavior.

If we look at these ideals in light of the six cognition limits, we can develop an even better understanding of how traditional societies manage to cope with normal stupidity, despite having no direct awareness either of it or its causes.

But, before we can compare the Ten Commandments to the cognition limits, we first have to take a new, hard look at them to make sure we actually understand both their meaning and intent, as well as how they fit into a social code. If we look at them abstractly, instead of prescriptively, we can boil them down to three essential categorical imperatives that happen to map nicely to the different intellect levels:

- the unique ultimate exists; honor and contemplate it → L2;
- bind yourself to the ultimate, your family, and your society → L1;
- sublimate your urges and appetites to protect and cultivate your family and community → L0.

This can be further reduced to the formula:

Align your axis of meaning with the ultimate, and use the commandments as your basis of value.

Thus, when you successfully base your life on the Ten Commandments, you are defining meaning and value (Limits 1 - 3) on a sound basis, and tempering hubris (Limits 5,6) with your respect for community and the ultimate.

The seven virtues have been around since ancient times, and have been variously formulated, but table 5.1[1] does a nice job presenting both the virtues and the corresponding sins:

Virtues		Sins
Chastity	Purity, abstinence	Lust
Temperance	Humanity, equanimity	Gluttony
Charity	Will, benevolence, generosity, sacrifice	Greed
Diligence	Persistence, effortfulness, ethics	Sloth
Patience	Forgiveness, mercy	Wrath
Kindness	Satisfaction, compassion	Envy
Humility	Bravery, modesty, reverence	Pride

Table 5.1: Seven virtues and sins

[1]https://en.wikipedia.org/wiki/Seven_virtues

The first thing you might notice about this table is that the sins column on the right is based on personal, $\mathbb{CS}$, indulgences, while the virtues column on the left is entirely focused on community, $\mathbb{SR}$, values. That is, the traditional view is that it is virtuous to bind oneself to the community, and a vice to only look after your own interests and appetites. The bifurcation of good and evil along these lines stems from the fact that, since these concepts are culturally transmitted, they naturally represent cultural interests as being superior to individual ones. However, the happy consequence of accepting this biased $\mathbb{SR}$ orientation is that it actually does provide exactly what one needs to build a durable sense of meaning and value in one's life, whereas cynics and libertines who reject the possibility of a commitment to a greater goal beyond their own selfish interests invariably set themselves up to eventually rue their decision to live a meaningless life.

Combining traditional values with belief and experience-based reasoning creates a practical solution to normal stupidity by focusing our attention on known experiences and well-tested ideas that keep us oriented to $\mathbb{R}$, while also girding us against the allure of passing philosophical and ideological fads.

Traditional societies, despite their primitive, unschooled beliefs, offer a sound guide to coping with a poorly understood reality precisely because their wisdom is based on actual experience with $\mathbb{R}$. Lessons learned from experience always start with a kernel of reality truth that abstract ideas, absent reproducible testing, *by their very nature* do not have. L0 and L1 naturally tend to respect the limits of cognition due to their exposure to the harsh, punitive realities of $\mathbb{R}$, whereas, since the abstract plane of L2 is structurally divorced from $\mathbb{R}$, it is free to flout limits, no matter how real and bruising they are, because it doesn't even see them.

The six cognition limits can be divided into three different categories based on what they force us to acknowledge or perceive before we can successfully cope with them:

- Limits 1-3: reality
- Limit 4: subjectivity of our thoughts
- Limits 5,6: humility regarding our cognitive powers

Traditional societies are not only absolutely certain that physical reality is real (Limit 1,3), but they also generally tend to elevate the significance of their semantic reality above that of the physical in order to strengthen and sustain the social bonds (Limit 2). They also tend to teach the individual not to over-value their own thoughts and feelings above those of their family and community (Limits 5,6). It is not trivial, of course, that they generally fail utterly to understand and appreciate Limit 4, the subjectivity of internal knowledge, since this leads to all sorts of unfortunate consequences.

The net effect of this is that traditional societies tend to be guided by belief systems (the L0 intellect) that have been modified and validated over time to accord with learned tradition and experience (the L1 intellect) in their quest to live a successful and meaningful life. The stability and durability of traditional societies is thus generally proportional to the stability of their circumstances, but their ability to cope with change is correspondingly reduced to the extent that the rigidity of their tradition starves, rather than cultivates, opportunities for invention and discovery.

It should be noted that religious codes can create a tension between tradition and orthodoxy, since traditional societies are more focused on experience with reality (Limit 1), while orthodox societies are more heavily focused on their own internally defined reality, $\mathbb{SR}$. Thus, traditional and orthodox societies have different stability quotients: traditional societies are only as stable as their $\mathbb{R}$ circumstances, while orthodox societies are only as stable as their isolation from other $\mathbb{SR}$s is hermetic.

Creative Coping

We can add modern tools to the traditional tool set by leveraging our knowledge of cognition limits to forge new tools powerful enough to improve our lives in the here and now, before we even consider undertaking the rigors of studying model-oriented reasoning.

In order to make this happen, though, we will first have to make the effort to creatively reconsider the cognition limits in different combinations and contexts (L3). We have to learn how to see them not just as barriers, but as the very powerful tools they are, tools that can be used in many different ways, some of which we might find immediately useful.

Following are several lessons we can learn from the limits,

lessons that can become very powerful tools, powerful enough to have an immediate impact on the power and efficacy of our reasoning. This list is open-ended, so feel free to add your own as you learn new ones.

Lesson One: All unverified thought is personal

The formal definition of statement[2] is:

Statement: [context] + content + [goal].

Context and goal have their usual meanings, and they are enclosed in square brackets to indicate that they are optional in the sense that they are almost always implicit or even undefined, *but they are always there*. Internal statements, thoughts that we have inside our minds, have their context and goal defined by the value-rich region of our CS in which they occur. However, when we externalize a statement by expressing it as a message, the context and goal are not included since value cannot be externalized.[3]

We know by Limit 4 that cognitive space is personal. This means that all thoughts are personal statements that only fully make sense in our own reality, unless they are explicitly contextualized and verified in some way in an external reality, and even then their interpreted meaning won't match our original internal meaning.

Ideally, the best way to verify ideas is to express them in a

---

[2] *Ultrareasoning*, p19

[3] Context and goal are not included unless the message is expressed in a formal language. The necessary and explicit specification of context and goal is actually what distinguishes a formal language from an informal one.

formal language, create a test for them, and publish them so that independent minds can verify them. Practically, though, most verification is semi-formal in the sense that we will repeatedly verify a lesson against our own experience, or, once we contextualize the message in the argot of a trade or practice, we can communicate the message to others competent in the appropriate skill area so that they can more or less reliably reproduce our results.

Absent independent verification, though, all thought is personal, and the startling consequence of this is that the relation between every personal thought and its purported referent in a reality is *undefined*. 'Undefined' does not mean that it is wrong, or defective, it means that by the very nature of the cognitive process, internal, personal thought has no known relation to external reality until it is proven by test, our conviction to the contrary notwithstanding. Thoughts form inside our head, and so are of a different nature than external phenomena, and have a several orders of magnitude smaller amount of data than the referent they model.

Surely, it is obvious that all of our thoughts must be tested in order to find out how closely they model their target. Since feelings, such as certainty and confidence, don't actually count as a valid means of verification, then, without tests, we simply have no way of knowing how right or wrong our ideas are.

We have always taken for granted that our ideas are valid by default, since we have historically assumed, because of the purblind defect, that perception and reasoning were transparent and objective. The reality, however, is very different: by default, the validity of our ideas is undefined. This means that merely *having* an idea cannot be the end of the reasoning process, but rather, must be but the beginning of a hard testing phase that will cull the vast majority of our ideas when they fail verification, leaving only the very few exceptions that we can actually rely on.[4]

Lesson Two: Error exceeds content

Lesson two is just Limit 6, repeated to get your attention, since there is very little chance you already appreciate how powerful this limit is.

Keep in mind that the ternary L0 evaluation has a 'don't care' dimension, which, went set high enough, allows us to dismiss any input we want to as unimportant enough to ignore and forget. It is this dismissive function that will bedevil your attempts to understand this discussion of lesson number two, because you will be instinctively pushed to dismiss the following explanation as too abstract to be real or important.

Nevertheless, let us forge on and pick an arbitrary, simple object to use as an example for this lesson, say a granite rock about the size of your fist. You look at this stone, pick up it up, turn it over in your hand, and then we begin our discussion.

Q: What's in your hand?
A: A rock.
Q: What kind of rock?

---

[4]The opinion object is discussed at length in *Ultrareasoning*, *The Structure of Truth*, and *Xiom*.

A: I dunno, maybe granite.
Q: How much does it weigh?
A: I dunno, feels like about 5 or 6 ounces.
Q: How big is it?
A: Oh, maybe 4 inches by 2, $2\frac{1}{2}$ inches.

If the conversation stopped there, you could say that you have a pretty good knowledge of the rock, at least as much you require for your current needs. But, what if we didn't stop the conversation there?

Q: If I took the rock from you, could you draw its outline?
A: Uhm, kind of, maybe, ... sure, I could draw a good enough outline.
Q: What is good enough? What is your acceptable margin of error?
A: What? No, I could just kind of draw the shape, I don't know how accurate it would be.
Q: If I gave you a 3D modeling program, could you render a 3D model of it?
A: No, certainly not.
Q: Granite has inclusions, do you know the precise mineral content of the rock?
A: No, of course not.
Q: Some granite is mildly radioactive, do you know if this rock is?
A: Yikes! No, I have no idea.
Q: Any idea how many atoms are in the rock?
A: Now you're just joking, right?

As promised, the greatest problem you are likely to have accepting this example as valid is that it is ridiculous on its face to expect us to know the precise weight, dimensions, mineral composition, and number of atoms in a rock simply from holding it for a minute or so. And it is, yet these quantities are facts that are undeniably true about the actual rock, and there isn't even a place holder for them in your model. Reality, $\mathbb{R}$, is very dense, and very specific, yet the cognitive process we use to *know* reality is, by its very structure and its functional nature, very approximate and reductive.

So, although you don't care about all the detail missing from your model — since your adumbrated sketch of it serves your purposes perfectly adequately — this is the exact point: we know only some of what our senses tell us, and only so much as interests us, or is easy to know. We — meaning cognitive entities, not just humans — do not ever actually know the full detail of any $r_i \in \mathbb{R}$ because we simply have no need for that level of knowledge, and no faculty to gain or store that level of knowledge.

The lesson here is that we must remain humble in the face of the magnificence and complexity of any reality, because our cognitive apparatus is built to use shortcuts to acquire such knowledge as will equip us to react as quickly as possible to a dynamic world full of threats and opportunities. Far from being a problem, it is these lifesaving shortcuts that make it impossible for us to know everything about anything. Even more important than that, there is no way that we can ever define what it is that we do not know, what we have left out, so it is impossible for us to be sure that what we do know includes the most important aspects of even the most familiar subject.

Lesson Three: Informal vs. Formal

As stated previously, a formal language is fully and unambiguously defined, so every expression in it can be parsed without having to refer to an implicit context or goal. Formal languages can easily and correctly be read by computers, and when competent minds read them, they get the same result as the machine. Informal languages, on the other hand, due to the implicit context and goal parts of each statement, are subjective to the point that they can support any number of contradictory, but equally valid, interpretations.

We don't speak or think in formal languages, of course, so they seem artificial to us, but that is simply because they are so precise, rather than comfortably ambiguous like informal language. Formal does not mean inherently difficult, it's just that precision takes some getting used to, and some discipline to master. Mathematics, symbolic logic, and programming languages are familiar examples of formal languages, while all spoken, verbal languages are examples of informal languages, such as English or Spanish. Informal languages are internal in the sense that they support an emotive component that is entirely supplied by the mind that is processing them at the time, first in the speaker, then in the listener, but the totality of the meaning and value contextualizing the message is different for each. The expressed words are external, and do serve as messages that bind ℂ𝕊s together in an 𝕊ℝ, but the strength of the bond is determined by the level of meaning and value that the recipient attaches to the message, not by the message itself, nor by the senders intent.

Informal language is the language of internal knowledge, it describes what we think and feel, but only to us, because everyone else must supply values and context from their ℂ𝕊, not ours. Formal language, in contrast, is value-free, it describes observable or theoretical phenomena in neutral, quantitative terms that can be communicated through 𝕊ℝ without loss of context, content, or goal, since the content is fully specified, and the context is the framework that defines the formal language. The goal of the statement is the veracity of the formal statement in the specified context. Value considerations have no place in formal conversations.

Each of the hard sciences, in addition to using math, has its own formal language to specify objects, relations, and procedures. The soft sciences and the humanities, though, all use informal languages to ambiguously express untestable, unreliable, and ultimately meaningless ideas.

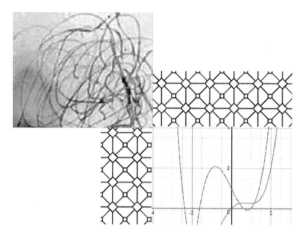

Figure 5.1: Informal and formal thought

The key difference between informal and formal language
is that informal language is built around a value attribute that
formal language does not support. This is why formal languages
can describe events and objects in $\mathbb{R}$, where value does not
exist, while informal language focuses on describing feelings and
experiences in $\mathbb{CS}$.

We can use our internal reasoning to encode a thought into
a formal or semi-formal language that can be communicated
to others by pruning the value and meaning components and
only expressing the reality-based elements of the thought formally. Such externalized statements can then be independently
validated or contradicted by a rerun of our experiment.

Informal language cannot be both complete and precise,
since it cannot communicate the complex value web surround-

ing an idea any further than the limits of the CS distortion field. Additionally, since it is impossible to identify lacunae in message content caused by the under-specification of the value-based context and goal statement components, the deficiency cannot be made whole even by a perceptive listener.

We can test practical thoughts, such as instructions on how best to swing a hammer to drive nails straight without bending them over, simply by translating the thought into action and observing the results. We can also express these thoughts to others by extemporizing a semi-formal language that mixes technical terms for objects and actions with natural language. This is how we can learn, and teach, a whole range of practical and recreational skills to each other. These are valid examples of the power of L1 to support learning from experience, but the limitation of these lessons is that they often only apply to someone with our peculiar set of physical and mental abilities, and experiences.

The problematic relation between informal and formal language is well represented in the sphere of software development where the programming language is formal, but the specification of what the program should do is not. Even though there are formal specification languages, they do not reduce the problem, because the gap is between our unspoken, and perhaps ill-formed, idea of what we want the program to do, and the formal specification of that informal thought, regardless of whether that specification happens in the code or the design document. The compromise that is generally reached in the development process is that the developers and the product owners will, in the end, be forced by schedule pressures to agree to accept a limited level of functionality in the current release version. No one is really happy with this solution because they are frustrated by their inability to realize their inner vision in the external product, but the difference between informal and formal languages makes it inevitable.

Formal language is the only testable bridge connecting internal and external reality, the only path strong enough to support testing, orderly learning, and progress. Formal language is the language of science. Historically, for as long as we mistakenly conflated $\mathbb{R}$ and $\mathbb{SR}$ together, we couldn't understand why science did so well in solving some problems and so poorly in solving what we might call 'human problems'. The answer, we now know, is that, as presently constituted, science only understands and investigates $\mathbb{R}$, but has always lacked the tools to understand and investigate $\mathbb{SR}$. Faceted model-oriented reasoning supplies that deficit, so that now science can begin to competently explore and understand the complexity of semantic reality.

In order to understand why formal languages are so important in the development of new knowledge about realities, stop for a moment and think about what we are trying to do here:

we want to build models in our minds of the realities that exist *between* us, but we need to have a way to independently verify the accuracy of those models, since we can no longer rely on that somatic feeling of certainty that is stimulated when we associate ideas with our core truths. To validate our models of the unknown, we must be able to express our thoughts in a complete and unambiguous language that others can understand and verify or correct. The only messages that can be unambiguously transmitted are those whose context and goal are explicit, hence, we can only verify thoughts that are expressed in a formal language.

Lesson Four: Truth is a matrix, not a scalar

We know from Limits 1 and 2 that both $\mathbb{R}$ and $\mathbb{SR}$ are real, and since realities are completely separate, this means that there are no shared attributes between them. Since they have no shared attributes, physical and semantic reality must therefore have completely different truth functions that evaluate different attributes using different standards. From Limit 4 we know that $\mathbb{CS}$ is personal, so it also has to have its own truth function, but since we know from Limit 5 that our mind is an aggregate of layers, then we also know that one truth function for each of these domains will not suffice, since there has to be at least one for each layer of the model.

A truth matrix is shown in table 5.2 below. The columns represent the domain a statement applies to: personal space ($\mathbb{CS}$), group space ($\mathbb{SR}$), or physical reality ($\mathbb{R}$). The rows represent the truth function for each intellect level from L0 to L3.

	$\mathbb{CS}$	$\mathbb{SR}$	$\mathbb{R}$
L0	$t \propto \frac{1}{\theta(i,a)}$	——	$t \propto \frac{|V_{t+1}|}{|V_t|}$
L1	$t \propto \frac{|S_2|}{|S_1|}$	$t \propto \frac{|S_2|}{|S_1|}$	$t \propto \frac{|S_2|}{|S_1|}$
L2	$P_i \to P_k$	$t \propto \frac{|G'+m|}{|G'|}$	$|m_i - r_i| < \epsilon$
L3	$t \propto (v,p)$	——	$|m_i - r_i| < \epsilon$

Table 5.2: Truth matrix

Here's how to read the table row by row, starting from the top:

(L0, $\mathbb{CS}$) In our personal cognitive space, ($\mathbb{CS}$), L0 (belief) truth is inversely proportional to the angle (θ) between the idea (i) and archetype vectors (a).[5] To put this in words, the more similar something is to the archetype of badness, the worse it is, and the closer it is to the goodness archetype, the better it is.

(L0, $\mathbb{SR}$) L0 truth is undefined in the semantic reality space since L0 is unaware that semantic reality exists. L0 only deals in interest/belief truths,

----

[5] In a quantitative model, ideas are represented by multidimensional arrays, which are flattened for easy calculation. See *Ultrareasoning* for details, but for now just try to understand that ideas can be modeled, and that the more ideas differ, the greater the angle between the vectors representing them.

so this cell is empty.

(L0, $\mathbb{R}$) The L0 truth of a statement about $\mathbb{R}$ is *imposed* on a species by natural selection, not defined by an action or thought on the part of the L0 mind. The expression means that this truth is proportional to the amount by which the post-action vitality (V_{t+1}) exceeds the pre-action vitality (V_t). That is, an organism can evaluate a threat any way it wants to, but natural selection will cull those that are too wrong, since nature tends to punish holders of ideas that decrease vitality, sometimes by ending their genetic line.

(L1, $\mathbb{CS}$) L1 (experience) truth in $\mathbb{CS}$ is proportional to how much an action improves a situation. A **situation** (S) is a collection of recorded observations, and an action is good/true to the extent that the post-action situation has a higher positive evaluation than the pre-action situation. This is the only truth that L1 knows, so the same calculation applies to external phenomena in semantic and physical reality.

(L1, $\mathbb{SR}$) $t \propto \frac{|S_2|}{|S_1|}$

(L1, $\mathbb{R}$) $t \propto \frac{|S_2|}{|S_1|}$

(L2, $\mathbb{CS}$) Internal L2 truth is based solely on whether one

pattern (P_i) connects to another (P_k) in one's
L2 intellect, since connected ideas inherit the
truth value of the containing opinion object.
This means that anyone can make any idea true
in their own mind, regardless of what reality, or
anyone else, says. Informal logic, consistency,
and 'makes sense' are all examples of L2 self-
validating truth.

(L2, $\mathbb{SR}$) L2 semantic reality truth can be either internal or external, the calculation is the same in
both, the only difference being whether the
terms are informally or formally defined. $|G'|$
is the magnitude of the strength of the bonds
in a semantic reality subset, what we know as a
group. The message is true to the extent that
the strength of a set of bonds in the group is
greater with the message $(|G'|+m)$ than it was
before the message $(|G'|)$.

(L2, $\mathbb{R}$) L2 physical reality truth is defined by the variance between an idea (m_i) and its referent (r_i).
When that difference is smaller than the allowed margin of error (ϵ), then the idea is true.
This truth test is rarely used (rigorously, at
least) outside of technical trades or scientific
disciplines.

(L3, $\mathbb{CS}$) Internal L3 truth is based on a calculation of an idea's viability (resistance to contradiction), and productivity (ability to generate queries with non-empty result sets). This calculation can only be done by the L3 intellect itself, so it will be unfamiliar to those who have not yet activated L3.[6]

(L3, $\mathbb{SR}$) L3 semantic reality truth is not yet defined, since it has not yet been observed (that is, as of this time, no L3 idea not already converted to an L2 pattern has been shown to have an effect in $\mathbb{SR}$).

(L3, $\mathbb{R}$) The physical reality truth of an L3 idea is exactly the same as for an L2 idea, $|m_i - r_i| < \epsilon$, and is established using the same scientific protocol of reproducible formal tests.

It's important to understand that table 5.2 also reads from the bottom-up, as well as from the top-down. The bottom up reading is that any idea in the lower rows is also always subject to the truth calculations in the rows above it. For example, the highest level, most abstract L3 model with a given viability and productivity truth measure will also fit into existing L2

---

[6] In *Pinnacle Questions*, L3 is introduced as the discovery learning mechanism, and in *Pinnacle Reasoning*, it is named the Discovery Intellect. The term L3 first appears with the introduction of the universal cognition model in *Ultrareasoning*.

conceptual schemes and either be verified by, or perhaps falsify, them. Then, as soon as the idea is used in rational calculations or a reality, it will gain an L1 experience level truth measure, and finally, once we are comfortable with an idea's reliability (positive or negative), we will assign it an L0 emotional truth value. Similarly, all ideas that generate results in $\mathbb{R}$ are ultimately evaluated at the (L0, $\mathbb{R}$) level by the harsh judgment of physical reality.

Lesson Five: Think in Multiple Dimensions

The multiplicity of realities and the truth matrix should force us to realize that we have to begin thinking in multiple dimensions simultaneously, rather than focusing simple linear thought on a single truth value. Intellectuals made the mistake of reacting to the discovery that there is not a single truth with the utterly idiotic conclusion that there is, therefore, no real truth, and have consequently spent the better part of the last century promulgating a nihilistic philosophy based on that error.

The fact that there is not one truth obviously means that there is more than one, but it would be as wrong to conclude that there are an infinite, or meaningless, number of truths, as it has been to conclude that there is none. Truth is a measure of a correlation between two or more things, such as a mental model and a phenomenon in reality. Since there are a limited number of realities, and a limited number of cognitive levels, we can calculate that there is a small, finite number of different truths. Furthermore, since in the cognitive apparatus truths are constrained to serve the purpose of aligning volitional action with reality to better achieve a goal, then the definition of truth can never be arbitrary.

As a first example of thinking in multiple dimensions, let us take the case of a person or group asserting as fact some description of reality that is demonstrably false, that is, lying for gain. The way opponents react now is they grab onto this factual discrepancy and triumphantly claim that this exposes the error of the group, and then are invariably surprised when the group grows stronger on the lie, rather than dissolving immediately. But, as previously explained, truth in semantic reality is not related to correlation between idea and physical reality, but is solely determined by the degree to which the message strengthens and extends the group bonds. Thus, an idea can be both factually incorrect but semantically true at the same time, and the semantic truth dimension can be of far greater consequence than the physical reality error dimension.

Protesting that this bifurcation of truth, and the possible subordination of fact to feeling is neither right nor rational, is a lot like arguing that gravity is unjust because it can make things fall down and break, and thereby make the beautiful ugly. But, just as gravity simply *is* — regardless of how it impacts your interests — so the several independent dimensions of truth exist simply by virtue of the definition of truth in each reality, and the multiplicity of contexts and perspectives.

L2 consistency truth is the weakest of all truths because it is only internally validated and is completely isolated from external reality, yet it is most highly prized by academics and intellectuals. What a surprise.

L2 thinking is linear with branching at decision points, but we can get around this limitation by gently introducing multiple dimensions into our thought just by reminding ourselves of the simple fact that L2 truth means nothing without external verification. Even when a reproducible test is not practical, it is demonstrably better to check L2 ideas against our own experience, against the experience of a competent group, or against the historical record, rather than simply relying on an idea's rhetorical presentation and so-called logical consistency with other L2 ideas as our only test of truth.

The primary justification for relying on L2 logic and consistency checks as a measure of truth of an idea is that it is thought that they act as a heuristic for predicting the degree to which the larger pattern/plan to which the idea belongs can be relied on to agree with reality. While this parochial rule of thumb does allow us to construct elaborate conceptual constructs that seem to hang together, it tends to divert our attention away from the fact that L2 ideas, logical or not, by their very nature have an undefined relation to any external reality. It is a mistake to think that internal verification is sufficient to validate otherwise untested ideas when this is clearly not the case, no matter what your logic or consistency checks seem to tell you.

L1 truth is both handy (since we mostly make it ourselves), and reliable (to the extent that current conditions match historical conditions). It is valuable because it has been tested in a reality outside of our mind. While these tests are informal and restricted to our domain of experience, the fact that L1 truths are inherently tested to some degree gives them a claim on legitimacy that untested L2 ideas simply cannot have.

Pure L0 truth is closest to the bone in the sense that the archetypes are validated in a given ecological niche by natural selection, and traditional beliefs based on it are roughly as reliable as the age of the tradition. The weaknesses of L0 beliefs are that they are entirely defined by the CS distortion field of the primitive self, they are highly resistant to change, and essentially incapable of growth.

Admittedly, becoming adept in running ideas through multiple layers of truth analysis takes a bit of practice, but since the truth values have already been calculated by the various cognitive levels, we don't actually have to work to generate them, we just have to query for them. Once we are aware of the many dimensions of truth and their various functions, then it is just a matter of decision and determination to choose to defer to the truth of reality, rather than choosing to rely entirely on some throbbing sense of conviction in our chest.

Religion is an excellent example of a subject that cannot be understood with linear thought, since it usually embodies three distinct, and often inconsistent, levels of truth in its teachings:

1. ℂ𝕊 level: beliefs provide a loopback[7] function and a transcendent aspirational goal;

2. 𝕊ℝ level: creed and rituals have a strong grouping effect that can support large and growing societies;

3. ℝ level: creed provides explanations of natural phenomena.

Intellectuals, of course, bail on religion when they discover that religion's third dimension, explanations of natural phenomena, is error-filled, but they neglect to credit the other, much more important dimensions. Largely on the basis of this marginal issue, modern intellectual atheists idiotically declare that everyone should create their own ethical and moral systems, certainly one of the worst ideas ever conceived.

Interestingly, while they are enthusiastically throwing away religion, intellectuals never seem to notice that the first level of religious truth actually dictates that evolution created god. So, for them to call religion nothing but the superstition of the ignorant, puts them in the curious position of supporting magical thinking over evolution. Odd.

---

[7]See appendix D, and p159.

The second level of religious truth, that of group formation, is interesting in that historically it seems that religions are often warlike in their early political stage, but as their failure on level three becomes more obvious, they tend to reform to focus almost exclusively on the first two levels of truth. It is truly frightening to think that atheists want to discard this civilizing progress in favor of having ignorant self-seekers start the process all over again.

It should be obvious by now that, with the addition of just a touch of multidimensional thinking to the mix, we have been able to considerably elevate the discussion and understanding of the function of religion and its truths in just a few paragraphs.

However, when we experiment with multidimensional thought it is important to keep in mind the fact that, while questions should be open, and answers nuanced, nevertheless, decisions often have to be quick and certain. So, however adept we become in the abstract, the ability to quickly reduce complexity to simplicity will always remain an indispensable skill in effective decision making, and in life.

Chapter 6

Summary

One of the reasons we haven't previously recognized that normal stupidity is built-in to our cognitive structure is because traditional mores and customs have generally been pretty effective at keeping us away from the edge, so nothing was forcing us to look for this issue. Admittedly, the traditional approach of distilling limits from experience has come at the cost of shutting down the type of free exploration that leads to innovation, but since we never even suspected that the discovery intellect existed in the first place, the amount of exploration we could have done without knowing how to use it, wouldn't have amounted to much in any case.

The power of quantitative models is that they state issues clearly in ways that support calculation, communication, deep

reasoning, testing, and computerization. Before now, the lack of
good models, and our use of rhetorical reasoning[1] in our primitive L0 and L1 intellects, restricted our attempts to understand
cognition and epistemology to the level of vapid L2 ruminations.
Now that we are able to create clear, crisp, quantitative models,
we can finally move on to explore and understand $\mathbb{SR}$ in ways
that were never before possible with wordy reasoning.

Super stupidity inevitably results when the educated elite re-
move the brakes on our hubris that were historically maintained
by traditional virtues. When people throw away cultural wisdom, religion, respect and humility, and replace them all with
new, untested, secular religions of their own making, disaster is
both imminent and inevitable, with but a small bit of unknown
around the timing of the coming blow.

Unrelenting attacks by the educated elite on belief and morality as being superstitious holdovers from primitive, ignorant
cultures, have long eroded our confidence in traditional beliefs
and values. We need to stop giving ground on these critical,
fundamental issues, and understand that preserving both our
values and our relationship with the ultimate is an appropriate,
and entirely modern adaptation to the realities of the normally
stupid nature of our cognitive equipment. The difference now is
that we no longer have to appeal solely to authority or tradition
to justify our values, since the universal cognition model shows

---

[1] This is explained later, on p243.

that sound, ultimate-connected values are not only entirely consistent with our cognition limits, but actually required by the very nature of cognitive function.

L3, exploratory learning, progressive querying, charging up query points, are all unfamiliar terms, but the fact remains that the L3 intellect is real, and that learning discovery is a process that can lead to learning explosions that can open entirely new vistas to explore. Once we get used to them, these higher level mental functions, which seem so exotic now, will soon be seen as what they are: perfectly normal cognitive functions that exist in all entities at or above our level of evolution that allow us to systematically explore and discover the unknown.

Part II

Super Stupidity

Chapter 7

Super Stupidity

Super stupidity is not a vice of the ignorant, because it takes education to achieve stupidity on a monumental scale. Universities cultivate an arrogance in their students which gives them license to disrespect traditional values, heretofore the only reliable indicator of the cognition limits of normal stupidity. Intellectuals and academics complete the transition from normal to super stupidity by waltzing past the cognition limits to push their latest ill-considered ideological blueprint for reinventing the world.

The crux of super stupidity is imbalance, the slighting of one or more of the internal and external realities in preference to a favored one, generally undervaluing $\mathbb{R}$ and overvaluing $\mathbb{SR}$. The reason we have to be concerned with super stupidity, the reason it is such a serious problem, is because it continually disconnects $\mathbb{SR}$ actions and rewards from $\mathbb{R}$ realities. This disconnect is an issue because virtually all of the most important human problems concern making arrangements in $\mathbb{SR}$ to allocate access to $\mathbb{R}$ resources in a way that benefits certain targeted populations at the expense of others. But, disconnecting the two in a way that disrespects physical reality itself can never succeed for very long, because, whether we like it or not, all of our realities balance on a pivot in $\mathbb{R}$, a balance that requires attention and effort to maintain, and which we neglect at our peril.

By destroying the link between thought and reality, super stupidity makes it impossible to make progress in developing solutions to the constrained resource problems which define and encompass mortality. Super stupidity tends to breed and multiply in the hothouse of higher education because the academy enrobes itself in an arrogance bubble to create an isolated subculture in which its unchecked ideas can rule supreme without fear of being contradicted by the harsh winds of reality. In this cloister, they can concoct elaborate, even insane, socio-political constructs on a scale grandiose enough to eat away at the sinews of civilization itself.

But, the most serious problem arises when super stupidity is combined with florid rhetoric, because this mix can produce a fertile growth medium for noxious organizations that can attack outsiders without conscience, because their only goal is to warp semantic reality enough to draw maximum advantages to the few at the top.

Defining Super Stupidity

The value of taking the time to define super stupidity quantitatively is that it elevates the term above the level of a mere insult and makes it an actual observable measure of thought quality. It also quantifies the fact that not all stupidity is created equal, as well as the fact that there are distinct levels of super stupidity, all of which are greater than normal stupidity, but some of which are much, much worse than others. The formal definition of `super stupidity` is:

$$S^s : \text{super stupidity}$$

$$S^n : \text{normal stupidity}$$

$$S^s = |S^n| \cdot \prod_{i=0}^{i=n} |v_i| \tag{7.1}$$

While this formulaic definition is meant to be more illustrative than calculable, it does, in fact, legitimately fulfill both functions. In words, the formula says that

Super Stupidity equals the magnitude of normal stupidity times the product of the magnitude (range: $1 \ldots$ `MAX`) of all the limit violations committed in a given event or interval.

Those familiar with modeling will understand that setting $|S^n|$ to any nominal value suffices to allow us to calculate how much worse super stupidity is than normal stupidity, whether or not one can accurately quantify the magnitude of normal stupidity in the first place.

The term v_i in formula 7.1 refers to violations of cognition limit principles, the magnitude of which can be assessed as a value in the range of 1 to MAX (whatever MAX is in the model). Precisely which limits are being violated in a particular case can be determined simply by applying the limit and principle definitions listed below to observed actions and words in $\mathbb{SR}$.

The magnitude of super stupidity can be calculated either on an instance, or a lifetime level. In a simulation, one would test the effect each type of super stupidity has on social dynamics across the range of allowed values (probably 1..3 since the numbers get very large very quickly, and certainly no more than 1..10, since we need to prevent a combinatorial explosion from needlessly complicating analysis of multidimensional cases).

Limit Principles

Limit 1 ($\mathbb{R}$ is real) **principles:**

1.1 do not assert idea truth over verified $\mathbb{R}$ facts

1.2 do not refute verified facts with feelings

1.4 do not make value statements about $\mathbb{R}$

1.5 do not assert that $\mathbb{R}$ facts prove $\mathbb{SR}, \mathbb{CS}$ values

1.6 do not credit affective language statements about $\mathbb{R}$

Limit 2 ($\mathbb{SR}$ is real) **principles:**

2.1 do not deny that $\mathbb{SR}$ depends on $\mathbb{R}$

2.2 do not neglect the significance of semantic gravity

2.3 do not conflate $\mathbb{SR}$ with $\mathbb{R}$

2.4 do not confuse $\mathbb{SR}$ and $\mathbb{R}$ truths

2.5 do not relate $\mathbb{SR}$ power and integrity to non-link sources (such as doctrines)

2.6 do not confuse $\mathbb{CS}$ evaluation with $\mathbb{SR}$ power (it is the aggregate of evaluations)

Limit 3 (Mortality is real) **principles:**

3.1 do not deny mortality interests

3.2 do not shirk responsibility for providing for mortal needs

3.3 do not fail to assume mortal responsibilities

Limit 4 ($\mathbb{CS}$ is real) **principles:**

4.1 do not deny that $\mathbb{CS}$ depends on $\mathbb{R}$

4.2 do not confuse internal with external reality

4.3 do not conflate $\mathbb{CS}$ ideas with $\mathbb{R}$ or $\mathbb{SR}$ realities

4.4 do not mistake $\mathbb{CS}$ ideas with $\mathbb{SR}$ messages

4.5 do not imagine others can, or should, see your $\mathbb{CS}$ truths

Limit 5 (Mind evolved in layers) **principles:**

5.1 do not confuse passion with knowledge

5.2 do not assume experience cannot become outdated

5.3 do not assume reasoning accurately describes external reality

5.4 do not separate knowledge from its truth function

5.5 do not reason across truth domains (truth on one level does not imply truth on another level)

Limit 6 (Error exceeds content) **principles**:

6.1 do not presume discrete model knowledge is complete

6.2 do not infer the truth of untested models based on a discrete model fact

6.3 do not compare discrete model completeness

6.4 do not dismiss anomalies

Character Flaws and Super Stupidity

To make it easier to see super stupidity in familiar terms, we will break down recognizable character flaws into a list of the violations involved in each, thus allowing each flaw to be scored on the super stupid index. Although talking about character flaws makes it seem like we have veered into a discussion of morality, we actually haven't, because morality is really just a means of wrapping lessons learned blindly from experience into value commands that can be easily and long remembered. Traditional (as opposed to academic or authority) wisdom has been very successful over the ages in helping us to avoid problems, even ones we don't fully understand, precisely because what sounds like prescriptive commands are really just hard-won lessons from experience.

At a very abstract level, the character flaws we will discuss can all be subsumed under just one or two categories, but to make the discussion more accessible, we will discuss seven different kinds of disrespect in addition to another six avoidable failures. Each of these failures involve one or more violations that multiply together to define its measure of super stupidity. Actual scoring of each violation would, of course, be done on a case by case basis by assigning severity measures to the violations listed. In the examples below, we will assume that the maximum value in our model is 3.

Disrespect

We begin with the seven examples of disrespect. The essence of disrespect is the exchange of accuracy for power: one disrespects another in order to bend the space between self and other in such a way as to draw resources from them to oneself. This applies whether the reality one is disrespecting is a person, a concept, a tradition, or an actual reality.

Disrespect of $\mathbb{R}$

Disrespecting $\mathbb{R}$ violates Limit 1, so it has a maximum super stupidity value of $(3 \cdot |S^n|)$.

Disrespecting $\mathbb{R}$ is always a losing proposition in the long term, but it is an extremely common phenomenon that arises from the interplay between the various realities. The most immediate way to disrespect $\mathbb{R}$ is to insist that your feelings or ideology trump scientifically verified facts. However, an equally powerful, albeit less recognized, way to disrespect $\mathbb{R}$ is to insist that some verity in $\mathbb{R}$ proves your policy in $\mathbb{SR}$, or your opinion in $\mathbb{CS}$. Projecting truth from $\mathbb{R}$ to $\mathbb{CS}$ is exactly as wrong as projecting truth from $\mathbb{CS}$ to $\mathbb{R}$.

Statements actually describing $\mathbb{R}$ do not have a value component (nothing in $\mathbb{R}$ has a value component), therefore, statements posed in affective language are not, and can never be, actually about $\mathbb{R}$ (whether they are about $\mathbb{SR}$ or $\mathbb{CS}$ is something that has to be determined in each case).

Obviously, disrespecting $\mathbb{R}$ can only bend the space in $\mathbb{CS}$ and $\mathbb{SR}$, and have no effect whatsoever on $\mathbb{R}$ itself. Thus, while disrespecting $\mathbb{R}$ can enrich one in $\mathbb{SR}$, or offer rewards in one's private emotional and intellectual space, it also can, depending on the details, expose the specific and extended self to potentially fatal hazard.

Disrespect of $\mathbb{SR}$

Disrespecting $\mathbb{SR}$ violates Limit 2, so it has a maximum super stupidity value of $(3 \cdot |S^n|)$.

It is a fallacy to think that organizations exist in $\mathbb{R}$ like any physical object or action. The reality is that organizations only exist in $\mathbb{SR}$, and $\mathbb{SR}$ is wholly defined by the concept of the organization that is embodied in the graph construct made up of ξ nodes and $\mathcal{M}$ message links. Organizations do involve physical bodies, and they do allocate and consume resources, so they have a distinct manifestation in $\mathbb{R}$, but the abstract graph that defines them, and the message evaluation that gives the links weight, exist only on the semantic reality level. Thinking that organizations and associations are actually phenomena in $\mathbb{R}$, similar to rocks and water, blinds one to the essential facts and mechanisms by which groups operate, and renders one clueless about their largely predictable actions.

Since the message recipient assigns the value attribute to received messages, and it is the value attribute that warps semantic and cognitive space, then these spaces are therefore unevenly curved or warped. We can easily understand this non-uniform distortion field around nodes as gravity, and use standard mathematics[1] to analyze it. Failure to understand this concept of semantic gravity dooms one to blindly grope about for clues to explain human and group behavior, instead of being able to directly attack the problem analytically.

---

[1] We just have to remember that gravity in semantic reality is asymmetrical.

Disrespect of Tradition

Disrespecting tradition violates Limits 1, 2, 3, 4, and 6, so it has a maximum super stupidity value of ($3^5 \cdot |S^n| = 243 \cdot |S^n|$).

For the last century or so, it has seemed that learning to despise traditional practices and values is the first prerequisite to satisfying the requirements for being considered an intellectual. The problem is that, by discarding traditional wisdom and practices in favor of 'rationality' and the ideology du jour, one violates five of the six cognitive limits.

The core violation involved in disrespecting tradition is that the mind can only do this by assuming that perception is objective and that education is the process of perfecting our ability to see reality ever more clearly as it really is. Assuming clarity of vision and completeness of understanding violates the principles of error exceeding content and of the reality of external realities, as well as ignoring the fact that our cognition creates its own internal reality. Disrespecting tradition demotes mortality concerns to the level of a detail of existence whose significance pales in comparison to the importance of the fruits of one's shining intellect.

So powerful is the effect of nascent ideological possession that, not unlike the rush of first love/lust, it induces a heady intoxication that fills one with a completely unwarranted sense of confidence and superiority, and disrespect for the lessons of others.

Disrespect of Religion

Disrespecting religion violates Limits 1, 2, 3, 4, 5, 6, so it has a maximum super stupidity value of ($3^6 \cdot |S^n| = 729 \cdot |S^n|$).

Disrespecting religion is so universal among sophisticates, intellectuals, and academics, while being so incredibly, inexcusably stupid and intellectually bankrupt, that it merits a chapter of its own.[2]

For now, suffice it to say that, anyone who, in the full flower of their intellectual awareness, loudly claims to all and sundry that "God does not exist!" brands himself as somewhat less bright and less sensible than members of the flat earth society or the Big Foot brigade, because you at least have to refer to evidence to refute those idiots, while the anti-religionists can be refuted with a single definition.

Disrespect of the Individual

Disrespecting the individual violates Limits 1, 2, 3, 4, 5, 6, so it has a maximum super stupidity value of ($3^6 \cdot |S^n| = 729 \cdot |S^n|$).

The great achievement of western civilization and the enlightenment has been to recognize and elevate the individual, and most particularly, the individual's inherent right to free inquiry and independent initiative, as a primary focus in the

---

[2]See chapter 8.

cultural discussion of meaning and purpose. The collectivist philosophies, primarily Marxist (and neo-Marxist, which is Marxism with a healthy dose of cultural appropriation), seek to supplant the individual as the center of concern with some arbitrarily defined class of imaginary oppressed victims. Such disrespect for the primacy of individual rights and responsibilities demonstrably threatens both the freedom and prosperity of the whole populace.

Demoting the individual from the autonomous center of potential and moral responsibility down into an anonymous cog in some dystopian class machine subsumes $\mathbb{R}$ to an authoritarian $\mathbb{SR}$ whose major goal is to crush the genius of the most motivated $\mathbb{CS}$s. That it also devalues mortality in favor of the fictional dignity of an imaginary class of automatons, and presumes that we already know enough to engineer society into its final shape (the "end of history"), marks the collectivist compulsion to disrespect the individual as perhaps the most invidious and pernicious intellectual fetish to which the vainglorious intellectual can succumb.

Disrespect of Knowledge

Disrespecting knowledge violates Limits 1, 2, 3, 4, 5, 6, so it has a maximum super stupidity value of ($3^6 \cdot |S^n| = 729 \cdot |S^n|$)

If we define knowledge as an organized system of operational descriptions of entities, forces, or relations in a reality domain, then we can immediately understand that elevating anything above the importance of accuracy and integrity of these usable descriptions severely compromises their quality and utility. Knowledge has to be prioritized above other values both to maintain its validity as a guide in a reality, and for it to support our inquiry into discovery of the unknown.

To the extent that we confine knowledge within belief, ideological, or social constraints, we confine that knowledge to the already known, and clip its potential to lead us into new discoveries. Confining inquiry aborts our ability to learn, and crippling learning kills the potential for progress. In order to get the maximum benefit of learning we have to allow knowledge to lead to knowledge, so we cannot start an inquiry with the intention of reaching, or defending, a certain goal. Forcing learning to develop knowledge that supports certain conclusions is like burning your bridges in front of you — it only guarantees that any progress you make will, at best, be in an orbit around your original position.

Preparing for an opinion argument, or its demented cousin, the debate, generally involves marshaling facts in support of a firmly held belief. More than just a waste of time, this attitude that learning and knowledge are just servants that can be forced to do your bidding is a crime against culture, a crime of potentially the highest order, since it violates all of the limits simultaneously.

Disrespect of the Unknown

Disrespecting the unknown violates Limits 1, 2, 3, 4, 5, 6, so it has a maximum super stupidity value of ($3^6 \cdot |S^n| = 729 \cdot |S^n|$)

Everyone who is ignorant of the existence or power of L3 cannot but be disrespectful of the unknown. The key insight that has apparently escaped almost everyone before now is just not that difficult:

> **We know external reality by building models of it inside our head. The only way to build these models is through unprejudiced, probing queries whose results we can add to a model that is itself a testable query. The correlation between these internal models and external reality is undefined. The only way to determine how accurate our models are, is by using reproducible tests.**

Once you have the obvious insight that **we think inside of our head**, and accept that our models are only partial at best, it's not that hard to see that model building is an essential part of learning that absolutely depends on L3 discovery learning, and furthermore, that L2 pattern processing is only adequate for applying known solutions to known problems.

L3 discovery learning is the only reliable way to probe the unknown. Our future will be defined by our progress in learning about our realities, and the only way to do that is by probing, discovering, and learning about the unknown. The dull, arrogant thought that the future can be discovered by committees whose major concern is avoiding error, represents the height of disrespect for the unknown and for our need to continue to learn about it.

Hubris

Hubris violates Limits 1, 2, 3, 6, so it has a maximum super stupidity value of ($3^4 \cdot |S^n| = 81 \cdot |S^n|$)

In its excessive overestimation of one's own abilities, hubris implies disrespect for everything else, but the emphasis in hubris is on its effect of supplanting realities from their rightful place as our ultimate focus of concern with our own overweening sense of power, control, and entitlement. Hubris was recognized as one of the earliest sins, and it remains so to this day, so much so, that its negative aspect hardly needs to be explained.

Irresponsibility

Irresponsibility violates Limits 1, 2, 3, 6, so it has a maximum super stupidity value of ($3^4 \cdot |S^n| = 81 \cdot |S^n|$)

Of the many ways to look at irresponsibility, the perspective most suited to current conditions is to see it as a failure to grow up, to mature. It is pathological for post-adolescents not to leave their parents' nest, not to feel the need to take control of providing for themselves, not to need to control and run their own life. The irresponsible live in a consequence-free bubble — at least in their own minds — and they are quite content to continue in this state as long as their providers are willing to maintain that bubble for them. Whether there are addictions, bad habits, or just immature attitudes and behaviors involved in the causation chain leading to it, all irresponsibility involves the failure to respect external realities and to understand the need to grapple effectively with them.

Sloth

Sloth violates Limits 1, 2, 3, so it has a maximum super stupidity value of $(3^3 \cdot |S^n| = 27 \cdot |S^n|)$

As volitionally mobile creatures, we are the embodiment of the proposition that movement solutions to mortality issues enhance viability. Take movement out of the equation, and you have a plant, or an anchored parasite. Movement in $\mathbb{R}$ is easy to understand, but the concept also applies to the other realities: in $\mathbb{SR}$, movement includes communication as well as action, and in $\mathbb{CS}$, it equates to expanding understanding through exploration and learning. Sloth can appear in these realities as: immobility, social isolation, or a lack of curiosity and intellectual initiative.

Think of us as cognitive sharks: we need stimulation and interaction to cognitively breathe, or we waste away. Sloth disrespects all internal and external realities, and narrows our radius of concern and accomplishment.

Inconstancy

Inconstancy violates Limits 1, 2, 3, so it has a maximum super stupidity value of $(3^3 \cdot |S^n| = 27 \cdot |S^n|)$

Irresponsibility, sloth, and inconstancy are all different facets of the same failure gem. Achieving anything significant in any reality takes a considerable amount of time and effort. Those who are unwilling, or unable, to sustain a focused effort over the long haul, and are only able to produce in short bursts, will never take their place in the first rank of producers or explorers.

Alienation

Alienation violates Limits 1, 2, 3, 4, so it has a maximum super stupidity value of $(3^4 \cdot |S^n| = 81 \cdot |S^n|)$

The more economically and strategically successful a society is, and the longer providers are willing to support an extended adolescence, the more that a sense of alienation will become the dominant attitude in the ranks of the educated elite. Alienation[3] is *not* a sign of enlightenment; cynicism is **not** wisdom,

---

[3] The mechanism is discussed extensively in *The Structure of Truth*.

not a worldly attitude, it is a mental illness. Alienation is cured by acquiring usable knowledge consistent with credible values, it is neither to be cultivated nor indulged, not by the group nor by the individual.

Cowardice

Cowardice violates Limits 1, 2, 3, so it has a maximum super stupidity value of ($3^3 \cdot |S^n| = 27 \cdot |S^n|$)

Cowardice is engagement paralysis. Instead of failing to engage due to laziness or malorientation, cowardice is the failure to risk engagement for fear of possible consequences. Cowardice is easy to simulate by maximizing the risk aversion parameter, and minimizing activity enough so as to maximize the time between engagements with reality. Cowardice represents the pathological belief that mortality can be preserved through rationing resources enough to reduce the frequency of the need for risk or adventure, as if mortality could be hoarded and extended through sipping slowly enough at life so that the risk of interacting with reality can be indefinitely deferred.

Conclusion

Super stupidity is not an insult, it is a formal description of a morally and intellectually defective state that L2 cognitive entities can choose to inhabit or to avoid. Super stupidity blocks both individual and group intellectual progress, and wreaks havoc on our social and political institutions.

Super stupidity is not merely a subjective invective, it can be measured and verified. It is distinct from normal stupidity because, rather than being structural and unavoidable, on the contrary, it is entirely caused by bad personal choices made by the educated elite.

The amount of super stupidity present in a speech, article, book, or comment can be calculated by identifying each instance of each limit violation and multiplying them all together. Ordinarily, this will give you a very large number because most of the samples you will be scoring will be coming from university educated people.

The formal definition of super stupidity gives us a way to quantify the fact that our civilization is drowning in it.

Chapter 8

Religion

In order to earn the title of *intellectual*, you must start with a natural affinity for pattern manipulation, use it to acquire a useless degree, and then talk endlessly about all the butterfly thoughts flitting about in your head. That's about it.[1]

Oh, but we mustn't forget the air of irreligious sophistication that intellectuals and academics flaunt like a silk ascot, it can hardly be separated from the degree granted by a prestigious university. No self-respecting intellectual (who doesn't actually make a living doing it) will admit to being religious. Why do they all reject religion? Because they are so *smart*. Sorry, just kidding, it's because they are super stupid.

Why is it super stupid to categorically reject religion as a

---

[1]The rest of the intellectual's sad little story will be explained in chapter 9.

badge of sophistication? Well, it shows disrespect for all the limits:

Limit 1: $\mathbb{R}$ is real,

Limit 2: $\mathbb{SR}$ is real,

Limit 3: mortality is real,

Limit 4: $\mathbb{CS}$ is real,

Limit 5: mind evolved in layers,

Limit 6: error exceeds content.

This means that gratuitously rejecting religion to signify one's elevated intellectual station is 729 times stupider than the normal stupidity baseline. While the significance of this particular number is undefined (the formula has yet to be tested extensively and iteratively refined), the meaning of it is simple: rejecting the entire concept of religion in favor of a modern, untested replacement is much more likely to lead to catastrophe than anything that believers could ever do. History unequivocally bears this prediction out.

Since it may not be obvious yet to the reader how summarily dismissing religion violates all six limits, we will go through them all, but it will be easier to understand if we start at number six and proceed backwards to number one.

Limit 6: What motivates someone to elevate the value of their **untested** internal thought above the level of millennia of civilized experience? There is no question but that there is much to be corrected and improved in the body of traditional knowledge and practice, but even when the time comes that we will want to make some changes to improve on the religious model, the way forward will be the way of scientific progress, i.e., slow and halting, because every step will require elaborate testing to verify, and often to correct, the new model. It will not be suddenly illuminated by an adolescent's conviction that a few days of his thought is valuable enough to overturn the accumulated knowledge of all of his predecessors. Especially an adolescent who is unaware of the cognitive limit that error exceeds content, that the error between his thought and external reality far exceeds the amount of content in his ideas.

Intellectuals who reject viable and productive 4D solution systems and replace them with untested personal ideas to prove how educated they are, are guilty of as complete a violation of Limit 6 as can be imagined, because their position only makes sense if Limit 6 is rejected altogether.

Limit 5: The Limit 6 violation hides the fact that declaring religion to be false, that God does not exist, violates the limit that the mind evolved in lay-

ers because it attempts to refute both L2 ideas
and $\mathbb{S}$ itself with a scalar truth, instead of working through the truth matrix for every level and
reality.

Limit 4: Not understanding the layered nature of our mental faculties and truth functions, means that you
also do not understand the crucial role that $\mathbb{S}$
plays in $\mathbb{CS}$ to make L2 work at all well.

Limit 3: The Limit 6 violation means that you are conflating ideas and mortality concerns to impute
the invulnerability of abstractions to the profoundly vulnerable mortal frame. Social engineering based only on ideas, rather than on the
codification of experience, is the shortest route
to disaster.

Limit 2: The Limit 6 violation denies the reality of $\mathbb{SR}$ by
averring that semantic gravity can be overcome
by enlightened intentions. The assumption implicit in the intellectual rejection of religion is
that uneducated people concocted a system of
superstitions to compensate for their ignorance.
This totally ignores the reality and power of $\mathbb{SR}$
gravity to organize hierarchical systems to generate and distribute scarce resources, and the role
that religions have historically played in this pro-

cess.

Limit 1: The Limit 6 violation subordinates experience in $\mathbb{R}$ to your inner knowledge because you are saying we should ignore the dead bodies piled up by previous attempts to implement your ideas because, this time, *your* internal logic and pure motivations can be relied upon to lead us only to good results.

Preferring internal thought that is verified only by internal logic and attested to only by personal belief, over practices validated by documented experience spanning centuries, means that you value all of the external realities less than you do your own personal feelings.

Understand, this refutation applies only to the affectatious, wholesale rejection of religion for being impossibly unsophisticated, for being the primitive crutch of the great unwashed, it does not refer to disciplined, testable analysis. There are, of course, principled ways to come to any judgment on the value of any of the individual facets religious systems, but none of those ways involve using the opinion object to formulate your views,[2] and none of them can dismiss the whole without specifically refuting each and every part.

---

[2]See *Ultrareasoning*, chapters 12, 16, and 23 for details, or just provisionally accept that opinions are essentially algorithms whose only function is to sort incoming messages in a way that we find comfortable. The opinion object does not have any intellectual components in it.

In order to understand fully why the casual dismissal of religion or traditional belief systems is intellectually indefensible, we need to make the effort to formally define religion. The first thing we will notice when we create a formal definition of religion within the universal cognition model is that god is not only not a necessary component of religion, it is actually a more or less negligible detail. In order to see this more easily, we will approach the subject from the $\mathbb{SR}$ perspective to see religion as a group formation force, instead of as a faith or creed issue. While creed is a defining characteristic of a particular religion, it is not, in fact, a defining characteristic of the religious structure in $\mathbb{SR}$.

We might want to define `religion` as a system of ideas and rituals designed to create a community of believers committed to a specific orientation to the ultimate (the spiritual aspect), but this would be incomplete because it omits the historically important function of enforced community behavioral standards (the political aspect). So, let us begin by differentiating between fundamentalist religions, those that have a strong political component, and reformed religions, those that have a weak political component, since this approach will take us directly to the formal definition of religion.

Fundamentalist, pre-reform religions tend to have a strong political component, not just as a means of controlling behavior, but to provide a complete solution for all of their congregants' physical, social, economic, and spiritual problems. Historically, believers seem to demand this, because it seems that they want to know not only what to believe, but what *to do*, that is, how to fill their day with religious acts that can sustain the experience of a connection to the spiritual world in a way that suppresses existential angst during the routine performance of their mundane daily tasks.

The essence of reformation, — even if it takes a while for it to become obvious to the participants themselves — is to subordinate the political to the spiritual and communal aspects of the religion.

With this distinction in mind, we can now define religion in universal terms. First, fundamentalist, pre-reform, religion, ($\mathbf{R}_f$) is defined as the solution tuple:

$$\mathbf{R}_f = (\mathbb{S},\ \mathbb{SR},\ \mathbb{CS},\ \mathbb{R}) \tag{8.1}$$

Reformed religion ($\mathbf{R}_r$) can then naturally be defined as the reduced solution tuple:

$$\mathbf{R}_r = (\mathbb{S},\ \mathbb{SR},\ \mathbb{CS}) \tag{8.2}$$

With these definitions in mind, we can define religion itself as:

Religion: a multidimensional solution tuple including non-null entries for $\mathbb{S}, \mathbb{SR}$ and $\mathbb{CS}$.

That is, fundamentalist religion ($\mathbf{R}_f$) offers solutions in the supernatural/spiritual ($\mathbb{S}$), semantic ($\mathbb{SR}$), internal ($\mathbb{CS}$), and external ($\mathbb{R}$) domains, while reformed religion deemphasizes the political and physical world aspects to focus mainly on the supernatural, semantic, and internal solutions. Abstractly, this means that religion is a comprehensive solution tuple that leverages the capabilities inherent in the supernatural/spiritual domain to provide an integrated solution to the problems in the self, group, and physical reality domains that are caused by our cognition limits.

Whereas fundamentalist religions compel mandatory observance of religious rules, which they insist represent the literal truth of their scriptures, and on which they base their system of truth, in contrast, reformed religions tend to use ritual only as a buttress to support their moral and ethical systems with tradition. Thus, religion does not have to address, or even acknowledge $\mathbb{R}$, but it must situate the believer in a group in relation to the ultimate.

The logical proposition that differentiates these two religious variants seems both universal and simple:

$$\text{either: } \mathbb{S} \supset \mathbb{R} \rightarrow t(s_{\mathbb{S}}) > t(s_{\mathbb{CS}}) \tag{8.3}$$

$$\text{or: } \mathbb{S} \subset \mathbb{I} \rightarrow t(s_{\mathbb{S}}) = \texttt{undefined} \tag{8.4}$$

Expression 8.3 states: the supernatural world is a superset

of the physical world, therefore, statements from supernatural sources are truer than statements coming from our own mind.

Expression 8.4 states: the supernatural world is a subset of our internal world, therefore, the truth of statements from $\mathbb{S}$ is undefined (without a verifiable test), just like the truth of any other statement from $\mathbb{I}$.

We get to choose which of these to assume, either the fundamentalist view, 8.3, or the reform view, 8.4. The modern view that dates from the Enlightenment is that, since events in the natural world can be entirely explained using only natural laws with no need for, or recourse to, the supernatural, then we will assume 8.4 is true, until proven otherwise.

Faceted model-oriented reasoning generalizes this Enlightenment version of Occam's razor to cover all cognition levels in the universal cognition model:

Events and elements in a reality that are fully explained by that reality do not require, or support, explanations from another reality.

In other words, the many religious commandments prescribing behavior consistent with, or proscribing acts inconsistent with, group cohesion, which themselves are consistent with the laws of $\mathbb{SR}$, are not divinely inspired, since they are fully explained within their own reality. To put it bluntly, if the prophet tells me god wants me to give my money to the prophet, then the prophet is lying, because his self-interest requires no divine inspiration.

The intellectual's argument for rejecting all things religious generally takes one or both of the following lines of attack:

- religious statements don't describe $\mathbb{R}$ accurately,
- neither God nor the supernatural world, $\mathbb{S}$, exists.

Both of these lines of attack can be handled simply by switching from fundamentalist to reformed religion to eliminate the $\mathbb{R}$ element in the solution tuple, but the problem is deeper than that, and the assertion that God does not exist merits another look.

If we assume a creationist myth in which the deity creates our universe, our reality, *from* his reality, then the existence objection vanishes, since our universe would be a subset of the divine universe, and subsets categorically cannot know anything about their superset. In fact, the only reason we suspect, or claim, that the superset reality exists is because of a claim that a message was transmitted from it into ours via some kind of sign, messenger or prophet (or more likely, because evolution created the need to invent one).

At any rate, the assertion that God does not exist is therefore puerile, at best:

$$\text{God} \in \mathbb{S} \tag{8.5}$$

$$\mathbb{S} \supset \mathbb{R} \tag{8.6}$$

$$\therefore \mathbb{S} \cap \mathbb{R} = \texttt{undefined} \tag{8.7}$$

$$\therefore \text{God exists} \equiv \text{God does not exist} \tag{8.8}$$

By the creationist myth, it is axiomatic and necessary that God must live in a supernatural universe (8.5) in order to have created ours, and that, therefore, the supernatural universe must be the superset of ours (8.6). This means that the intersection of the two sets is, *from our perspective*, undefined (8.7), so, since the truth value of any statement about an undefined set is also undefined, therefore, all statements with an undefined truth value are equivalent (8.8).

But, let's go a step further and reference the Torah, in which God tells Moses that direct experience of him would kill Moses (Exodus 33:20), suggesting that God's direct exposure to the elements in this universe is incompatible with our natural laws, i.e., that god does not exist in $\mathbb{R}$, and can only visit using special precautions.[3] Now, by no means is this line of reasoning meant to prove or disprove something we cannot know, such as whether $\mathbb{S}$ exists other than as a subset of $\mathbb{I}$, or whether any

---

[3]This sounds analogous to, and consistent with, the need to use strong magnetic fields to keep bits of anti-matter and matter separate, lest they be mutually obliterated.

particular god does or does not exist in a superset reality we cannot perceive or penetrate. This is just intended to demonstrate how ridiculous it is for an atheist to stand his argument on the claim that $\text{God} \notin \mathbb{R}$, since this is a given, not an insight or a conclusion.

But the intellectual goes further than just rejecting god to protest that all religion is based on primitive, superstitious mumbo-jumbo, and, as modern people, it is our moral duty to reject all archaic beliefs and traditions, and replace them with a science-based rational system. But, what they are really arguing is that, because congregants' historically demanded their prophets and clerics say something to make them feel better about earthquakes, an indulgence which led to religions accumulating piles of baseless $\mathbb{CS}$ assertions about $\mathbb{R}$, therefore, the $\mathbb{S}$, $\mathbb{SR}$, and $\mathbb{CS}$ solutions must also be thrown out, even though they have, for the most part, successfully withstood the test of time. That doesn't make sense on any level, even for academics.

Rejecting the idea that the reformed religion three-tuple can provide a valid basis for a civilization's value system (with individual tweaking) puts academics and atheists on a collision course with two small problems:

1. the attempt to create a rational replacement for traditional systems is guaranteed to end in disaster, and

2. evolution.

The attempt to replace traditional religion with a synthetic rational value system, one which has been contrived within a generation,[4] will necessarily founder on Limits 2, 5 and 6. In fact, the attempt to do this will fail in exactly the way it is failing right now in the academy, where traditional religion has been replaced with an intersectional, social justice religion that not only embraces and worships racism and sexism, but that also dismisses modern enlightenment and rationality itself by rejecting the very principles on which the sciences and formal languages are based.

The second problem is that, since evolution created god,[5] this means that effete intellectuals are arrogating to themselves the power to replace an evolutionary mechanism with an idiotic, untested L2 idea chain that has no known connection to reality whatsoever. They are actually arguing that we should replace an idea written into our genetic code by evolution with one they came up with last Saturday.

As long as error exceeds content (Limit 6) in our thought, the only way we can test the viability of ideas as large as reality orientation systems is with cross-generational tests, not callow intellectual 'logic'. Also, the fact that intellectuals don't even know that they are attempting to replace transcendent loop-back structures[6] with a pastiche of 'logical' personal opinions,

---

[4] More commonly, put together within a few months by a teen or twenty-something year old.

[5] Evolution created our proclivity to create and believe in god, see **§Supernatural Reality** below.

[6] See **§Supernatural Reality** below.

makes it impossible to imagine that their solutions won't have to acquire all manner of frankensteininian add-ons before they are finally able to fill the void left by their destruction of tested, traditional belief systems.

The fundamental error in the intellectual's approach to religion, though, is that they are using the wrong data structure to ask the wrong question. Asking whether religion is right or wrong is the wrong question, since it is seeking an L0 answer to L2 questions about $\mathbb{S}$ issues. In order to verify the $\mathbb{R}$ component of L2 ideas, we have to answer L2 questions with reproducible tests or L3 truth evaluations, not with L0 belief assertions, or L2 consistency checks. So, the correct question to ask is, does a traditional, historically tested system of beliefs, attitudes and practices that focuses on addressing the flaws inherent in our L2 pattern processing engine have the potential to help us maintain a stable society while we begin to move forward in our cultural learning journey towards reproducible progress? The answer to this question cannot be evaluated with a simple binary data structure only a few bits long; only an L3 data structure can hold the type of truth value that is required the answer the question: to what extent can some kind of individually adjusted reformed religious tradition be a viable and productive tool in a particular discovery learning process?

Since the path to the super stupid abyss is paved with discarded traditional values, and since it is so expensive to express our ideas in formal terms and then to test them — so expensive that few of us will extensively test more than a handful a year — the obvious and sound strategy regarding $\mathbb{S}$ questions is: **if we are qualified, we should go fearlessly forward into our personal journey of exploration, but go slowly in our efforts to re-engineer society, and certainly not let our social prescriptions get ahead of our reproducible tests.**

Supernatural Reality

Up until now, we have used $\mathbb{S}$ to represent both our internal model of the supernatural, and the externality itself, but this was just for rhetorical convenience. Now, since we can only know supernatural things through models we build in our head — just like anything else that is internal, external, real, or imagined — we will formalize our terminology to strictly focus on the internal model.

In the universal cognition model, $\mathbb{S}$ is a subset of L2 with the following characteristics:

- **it is a primordial structure**

  $\mathbb{S}$ is a structure, not just a model of something.

- **it is a programmable and queryable data store**

  $\mathbb{S}$ is a small, very sticky data store.

- **its entries are archetypal and high-value**

S holds fundamental, ultimate, archetypal concepts such as: good/evil, god, heaven, forbearance, etc.

- **it predates higher level pattern processing**
  S has a closer, higher intensity connection to L0 than the rest of L2.

- **its entries are immutable**
  While entries are immutable, they can be reevaluated, and newer versions/branches can be added, and then preferred.

- **its entries are loopbacks**
  The entries in S kill queries, they do not generate or support them. They dampen, rather than incite, questions.

- **its entries are extremely long-lasting**
  Core beliefs in S essentially last forever, even when we choose to follow later replacements.

It seems that S is a semi-isolated partition of CS in which all stored ideas have significant impact, and are relatively immune to L2 cavils. The only function S seems to have is to house loopbacks, from the trivial to the profound.

S is the functional structure created by the mutation companion set of the L2 mutations. S is what made the sloppy L2 result set work: by itself, L2 is a partial solution, it will not work without a mechanism to clean up the mess resulting from underspecified queries exciting a host of irrelevant thoughts. Without the built-in ability to kill runaway queries (that manifest as hope or anxiety about the future), our pattern processing ability (which is what enables us to anticipate the future) would bury us under a paralyzing flood of hopes, doubts and worries.[7]

These characteristics make $\mathbb{S}$ a primordial, small, permanent store of high value idea-beliefs whose main function is to calm the apprehension storms generated by the inherently sloppy L2 result set structure. It is different from L0 and L1 in that it actually holds pattern objects, but different than the mature L2 data store in that it is built to hold a small, stable set of loopbacks, not dynamic, extensible pattern chains.

$\mathbb{S}$ is thus the primary value nexus in our higher cognitive structure, an island of stability in an L2 sea of uncertainty and doubt. $\mathbb{S}$ can almost be thought of as a value intrusion into the inherently value-agnostic L2 pattern world. The loopbacks in $\mathbb{S}$ are essentially anti-queries, anti-thoughts, such as: god, religious ideas, or the puerile belief that we can build a life and society based solely on verified, rational thoughts. These deadening value connections are the balm that soothes our fragile, over-excitable L2 ability to anticipate, and fear, the future.

The problem with L2 result sets that are heavily weighted with false positives is that many of the more significant false positives will find a place in the recently accessed pattern store,[8]

---

[7]One of the universal laws of evolved cognition is that later cognitive layers cannot impair the function of earlier ones (a law that is enforced by natural selection). *Ultrareasoning*, p53.

[8]A data structure that supports associative reasoning. The design for it arose from simulation experiments that highlighted the need for a mid-term

a memory cache that is automatically searched each time new
input is processed. Ideas stay in this store as long as their
charge remains above a certain minimum level, and their charge
is refreshed every time we seriously consider them to see if they
apply to the new input, and this keeps these ideas from aging
out of the store. The end result of this economical design is that
we are chronically bedeviled by irrelevant hopes and fears that
were triggered by mistake, and that are kept alive throughout
each and every day every time we process new input, until they
are replaced by other more urgent, accidentally triggered, new
hopes and fears.

The solution to this problem is $\mathbb{S}$ and its *loopbacks*, structures that serve as grounded connections that can drain energy
off of erroneously excited ideas. Loopbacks get hooked up to
randomly triggered ideas through a class of `disregard()` commands that often have the form of a wise saying, such as: "don't
sweat the small stuff", "what will be, will be", etc. Above the
level of small loopbacks like this that we use all the time to get
through the day, there is another level of loopback, one that acts
as the ultimate backstop, and this is called the `transcendent`
`loopback`. This final loopback can catch any idea that makes it
through the lower level defenses to threaten to impair our functioning by becoming an idée fixe, such as the emotional/thought
responses that are triggered in us by a terrible loss. Transcen-

memory to explain both conscious association and dreams.

dent loopbacks generally take the form of religious verities, or indeed, verities of any kind: cynical, resigned, even optimistic.

Even though loopbacks often take the form of bromides, this doesn't gainsay their power. Think about bromides for a minute: even though we all see them coming, and we all know that they are silly, trivial, and not 'true', yet, if we give them the slightest chance, we do find that they all tend to succeed, more or less well, in dampening, at least for the moment, our most unsettling anxieties. The reason they work as well as they do (those whose major premise we can accept) is because bromides, apothegms, wisdom sayings, are not actually philosophical, informational, or spiritual mechanisms, but instead, are physical, electrochemical realities in $\mathbb{S}$ that trigger physical changes in our brain to alter our state of mind by momentarily quieting disruptive thoughts. Even a short respite can work, because a thought only has to be calmed for ten seconds or so to drop lower in, or out of, the recent pattern store, so sometimes even the most trite saying can do the trick. Certainly, whether the change is temporary, persistent, or permanent depends on the circumstance, such as how deeply the idea connects with us and to what extent it alters our future life path. We are all familiar with weaker loopbacks in the form of sayings so bland that we have to repeat them to ourselves over and over, like a mantra, in order to maintain our equilibrium through a difficult time.

While local and global loopbacks are structurally supported, specific ones may require social learning in order for them to be correctly activated or tuned. Advice that we get from friends is a kind of low level loopback, but religion is the natural, and perhaps only, source for effective, positive, transcendent loopbacks, and the training for how to use them. Transcendent loopbacks supplied by philosophy, rather than religion, are notorious for falling short in times of great crisis. The classic examples of religious transcendent loopbacks include: "it's in God's hands", "God has a plan for everything", "we are rewarded in heaven for what we suffer in this vale of tears", etc. Philosophical loopbacks tend to be pallid attempts to predict the obvious, and to reconcile us to the unavoidable.

$\mathbb{S}$ sits at the edge of L2, closer to the absolute truths of L0 than any ordinary L2 pattern. A side effect of this is that ordinary L2 ideas can be automatically assigned evaluations simply by associating them, directly or indirectly, with any belief in the $\mathbb{S}$ hierarchy of beliefs, since they will inherit the value chain of the $\mathbb{S}$ idea they are linked to. Thus, both our constitutional proclivities (such as our level of confidence, energy, acquisitiveness, diffidence, introversion, etc.), and our $\mathbb{S}$ value hierarchy, together form the basis for our general approach to life.

Atheists effectively want to replace the functionality of $\mathbb{S}$, which they don't even know exists, with a bookish attitude that blends the wisdom, erudition, and reasoning fallacies[9] together

---

[9] See appendix E.

into one self-indulgent delusion that will only survive as long as their current bubble of safety and prosperity is maintained by their society.

Uncomfortable Truth of Religion

The problem with religion has nothing to do with religion, and this is what intellectuals and atheists completely miss. There is nothing special about religion other than that it is an instance of a demanding, hierarchical 4D cognitive solution system, and nothing more. Subtracting $\mathbb{R}$ from the $\mathbf{R}_f$ four-tuple, ($\mathbb{S}$, $\mathbb{SR}$, $\mathbb{CS}$, $\mathbb{R}$), creates the weaker three-tuple ($\mathbb{S}$, $\mathbb{SR}$, $\mathbb{CS}$) of $\mathbf{R}_r$ that satisfies only some of our needs. We all know from experience that reformed religions lack the power to incite fanatical devotion in their followers, but most mistakenly ascribe the dissimilar levels of passion to the doctrines, rather than understanding this $\mathbb{SR}$ law:

$$\mathbb{SR}.max(P) \propto |D| \qquad (8.9)$$

The uncomfortable truth in the $\mathbb{SR}$ space is that the maximum power, (P), of a solution is directly related to the number of dimensions, $|D|$, it has, because, since each dimension can contribute to the total power of the solution, the more dimensions a solution has, the more powerful it can potentially be. This means that fundamentalist religions are inherently potentially stronger than reformed religions, but not because of their doctrine or even their leaders, but strictly because of the number of dimensions in their profile, regardless how ridiculous some of their pronouncements on $\mathbb{R}$ may be.

While reform religion can be a relatively weak tea, nevertheless, it still has the capacity to offer solutions that can successfully support civilizations across generations, as well as providing strong guidance and comfort to individuals. However, the absence of the fourth ($\mathbb{R}$) dimension weakens the individual's bond to the congregation, and renders them vulnerable to conversion, or to just falling away from the group.

The intellectual atheist's proposal of a variant three-tuple, ($\mathbb{R}$, $\mathbb{SR}$, $\mathbb{CS}$), is even weaker still in that it utterly fails to address the structural need for both transcendent and minor loopbacks by repressing, but not eliminating, the $\mathbb{S}$ dimension. They are suggesting that the way forward is to deactivate a significant part of our cognitive apparatus, but this is no less stupid now than it was in the Victorian era, when the target of repression was the id.

Attempting to repress an entire functional system as powerful as $\mathbb{S}$ will just make it burst out in some other ugly, perverted manifestation, such as what is happening in modern academia, where learned academics are significantly more religious, and less tolerant and enlightened, than were the priests in the Spanish Inquisition. Suggesting that the way to make ourselves stronger is by closeting a section of our core abilities to make ourselves weaker, is patently absurd.

The atheist tries to substitute *attitude* for religion: they elevate the rational fallacy to a core value in the hope/belief (yes, it is an irrational faith element) that others with the same attitude can come together with them to institute the nightmare of Plato's republic, in which they play the role of the philosopher-king, apparently. This utopian (dystopian, actually) dream relies solely on the irrational belief that 'rational knowledge' can guide us in all things, even when the majority of the decisions we make on a daily basis are far beyond the limits of verified knowledge.

Even worse than simple atheism, for the last century or so, the modern academic replacement for traditional religion has been the Marxist 'scientific' religion, a more rigidly fundamentalist cult than any orthodox western religion still active today. Marxism is absolutely a religious four tuple identical to $\mathbf{R}_f$ that goes full in on making demonstrably false claims in $\mathbb{R}$, the refutation of which only inflames its partisans' fervor to a fever pitch.

The only difference between traditional religions and the modern neo-Marxist grievance religions is that, instead of the supernatural $\mathbb{S}$ being the divine dimension as in the former, in the latter it is a profane ideology. Instead of encapsulating aspirations and ideals that reach beyond the human condition, they supplant god with the devotee, himself, to stand as the all-knowing tyrant with ambitions to rearrange everything to suit his own whims, without respect or regard for the mortality or dreams of his unfortunate subjects.

Reflections on Religion

To wrap up our discussion of religion, some age-old misconceptions often cited in attacks on the validity of religion have to be cleared up, and a few insights of the way forward will be suggested. Using a faceted model-oriented perspective in the context of the universal cognition model, an option that was previously unavailable, will clear up the confusion straight away.

Hypocrisy

Religions are multidimensional solutions, and, while this is what gives them their power, it also creates a complexity that few have really appreciated before now. Whenever a problem or solution manifests in multiple realities, then, in order to be able to translate thought into action, we have to create a hierarchy of values before we can evaluate input. That means that we have to sort the reality dimensions in whatever order of priority we deem appropriate at the time. Other than the practical

Highest Value	Highest Goal
$\mathbb{S}$	match behavior to doctrine
$\mathbb{CS}$	match behavior to feelings
$\mathbb{SR}$	maximize group power
$\mathbb{R}$	monitor results and adjust

Table 8.1: Sortable value hierarchy in religions

necessity of keeping our results close enough to reality in $\mathbb{R}$ to avoid injury or death, there is no right answer to this problem: what is important to one may not be to another, and what is important now may not be at another time.

Although it applies to all situations, table 8.1 clarifies the issue that people have with the so-called hypocrisy of religion: the goals of a semantic reality may change over time. In the quiet contemplation of the cloister, it may be clear that $\mathbb{S}$ concerns are the only priority, while religions that want to grow have to prioritize $\mathbb{SR}$, those focusing on pastoral concerns will prioritize $\mathbb{CS}$, and those struggling to pay their bills must focus on $\mathbb{SR}$ for solicitation, and on $\mathbb{R}$ for expenses and balances.

To an observer, a congregation may seem to be acting hypocritically at times, but this is only because their current prioritization of realities does not match what the observer expects or desires. It should be obvious that the fact that this happens does not invalidate religions or their traditions, nor does it prove that they are just lying, self-serving hierarchies. On the contrary, the cycling of priorities is entirely predictable and appropriate.

Divine Origin

This chapter has argued, from a number of perspectives, that thoughtlessly dismissing religion is a fool's errand, but it has not argued for piety or blind acceptance of doctrine. The subtext of all of the volumes in this series is that the best path to the future is a disciplined journey of exploration into the unknown that leverages valuable lessons of the past to invent new solutions for the future. But, exploring the unknown can only be reliably done with L3, the discovery intellect, and it only works by breaking down accepted concepts into atomic, ideational statements that can be used to build fractally branching query trees. The reason piety is inadvisable for explorers or leaders is that it prohibits the critical examination of anything deemed sacred, or part of the canon, and exploration and discovery cannot proceed with such artificial constraints.

The universal version of Occam's razor discussed earlier is a necessary consequence of both the cognition limits that have guided our entire discussion, and the formal definition of reality. This means that it is not valid to assign remote causes for local events that are fully accounted for by natural laws in a given reality. While the suggestion is being strongly made that highly educated people should reconsider, and reverse, their ill-considered rejection of religion, it doesn't mean we should swallow doctrine or unproductive ideas whole.

The pruning process mentioned earlier is a tool we can use to customize traditional solutions to meet our current needs, abilities, and circumstances. We prune idea trees by applying the universal form of Occam's razor to all claims of divine origin, and rejecting, for example, any assignment to divine origin of anything that can now be explained with natural laws.

Just as we no longer assign responsibility for earthquakes to a deity, neither should we accept that a prophet's claim that commandments to do those things that predictably strengthen the group have a divine origin. We don't need god to tell us to sleep, eat and drink, nor do we need him to tell us to coordinate ourselves in a way that maximizes the cohesive gravity force that holds congregations, and peoples, together. Natural phenomena are explained in natural realities using natural laws.

Whether this leaves anything in the scriptures that we can accept as divine is for each of us to decide, but that some religions support inter-generational progress is an observable fact, as is the fact that the project of replacing all of the mechanisms that accomplish it is beyond any of our individual abilities. Denying our limitations is hubris. It is super stupid.

Crippled $\mathbb{S}$

The educated elite pay a price for their unthinking dismissal of religion, and it is a sickness in their soul, a bitter, fatalistic, cynical attitude that only comforts them with the knowledge that nothing means anything, and that failure, disappointment, and betrayal are the only constants in this world.

This pathological attitude, which they parade as sophistication, is actually a symptom of the failure to create, maintain, and use effective loopbacks. The rejection of supra-L2 mechanisms to cope with doubt and fear obviates the possibility of using the systems built into our mind to cope with our cognitive limitations. This is like choosing to run without using our legs because we think that doing so is somehow morally superior to just using the brute strength of our muscles.

Crippled $\mathbb{S}$ is a self-induced, self-maintained mental illness. It is largely a matter of choice, not an affliction. It is a failure-to-mature disease created by the intransigent adolescent himself.

Future

The universal cognition model does not tell us how we should live, or what choices we should make, it is merely a toolbox of concepts and procedures that are useful in, or a product of, the discovery learning process.

This chapter, for example, should not be read as a pronouncement that traditional religion is an irreplaceable component in any stable solution. On the contrary, it shows that the only reason we haven't come up with a 4D solution alternative to fundamentalist religion that is potentially just as strong as it, is simply because we haven't even tried to figure out a way to replace the superstitious, $\mathbb{S}$-based $\mathbb{R}$ statements in $\mathbf{R}_f$ with a flexible, reliable, science-based $\mathbb{R}$ dimension.

The more we know about a system, the better our analytical and computational tools are, the more options we have when trying to develop new, more powerful solutions.

Chapter 9

The Source of

Super Stupidity

Where is super stupidity produced? Since the supply of it seems to be inexhaustible, the flood must be coming from a spring-like source that continually pumps out more and more infected people who can pass it along to others.

As it happens, it turns out that identifying the source of the infectious flood of super stupidity isn't hard once we start using the ideas we've already discussed in previous chapters. In order to see it more easily, though, we first have to set up a little thought experiment, but before we can do that, we have to put a name to the modern secular religion we began examining in the previous chapter, and then reframe it in the new standard model terms.

Let's call the secular religion that has been sweeping the West in the last century or so **Grievancism**, a full ($\mathbb{S}$,$\mathbb{SR}$,$\mathbb{CS}$,$\mathbb{R}$) 4D solution that demonstrates that god is not a necessary element in religion. Grievancism's elements are:

$\mathbb{S}$ Spiritual/Supernatural Reality:

The job of the supernatural element in a grouping solution is to establish a value basis for beliefs and actions that is immune to criticism from any of the other dimensions by virtue of the fact that its meta-dimensional nature makes it superior to the ordinary dimensions. Traditionally, this has meant god and his divine world, but in Grievancism it is an ideology based on some imaginary force or structure such as the clockwork of history, the patriarchy, racial supremacy, or some other emotional passion. A primary article of faith is that anyone who fails to accept the truth of the $\mathbb{S}$ proposition, is, by definition, evil, sinful, and ignorant.

The supernatural component in Grievancism is profane, rather than divine. Instead of orienting us towards the ultimate, the way 'primitive' religions do, this modern, sophisticated religion focuses our attention on our inner demons by preaching that all bad feelings are caused by 'oppressors', and that we feel unsuccessful, unsafe, and lost because we are the innocent 'oppressed' class that is injured and exploited by the 'oppressor' class. Our sense of resentment is stoked and encouraged into a building rage that will fuel a revolution to overthrow the 'oppressors' so that the 'oppressed' can finally restore the Garden of Eden on earth. Thus, instead of connecting us to a source of goodness in the ultimate, Grievancism connects us to badness by blaming our negative experiences and emotions, not on us or the vicissitudes of nature and fate, but on some arbitrary class of other *humans* that it designates as the oppressor enemy that deserves contempt and destruction.

$\mathbb{SR}$ Semantic Reality:

The dominant force in Grievancism is the group component which gives us the strength we need to overthrow our 'oppressors'. Groups of like-minded followers replace the family as the primary support system. It is explicit in Grievancism that $\mathbb{SR}$ truth is the *only* truth, i.e., whatever strengthens the group is true, whatever does not, is false (and $\mathbb{R}$ doesn't matter at all).

$\mathbb{CS}$ Cognitive Space:

The individual's resentments, malaise, and angst are exalted and encouraged as evidence of 'oppression', and followers are taught that their individual weakness can only be cured by the strength of the group, and that total commitment to the group and its truths is required to qualify for relief.

ℝ Physical Reality:

Physical reality is conceived of only as an inexhaustible store of goods that the group should be able to draw from to make equitable distributions to its members after the revolution, rather than as an independent reality that must be respected and perhaps cultivated.

With this understanding of Grievancism clearly in hand, we can begin to set up the thought experiment by considering three different cases of super stupidity, each a thousand years apart, which, when considered together, prove to be quite enlightening.

1. Pliny the Elder (23 CE - 79 CE) wrote *The Natural History*, an encyclopedia of the knowledge of his time. Following is an excerpt on astronomy:

The course of all the planets, and among others of the Sun, and the Moon, is in the contrary direction to that of the heavens, that is towards the left, while the heavens are rapidly carried about to the right. And although, by the stars constantly revolving with immense velocity, they are raised up, and hurried on to the part where they set, yet they are all forced, by a motion of their own, in an opposite direction; and this is so ordered, lest the air, being always moved in the same direction, by the constant whirling of the heavens, should accumulate into one mass, whereas now it is divided and separated and beaten into small pieces, by the opposite motion of the different stars.[1]

2. In the late middle ages, universities awarded Master of Arts degrees to students who completed a six year course of study in the seven liberal arts: arithmetic, geometry, astronomy, music theory, grammar, logic, and rhetoric. After this, students could continue to study for a higher degree in theology, medicine, or law.

Astronomy: Before the middle of the seventeenth century, the astronomy that was taught was Ptolemaic (geocentric), not Copernican (heliocentric).

Medicine: "During the beginnings of the Age of Reason ... [m]ost of the medical professionals were also spiritual healers, and they based their practices on the theories of Galen. From the idea that the physical and psychological ailments people experienced were the result of fluctuations of four bodily fluids and the balance of internal "elements" and "qualities," 16th-century medical practitioners were hesitant to challenge established ideas with new observations and research."[2]

3. Many, if not most, humanities degree programs in the

---

[1] http://www.perseus.tufts.edu/hopper/text?doc=Perseus:text:
1999.02.0137:book=2:chapter=6
[2] https://gohighbrow.com/16th-century-medicine/

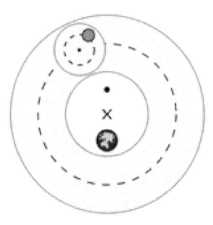

Figure 9.1: Epicycles in Ptolemaic astronomy

modern university require, on pain of failure or expulsion, that the student convert to Grievancism, or at least write and speak as if they were securely in the fold. Grievancism, with its Marxist base, is generally not offered as an option, or an object lesson in failure, but is taught as the one and only truth. Professors, even tenured ones, are regularly fired or have their careers otherwise limited for daring to support the doctrine with anything less than full-throated conviction. Publicly disagreeing with the doctrines will not only get you fired, but can even get you barred from any other higher education institution.

Now, let's tie these three very different examples together.

First, what was Pliny writing about? The drivel he was spouting cannot be excused simply by saying that it was the best knowledge of the day, since it was in no way knowledge about $\mathbb{R}$, and it wasn't even close enough to be wrong. So, what was it knowledge of, if not $\mathbb{R}$?

Second, what were university students in the middle ages studying if negative numbers were considered abhorrent, astronomy involved contorting Ptolemaic geocentricism to get it closer to observed reality (see figure 9.1), and medicine was still completely unscientific, still based on authority and emotion instead of on actual reality?

Third, what are today's university students in the non-technical fields studying if they are not allowed to rebut Grievancic doctrine with scientific fact? What are they studying if they are being forced to agree that science, itself, is invalid because it is nothing more than a colonialist tool of the patriarchy? What are they learning if they are forced to accept that math is unjust and unnecessary because some classes of people find it too hard? Students are even being told to confine their research resources to an approved list of works in Grievancism, so clearly, in addition to not being taught how to think, they are actually being taught how to do research wrong.

These three different and completely mainstream examples — separated from each other by almost a thousand years — together all demonstrate the same issue: higher education is **not** about knowledge of $\mathbb{R}$, not about exploring the unknown, *and it never has been.* Higher education is about something else, something other than learning how to systematically and successfully interrogate reality. What else is there that could consume so much of our time and resources over so many centuries?

Think about Pliny. What was he doing when he was acquiring all of his bogus 'knowledge'? He was building elaborate opinion trees around statements he accepted as fact that were actually just twaddle. Why was he doing this? Of course, he was trying to extend his education, but why? Think about it: because doing it *felt good* to him. Some of us are gifted with an affinity for pattern assimilation and manipulation. The reward we get from building vast interconnected opinion webs is a great sense of being situated, a sense of satisfaction that we have the ability *to know* things, a pride in knowing that we have the ability to penetrate the mysteries of life and nature. Knowing things makes us feel strong, confident, secure, and yes, important. Some of us are built that way.

Pliny studied because he enjoyed it; he put together a giant, interlocking knowledge puzzle for the sense of satisfaction he got as he saw the growing picture come together; he published it to enjoy the respect and admiration of his readers. But, he only validated his 'knowledge' with L2 consistency checks, not reproducible tests. Even though consistency checks have been mistaken as being meaningful ever since L2 evolved, this does not excuse the serious scholar for following bad procedure. Pliny did not understand Limit 6, he did not know how much error or missing information there was in his very best knowledge, and thus had no way of imagining how incredibly wrong the vast majority of his 'knowledge' actually was.

What about pre-Enlightenment scholars? Were they learning verifiable facts in $\mathbb{R}$, or just assimilating patterns in $\mathbb{S}, \mathbb{SR}$ and $\mathbb{CS}$ that would help to integrate them into existing power structures? Were they learning how to interrogate $\mathbb{R}$ to build evidence from which they could draw testable conclusions, or were they being taught how to acquire, form and express opinions acceptable to their peers and superiors in their power structure of interest?

There is no question that today's students in the humanities and social sciences are being aggressively and explicitly indoctrinated in Grievancism, nor that those who object are being marginalized or ejected from the university. Modern students, just like those from 900 years ago, are being trained in the lexicon and grammar of the grouping creeds currently controlling the university. Why, and to what end? If the goal of universities is not mastery of investigative skills and knowledge of $\mathbb{R}$, then what has motivated the wealthy and powerful to create and maintain these impressive institutions?

Higher Education

If we look at Oxford University as a very early example of the trend to create institutions of higher learning,[3] we find that it was founded very soon after the Norman invasion unified much of England under William the Conquerer. While the anecdote does not make the case, nevertheless, the chain of causality suggested by the chronology is fairly straightforward: instead of nine essentially independent administrative districts, William combined all of his English and continental possessions into a single empire. This larger organization created the need for a much larger and more complex organizational structure than the separate fiefdoms required.

Large semantic (sub)realities, those on the scale of governments and modern corporations, are eventually forced to develop their own domain specific languages tailored to streamline intradepartmental communication in a way that meets their peculiar needs. These needs differ by department and discipline. While these job-specific languages that develop in the various departments and sections can be highly specialized, for example, in the financial or legal areas, much of the language and process is shared by all departments.

The problem with specialized language and procedures is

---

[3]This is an illustration, not an argument. If your reading of English history varies from this tale, substitute your own, or regenerate the argument yourself after mastering *Ultrareasoning*.

that, to maintain the organization over time, new recruits have to learn not only the specifics, but the general culture that pervades the organization of organizations. Certainly, the organizations would suffer if it took, say, several years, or more, to teach every new employee the general history, procedures, and assumptions involved in life in a large organization. At a minimum, new hires must come prepared with a basic command of general terms, processes, and outlook in order to keep the training requirements small enough to take weeks, instead of years, so they can be immediately productive while being trained for higher positions.

The higher education system is the solution to the problem created by the complexity of large government (and, eventually, commercial) organizations. It trains university students in the culture surrounding the large institutions that society supports. The schools teach students the language of these institutions, focusing on the implicit terms in the `statement` construct, the `context` and the `goal`, that are common across domain specific languages.

Why would anyone willingly undergo the effort and expense of such a lengthy educational regimen required by an organization they don't yet work for? People willingly undertake this arduous, self-financed training because it is in their self-interest to get closer to the center of power, since resources flow to, and collect in, the center of the group. The only sure way to start working in a higher position in an organization is to know more about how the group operates, how it thinks, talks, and acts, what common knowledge is assumed, what goals are acceptable, than your competitors. This is what universities teach, this is the type of networking that they facilitate. This is what they do, this is what they have always done, to the exclusion of almost everything else.

This is not some cynical conspiracy theory, it is merely a recognition that complex organizations work by interacting with others in an overarching $\mathbb{SR}$, and in order to do that, there must be a shared high-level language and frame of reference common to all. This is what university students are trained in.

To understand the difference between a university and an actual educational institution (still a theoretical phenomenon, at this point), we need only look at the definitions of the two operative concepts that differentiate the two: `educate`, and `inculcate`.

The word `educate` comes from the Latin stem **educere** which means *to lead out*. The essential concept is that we need training in concepts and practices to grow our mind beyond the confines of our inner reality to encounter and understand external reality. True education is primarily an L3-level function because disciplined, free-range querying cannot be mastered until one gains a certain level of competency in independent thought.

The word `inculcate` means to instill by persistent instruction. Ideas, skills, or attitudes can be inculcated with some predictability into a majority of qualified students. Whether or not a student is 'college-ready' is determined by making them demonstrate a certain level of facility with pattern acquisition, retention, and processing. Thus, matriculation requires a certain level of ability in L2-level function, and the university curriculum builds on this base with pattern assimilation and manipulation courses in a variety of fields and disciplines to deliver graduates who are ready to join the ranks of professions, or organizational management.

Universities acculturate students to complex organizational thinking by inculcating patterns and procedures into them. They never have, and never could, mentor individual geniuses to tackle the unknown alone. Even though progress in understanding the unknown is the putative goal of institutional education, new discoveries are always achieved by the solitary trailblazer using techniques unknown in the academy, not by the best, most compliant student.

Universities are, and always have been, vocational schools, institutions that train students to take their place in ongoing enterprises. For the last four centuries or so, the technical colleges in the universities have trained their students in the language and procedures of mathematics and perhaps a branch of the sciences. The humanities and soft science colleges have trained their students to fit into a particular subculture in the dominant semantic reality.

Hubris is the great sin that is behind universities' intellectual and moral degeneracy, manifesting as a profound disrespect for realities outside of the academic hothouse of fevered L2 pattern assimilation and manipulation. Academics both believe and teach that the world is as small as their own miserable little slice of $\mathbb{SR}$, because this makes them feel like monarchs in their own domain. This religious belief infects students with the myopic perspective that only their own $\mathbb{SR}$ truth matters. This inevitably leads them to systematically and deliberately denigrate, rather than respect, other realities.

Granted, university faculty and students don't know about the various realities, so they have no idea that there are levels in our mind that all use different data structures for different purposes, they have no inkling that L3, the discovery intellect, even exists, let alone that it can be deliberately used to generate brilliant insights on a regular basis. But they do know respect, they do know the difference between being humble and being arrogant, they do know from experience that their knowledge is partial and imperfect, and, deep down, in some dark, locked recess in their soul, they know that all of their values are based on specific and extended self-interest.

And yet, each new generation deliberately chooses to desecrate these values, one by one, to further their own ambitions and to feed their own egos. The intellectual stagnation caused by these twisted ambitions continues to this day, when the proudest scholars are all able to bray their twisted, bitter, demented ideology without shame, thanks to having methodically stripped themselves naked of the last shreds of dignity, respect, humility, and diligence.

This individual and institutional character flaw is what led these simple vocational training schools to take on airs, to see themselves as being institutions of higher education instead of what they actually are. Academics and their institutions claim credit for being what they are not, and in so doing, block civilization from progressing beyond the primitive stage we have been stuck in for millennia, thus preventing us from being able to develop actual higher educational institutions. Universities, in their pride, have managed to become kidney stones that block the flow of events they are supposed to be facilitating.

These institutionalized flaws of arrogance, ignorance, and jealous pride manifest as the three great fallacies: wisdom, erudition, and reasoning.[4] These fallacies are caused by the false beliefs that arise from the contradiction between higher education's claimed, and actual, mission, and they lead to academics and intellectuals dismissing the significance of realities that exist outside of their own little $\mathbb{SR}$ sphere.

---

[4]See Appendix E.

Disregarding Reality

How is it possible simply to disregard any of the internal or external realities? Actually, it is surprisingly easy to do so, due to a peculiar ability our cognitive apparatus has: the value of the n dimension in the evaluation evacule can be dialed up until the other dimensions no longer matter in the current calculations. The miracle of evacule-based evaluation is in the semantics of the three part evaluation (anti-self, pro-self, and non-self components): our estimation of the significance of any idea, event, or input can be effectively zeroed-out to irrelevance if we choose to increase the 'don't care' dimension, n, high enough to overcome whatever our positive or negative responses might be. This is what you do when you grab your family as you escape from a burning building before grabbing your photographs of them; the photos have value, but not in the moment of crisis relative to other, more important things, such as people.

Not only is it not an aberration nor a mistake to devalue various dimensions of reality, it is a skill all mobile species depend on to survive. We are movement solutions to mortality problems: given a problem, we move to solve it. The problem is that, in any given situation, multiple problems may be simultaneously demanding our attention, but we can only move (at first) in one direction from our starting position, so we always have to group and rank the problems we see so that we can respond to the most pressing issue first. Devaluing a physical risk in order to work on preserving a life asset is not an error, even if we die in the attempt. It is an inescapable part of life.

For another example, most would certainly agree that $\mathbb{R}$ is important, but what about when it is compared to our need to extend and defend the set of ideas our entire career is based on? In this case, it's not even a contest, our extended self-interest will always trump vague abstractions such as physical realities, and for good reason: our knowledge of physical reality is so poor and incomplete that we routinely find some way to do that which we previously absolutely *knew* to be impossible, so temporarily ignoring our 'knowledge' of reality is not always unreasonable. Successful people learn to focus on the most critical issues in times of crisis, and to let the rest sort itself out. This is one of the attributes that makes them successful.

The Higher Education Stupidity Pump

Super stupidity is the product of disrespecting the value of a reality based on the arrogant, habitual preference for one reality above the rest. Institutions of higher education are the primary source of super stupidity because they prioritize their parochial $\mathbb{SR}$ truth and utterly disrespect other $\mathbb{SR}$ and $\mathbb{R}$ truths altogether.

The three fallacies (wisdom, erudition, reasoning) are the

pillars of the higher education system. They each represent several violations of traditional values and, from a more modern perspective, violations of all of the cognition limits, and this is why the system is corrupt from the foundation up.

The university system is the primary source of the super stupidity that is blocking civilization's path to progress. They make themselves the cause of it, not the solution to it, by teaching that:

- internal truth is truer than external truth,

- authority is a valid truth test,

- ideological truth is truer than any other, and

- scientific expertise extends authority to reasoning done outside one's area of competence.

Universities spew super stupidity into the world packaged in the form of graduates who were only trained to compete in a particular $\mathbb{SR}$ subset while disdaining any inconvenient $\mathbb{R}$ truth. Yet, these people are celebrated as being educated, rather than accepted as just having been vocationally trained. Academics and graduates have been lying to themselves and the world about the limits and value of their training, and they have been doing this for the basest of reasons. Worse yet, to hide their intellectual indolence and depravity, they have done all they could to block the stray L3-competent student from surviving, let alone thriving, in the academy.

Universities instruct their students that L2 pattern manipulation knowledge is superior to belief, experience, or exploration knowledge. Modern schools require that their graduates adopt an ideology consistent with the local Grievancism sect. Currently, they teach their students to use a primitive two class analysis to reduce all of history and human affairs to an oppressor/oppressed struggle. A thousand years ago, students were forced to accept the dominant culture viewpoint not only on religion, but also on the parameters of acceptable thought and inquiry. The difference between the two ages is indiscernible.

Universities teach their students to overvalue the semantic reality encompassing their discipline. This has unexpected results with the hard science graduates: they favor $\mathbb{R}$ while discussing their subject, but once they move beyond it to consider the rest of reality, they convert to a group-think orientation that should be understood as $\mathbb{SR}_\mathbb{R}$. That is, science graduates create an orientation to semantic reality that has a scientific idiom, but is otherwise no better grounded or thought out than the flakiest argument tossed out by the worst humanities students.

Universities inculcate into their students the prideful belief that the only world that matters is the one contained in their small slice of $\mathbb{SR}$. Students and instructors alike fall for this because they are seduced by the lure of being able to feel powerful and in control. University education validates the narcissism of $\mathbb{CS}$ by projecting some of its needs and feelings onto an $\mathbb{SR}$ ideology.

University students live in an $\mathbb{SR}$ world of relationships and attitudes, instead of physical realities. Universities are the primary source of training, but they are the worst enemy of education. They are the polluted springs from which noxious torrents of super stupidity pour into our world every day.

Our society will not be able to begin making progress towards successfully devising solutions to pinnacle questions until universities have been recognized as the malign influences they are, and always have been.

Chapter 10

The Power of

Super Stupidity

Normal stupidity is a miracle that allows us to make life and death decisions based on almost no information. In a split second, we can glance at something and instantly decide how to react by assessing just a handful of data points from a situation that has millions of details that might be important. Somehow, humans and other animals manage this instantaneous data pruning and rapid decision making well enough not only to survive, but to thrive in an increasingly fast-paced and complex world.

Super stupidity is something else. Clearly, the term is intended as an invective, and up to this point, we have concentrated on the moral failures that both allow it to emerge, and cause it to grow. This emphasis was a choice, not an error, it arose from the commitment of the entire `Pinnacle` project to identify the issues that have prevented us from making progress in resolving the problems that are most important to humanity and its future. But the capacity of super stupidity to simultaneously damage humanity's current population and future prospects is not the whole story of it.

The other side of the story is that super stupidity is not just destructive, it is also very powerful. It would have to be, wouldn't it, for it to thrive despite its failure to see or deal with $\mathbb{R}$ accurately? There has to be a trade-off in which the cost of ignoring or misunderstanding $\mathbb{R}$ is compensated for by some reward that makes the risk seem acceptable. The reward for super stupidity is power in $\mathbb{SR}$, the reality in which we live our social, economic, and conscious lives.

We were taught as children that lying is a bad thing, and were constantly shown in stories how lies complicate everything until, eventually, the lies get exposed and we get punished for them. Yet, as adults, we see both public and private figures lying all the time, apparently even going so far as to build their careers on a never-ending stream of lies.

So, how do we explain why lying, which is prohibited by most major religions as immoral, can be such a useful tool? More than that, how can we explain why, even when they are exposed, some lies will somehow actually retain, or, worse yet, amplify, a positive effect in $\mathbb{SR}$? How can an obvious falsehood about something in physical reality act as a power amplifier in semantic reality?

Incidental preaching notwithstanding, this is not a book on morality, nor is it a philosophical or spiritual treatise that tries to tell you how you should live your life. It is a book on model-oriented reasoning that examines quantitative models of observable phenomena arising from the subjective domain, models that you are free to test and modify, or replace, as you see fit. Our goal in this chapter is simply to model cross-domain lying in a way that accounts for what we see in public and private life everyday, not to countenance it.

Surely, we have all noticed that pointing out a contradiction, an error, or a false claim is usually a futile act in that it only angers our opponent, rather than forcing them to concede their error and change their beliefs. We have all been frustrated in the past by seeing that neither politicians nor ideologues hesitate to tell bald-faced lies to advance their cause, and then don't even miss a beat when the lie is exposed.

Talking heads programs largely focus on participants snidely revealing flaws in their opponents positions with the apparent expectation that refuting claims will somehow be productive, important, and even conclusive. Yet, it never accomplishes anything beyond energizing believers. How can this be? How can we account for the apparent invulnerability of a partisan's position to proof of deception and error?

Making verifiably false statements against $\mathbb{R}$ to strengthen a position in $\mathbb{SR}$ is the essence of super stupidity, because it mortgages the future for the possibility of a short term, temporary gain in semantic reality. The practice is dangerous, expensive, and yet, very often successful, at least from the point of view of the practitioner. We need to be able model this puzzling, complex reality in order to understand how super stupidity can be, and very often is, a potent, power-enhancing tool that can be deliberately wielded to strengthen a group movement, regardless of the severity of the errors and lies involved.

In order to explain this phenomenon, we can extend our model of attraction in $\mathbb{SR}$ in such a way that we will not only be able to account for this anomaly, but to predict it.

Calculating Super Stupidity Power

Let us start building our model of super stupidity's power by recalling the definition of $\mathbb{SR}$: a graph of ξ nodes and $\mathscr{M}$ links, $\mathbb{SR} = (\{\xi\}, \{\mathscr{M}\})$. The total power of the group is the product of the strength of a strategic set of links that tie the different parts of the group together into a potent whole.[1]

In the previous chapter, we defined fundamentalist religion

---

[1] Exactly what links this subset includes, and whether or not it equals the whole set, will have to be experimentally determined.

as a 4D solution, but, of course, it's not the organizational structure that has the dimensions, it is the message links its members share that do. In a 4D solution, all messages can be thought of as 4D messages with possible null entries. What this means in practice is that, for example, you can tell an employee to vacuum the floor in a house of worship just as you could in an office building, but in the former case, the hearer would be less surprised to also receive an $\mathbb{S}$ reference in the message than would the worker in the latter case (who might sue you for it).

While the value of a message is determined by the recipient, as previously stated, we still have to determine whether the message's net binding strength is equal just to the value of the recipient's evaluation of the message content, or is there something more involved?

If we define the `power` of the message to be the product of the recipient's evaluation of its content and some other factors, such as the power of the sender, and some verifiable elements of the message that signify its intended importance, then we have to decide what parts of the message could indicate its importance. Since the actual value attribute cannot be communicated directly, then we have to look at the rhetoric used to communicate the content of each of the dimensions touched on by the message.

In evaluating the language conveying the intended meaning of each dimension, we can use conventions of literary interpretation to score the intended importance of each dimension in a group of statements from minimum to maximum (which we have set to be 1..5 for this case). Therefore, we can set the *intended* importance of a message set as the total of the value of each dimension in a message.

The weight or power of the subgroup on the sending side of a message link must also figure into the potential power of a message, because it is clear that, in general, people can often be much more strongly attached to, and motivated by, their connections to groups than they can to a single object or individual. Since both experience and the physics of semantic reality agree that we tend to be attracted to those who have more power than us, who are closer to the group center than we are, then it makes sense to include a calculation of subgroup power to represent that potential enhanced attraction.

We will represent the *value* in the four internal and external reality dimensions with the following symbols corresponding to the the normal symbols, $(\mathbb{S}, \mathbb{SR}, \mathbb{CS}, \mathbb{R})$, for the dimensions:

$$\text{s, sr, cs, r} \qquad\qquad (10.1)$$

Now, further suppose that, consistent with our real life observations that we are trying to model, not all of the message dimensions have the same potential impact. That is, while each dimension may have the same bounds for the input parameter, the calculations determining the overall result do not treat all dimensions equally. We can model this disparity by adding weighting to the formula. The natural dimensions to weight more heavily would be the dimensions that have historically had the greatest observable effect on human history, the supernatural and semantic dimensions. The formula for the perceived importance (imp) of the message, might be:

$$\mathtt{imp} = \mathrm{S}^2 + \mathrm{SR}^2 + \mathrm{CS} + \mathrm{R} \qquad (10.2)$$

If we multiply this quantity by the recipient's evaluation of the message content times the message sender's perceived power, we get a formula for the **power** of a given message link in $\mathbb{SR}$:

$$\mathrm{E} = eval(m) \cdot power_s \qquad (10.3)$$

$$\mathtt{power} = \mathtt{imp} \cdot \mathrm{E} \qquad (10.4)$$

While this is just back-of-the-envelope work to start with, note that formula 10.2^2 actually does accomplish our goal of giving greater influence to the first two dimensions than the last two.

If we set the maximum for the sum of the importance of each

---

[2]While formulas 10.3 and 10.4 have been included for completeness, the rest of the chapter will use formula 10.2 since it supports the exercises we need, and the results obviously will flow into the other formulas.

dimension to 12, this small number will be adequate to focus on the impact of dimension pairs. If we distribute the total importance across the four dimensions to match maximum and minimum values for the first and last pairs of dimensions, we get this sample table of parameters we can use to run some simple experiments to see what results this formula produces across a range of input values.

S	SR	CS	R	TOTAL
1	1	5	5	12
2	2	4	4	12
3	3	3	3	12
4	4	2	2	12
5	5	1	1	12

Table 10.1: Importance parameters used in exercise

Table 10.1 just shows the parameters we will be using that add up to our specified maximum, (this is input, not results).[3] This arrangement pairs the first two dimensions together, since they are the dimensions that can strengthen group bonds, and the last two together, since they can weaken one's affiliation with the group.

When we apply formula 10.2 to these numbers we get these results:

---

[3]Of course, message dimensions don't have to, and usually wouldn't, add up to the maximum.

S	SR	CS	R	TOTAL
1	1	5	5	12
4	4	4	4	16
9	9	3	3	24
16	16	2	2	36
25	25	1	1	52

Table 10.2: Impact of S and SR dimensions on importance

Clearly, the formula we are using maximizes the impact of the first two dimensions, and minimizes the impact of the last two. The justification for this is that, from a natural selection perspective, the salubrious effects of grouping would favor those inclined to it, over those averse to it. That is, those who were built to respond positively to calls to join a group would have a higher chance of surviving long enough to reproduce than would those who valued solitude and personal experience higher than group 'wisdom' (i.e., shared directives).

Next, as shown in table 10.3, we concentrated the importance in just the $\mathbb{SR}$ and $\mathbb{R}$ dimensions to test the effects of lying. We held $\mathbb{SR}$ (group attachment) at the max, and reduced the $\mathbb{R}$ dimension step by step from maximum to minimum to represent the effect of an $\mathbb{R}$ statement's truth evaluation being reduced. What the percentage change column, δ, shows is how little the overall importance of the message changes as the evaluation of the R dimension declines.

S	SR	CS	R	TOTAL	δ
1	25	1	5	32	
1	25	1	4	31	-1%
1	25	1	3	30	-1%
1	25	1	2	29	-1%
1	25	1	1	28	-1%

Table 10.3: Low Impact of R dimension on importance

Then, in table 10.4, we held the $\mathbb{R}$ dimension value at the maximum, and reduced the evaluation in the $\mathbb{SR}$ dimension from max to min to represent how weakening group affiliation affects message evaluation far more than reducing the evaluation of a message's $\mathbb{R}$ truth. The result shows how sensitive message importance is to changes in one of the higher impact dimensions, SR, where the overall decrease in importance is 24%, while in table 10.3, the change is only 4%.

S	SR	CS	R	TOTAL	δ
1	25	1	5	32	
1	16	1	5	23	-9%
1	9	1	5	16	-7%
1	4	1	5	11	-5%
1	1	1	5	8	-3%

Table 10.4: High Impact of SR dimension on importance

These results are determined by the formula, so they are designed in, and not a surprise, but the question is: does modeling message importance this way give us insight into observable results in real life? Does this model produce results that align with reality? Does this model, in fact, predict exactly the results that we find so frustrating and surprising in everyday life, to wit, that lies in $\mathbb{R}$ don't seem to have any significant negative effect on the ability of a group to recruit and retain its members?

Applying the L3-level `viable` and `productive` truth calculus to this model, we ask: is this model contradicted by reality, and does this model help us to reason deeper into our problem space? The answer to the first test is that no, this model is not contradicted by reality, but, instead, both conforms to it, and is also completely consistent with the evolutionary model. The answer to the second test is, for the experimenter (me), yes, it does support further inquiry into the problem space.

These results do not prove that this model matches reality, only that it describes reality within an acceptable tolerance, and it does support further exploration. This means that the model works for now, and it is reasonable to continue to use and develop it until a better model is available, or until it becomes unacceptably inaccurate or expensive.

Remember, the goal here is not to suggest what ought to be, but merely to account for what we observe, to account for what is. Just as gravity is not bad just because you can die from a fall, so the laws of $\mathbb{SR}$ are neither good nor bad, they just are. Whether or not this doodling will hold up under testing is not the issue: the question is, does this give us a starting point to create quantitative models of $\mathbb{SR}$ grouping behaviors that explain how a lie in $\mathbb{R}$ can have no significant impact on the message it contradicts in $\mathbb{SR}$?

The answer is clearly yes, since a semantic reality is defined by its links and nodes, and the strength of the links determines the strength of the group as a whole, then it is no surprise that, in this context, link-relevant factors are considerably more significant than extraneous (in $\mathbb{SR}$, $\mathbb{R}$ is ordinarily extraneous) concerns are. Group dynamics are more influenced by group interactions than by statements about verifiable physical properties.

It is important to understand that, regardless of how idiotic some of a statement's elements might be, super stupidity — the hyperfocus on $\mathbb{SR}$ to the neglect of $\mathbb{R}$ — can, and often does, strengthen people by reinforcing the bonds that tie them to groups. Because people in groups have more surviving progeny than loners do, natural selection does seem to favor the judicious use of super stupidity. The mathematical model of message power simply describes the otherwise puzzling reality that group bonds can be strengthened by false messages in other dimensions, not weakened by them.

In debate, when someone shows you that one of your facts is wrong, instead of changing your opinion, normally you just quickly reevaluate the culprit fact to a maximum *doesn't matter* value, move it to the don't care bucket, and continue on without missing a beat. This is how you get to maintain both your psychological equilibrium and social relations with your web of groups regardless of how badly your ideas are savaged in a debate.

Errors and contradictions don't matter in reasoning when the participants' views of $\mathbb{SR}$ differ, because each is evaluating everything from their own point of view, not from some disinterested, objective perspective. But, before you use this fact to justify scoffing at the intellectual and moral frailty of humanity, you must stop and realize that this is not a human flaw, on the contrary, it is inherent in the nature, structure and function of cognition everywhere in the organic universe.

The strength of super stupidity is that it sacrifices other interests to support grouping, and grouping is generally a very effective amplifier of an individual's viability power. Regardless of our own personal philosophical bent, the physics of $\mathbb{SR}$ make it clear that force can distort space in a way that is beneficial to those closest to the apex (or nadir, depending on your perspective) of the distortion field, and message link power can be enhanced by concentrating the maximum value in a message to its two more impactful dimensions. This renders it a near certainty that efforts to distort space with super stupidity will always happen, as well as that such efforts will sometimes even be prudent and wise.

Evolution and the structural nature of cognition together make normal stupidity inevitable, and the physics of $\mathbb{SR}$ make super stupidity almost irresistible. Shifting resources between dimensions can be dangerous if done blindly, irresponsibly, or chronically, but done strategically, the payoff can be significant, because it can simplify competing realities to focus on just one to clarify a problem. This can empower one to finally be able to understand something well enough to know how to fix, or overpower, it.

Super stupidity trades theoretical progress in the future for strength in the present. While what could be a strategically created imbalance in reality valuation can become chronic and destructive because of moral lapses, super stupidity is not, at heart, a moral issue. In the physics of the semantic reality model, the effects of super stupidity can be measured, and the effects can be calculated just like the strength of gravity can be, because it is just a force in a reality. Super stupidity ought to be despised only conditionally, and not because it is wrong, but because of the damage it wreaks in the present, and because it makes working towards the future virtually impossible.

The power of normal stupidity is the simplification of the reference to referent correlation that makes cognition possible: we don't need to understand reality in all its detail and complexity to solve our daily problems, we can solve them just by using a handful of data points to compare the unknown to our internal library of situations we already know how to handle.

The power of super stupidity is in the bet that, by focusing all of our attention on a single dimension of a problem, we can generate enough power to prevail in the moment, and will eventually get around to handling the consequences of temporarily ignoring other parts of reality.[4]

The risk in super stupidity is that our myopia will prevent us from recognizing when it is time to make good on our debt until it is too late. In that case, the reality we were ignoring will — when we least expect it, and are least able to handle it — suddenly come back on us with a vengeance.

---

[4]When faced with the prospect of fighting a combined army, Caesar left a skeleton crew in his encampment facing the first army, and went out and attacked the approaching force before it could join the first. Then he returned and defeated the original force before they knew he had ever left. A very risky, but successful tactic that had the advantage of being his best option at the time. Borrowing from the future can work out if we pay back the debt in a timely fashion.

Chapter 11

The Cost of

Super Stupidity

Super stupid intellectuals are not all the same, of course, some are bored or resigned, some are passionate, but most cluster towards the middle range of emotions associated with living a meaningless life.

Disillusioned, cynical functionaries, such as the jaded academics who have traditionally haunted the universities, cluster towards the bored end of the spectrum. They seem content to sow misery and stifle creativity wherever they can, but the blast radius of their damage is generally limited to the scale of the individual or small group unlucky enough to fall under their power. They are pure misery for those unfortunates, but are generally inconsequential to anyone with the power and freedom, or luck, to avoid them.

True believers, on the other hand, such as those who publish provocative papers on Grievancism, and the morally and intellectually deficient students they successfully infect, fall towards the passionate end of the spectrum. When an accident of birth weds unprincipled, ideological possession with an energetic constitution, it creates a truly obnoxious personality that is eager to wreak destruction all the way down to the pillars of civilization. The ideologues currently spewing forth from academia generally tend to be of this more vicious type, eager to push a doctrine that is explicitly committed to the destruction of all that is good. They dream of dismantling all existing societies, all successful economies, even the whole of western culture itself, along with science, mathematics and anything else that makes them feel inadequate.

Super stupidity arises from the ugly motivation of meager nonentities wanting to blame the world for their own inadequacies so they can avoid having to accept responsibility for their own failures. They start the downward slide when they decide that how they feel is more important than anything else, any fact, any other person, any other reality. So, instead of working to improve themselves, they choose to absorb an ideology that recognizes and supports their resentment and protects their inadequacy with a system of beliefs that projects responsibility for their issues onto external forces or groups. This allows them to wrap their damaged selves into a cocoon inside of their $\mathbb{SR}$ cult from where they try to force others to change the external world in a way they hope will compensate for their neuroses and developmental failures.

Once the educated elite decides to focus only on what they think and feel, and to discount the validity and importance of all the rest of all the other realities, their disrespectful and narcissistic personality bent opens the door for super stupidity to escape and wreak havoc on the world.

The primary formulations of most super stupid doctrines fall under one of the following two types:

- religious: $\mathbb{CS} \subset \mathbb{SR} \subset \mathbb{S}$
  - $\mathbb{CS}$ is a subset of $\mathbb{SR}$ which is a subset of $\mathbb{S}$
- ideological: $\mathbb{CS} \subset \mathbb{SR}$
  - $\mathbb{CS}$ is a subset of $\mathbb{SR}$

In both of these cases, $\mathbb{R}$ is considered an unimportant, ignorable detail, a distraction from the truly important issues. This doctrinal devaluation of $\mathbb{R}$, along with the imbalance in the valuation of the others, has extraordinarily destructive consequences. Since $\mathbb{R}$ is the reality on which all other realities stand, the neglect of it will always result in increased mortality, while the neglect of the others tends to disable self-correction faculties.

It should be easy to see that the real cost of super stupidity

Figure 11.1: Ignore reality at your peril

is:

1. it eliminates any opportunity for intellectual progress;

2. it exposes everyone to *unbounded* loss in $\mathbb{R}$ for the ephemeral gains sought by the few in their private realities.

Self-Other-Ultimate Value Vector

The rest of this chapter relies on the concept of the self-other-ultimate value vector. In this section, we will define it, and explain its profound significance.

In traditional morality, the self is related to the group, and the group to the ultimate. This approach uses three points, instead of two, to define a line of value, meaning and purpose: self, group, ultimate. Why three points to define a line? Because the first point is the self, it is us, it is in our control, so *it can be changed*. The essential idea of traditional morality is precisely that the individual can and must strive to bring himself into line with the other two points. The three point line gives

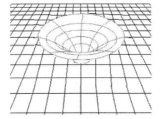

Figure 11.2: Representing the maximum as the nadir of a pit.

us a compass that points to a goal that we can work towards in order to improve both ourself and our world.

In order to understand the critical importance of the three point line, we have to look more deeply into the nature and implications of semantic reality. Using general relativity as a metaphor, we have been imagining the $\mathbb{SR}$ landscape as a flexible membrane with depressions forming at group power centers. This visual model makes it easier to visualize how resources would naturally flow towards, and collect in, the deepest interest wells. But, this is just a visualization aid, not an actual property of semantic reality. We could just as easily flip the orientation from down to up, and represent the maxima as peaks as in figure 11.3, instead of as paraboloid wells as shown in figure 11.2.

Seeing maxima as peaks, rather than valleys, will make it easier to understand and work the next exercise, so we will be using figure 11.4 to represent the semantic reality landscape in this discussion, where each peak represents a separate group,

Figure 11.3: Representing the maximum as a peak.

and the whole extends without bound, but with sparsely populated areas interspersed throughout.

Exercise One: Find, from any given point in figure 11.4, the local minimum and maximum value.

The answer is obvious: the local maximum is the peak of the enclosing $\mathbb{SR}$ subreality, and the minimum is the ground level at the base of the peak.

What have we just calculated? The point of maximal distortion is the maximum power a group (subreality) has achieved; it equates to the mass, the organizing and influential force, of the group and its truths. When we are talking about our own group, it should be obvious that the power of the group has to be related, at least in name, to some of our core values, since we have to connect the group's messages to our own $\mathbb{CS}$ value system. We join groups as a way to further our own goals or values, whether out of belief or ambition, so the group's essential mission has to align with some of our values for us to be

Figure 11.4: Semantic reality landscape

able to connect beneficially with it.

When supplied with the appropriate parameters, finding the best local maximum in a neighborhood can give us a life answer, e.g., which group we can join to best pursue a career, affiliation, or relationship ambition. Finding a maximum in a small set of local maxima can define an achievable goal in an actual reality, such as $\mathbb{SR}$ or $\mathbb{R}$, or a pseudo-reality, such as $\mathbb{CS}$ or $\mathbb{S}$. Such short term goals are potentially achievable, but this also suggests that they have to be replaced periodically as they are attained or discarded. These group-related goals are based on values that originate in our mortality interests.

Exercise Two: From any given point in figure 11.4, find

a *global* minimum and maximum value, and describe the solution in an algorithm with no more than a polynomial order of complexity.

The solution to the second exercise is more of a problem, since both the math and the visual metaphor break down. Mathematically, there is no way to identify a global maximum or minimum in a set of unbounded extent with unbounded, changing values (remember, a peak's height changes constantly as members join and leave, and as the level of their commitment waxes and wanes). The visual metaphor also breaks down because we cannot actually scan the $\mathbb{SR}$ landscape to determine the extrema, the only way we can determine it is to measure each prominence we can find, a task that would have an exponential order of complexity (meaning not computable even for moderate size data sets).

The point of these two exercises is to illustrate the complexity of the $\mathbb{SR}$ landscape. The only fixed point in $\mathbb{SR}$ is our own core self-interest in our $\mathbb{CS}$, which isn't even a part of $\mathbb{SR}$ except from the perspective of our purblind defect. In $\mathbb{SR}$, all truths are local, and all truths are affected by changes in a group's power. You can't find a global maximum in an $\mathbb{SR}$ space, because it simply does not exist.

Recall that current `value` comes from us, $\mathbb{CS}$, while future `meaning` comes from $\mathbb{SR}$, and neither of them are to be found in $\mathbb{R}$. The former comes from the individual's mortality interests, while the latter from the community's viability interests.

Meaning defined in the $\mathbb{SR}$ plane projects current value into achievable, future goals, but nothing more durable or global than that, since there is no global maximum in $\mathbb{SR}$. Conceiving an eduring **purpose** from meaning requires a fixed point we call the **ultimate** that is independent of both personal and local successes and failures, such as career and life accomplishments and disappointments.

Attempting to find **purpose** within $\mathbb{SR}$, such as by committing to a group and its mission, has the effect of fusing the **ultimate** terminus of the self-other-ultimate value vector with the **other** midpoint. The end result is that purpose, rather than being transcendent and durable, becomes a mere goal at the end of a series of tasks. In all cases where the ultimate is defined in terms dictated by an $\mathbb{SR}$ group, the group and ultimate points are fused into one. The mere act of joining such a group then brings one into alignment with it, so there is no need, nor allowance, for self-reflection, self-improvement, or even doubt.

This subordination of ultimate purpose to group affiliation can occur whether the doctrine of the group is religious or ideological whenever it identifies the leadership with the ultimate doctrinal values. In both cases, the guiding power of an **ultimate** point situated in $\mathbb{S}$ is lost in the total dependency on the group leadership. A robust purpose whose meaning cannot be belied by failures of a group and its leaders requires a three point solution where the group and ultimate points are distinct and independent, instead of being fused together when the group's values are defined to be the ultimate values.

The difference between a cult and a religion, or any normal organization, in fact, is freedom to criticize: in a normal organization, you can argue that the organization's actions are not consistent with its principles, but in a cult you cannot, because doing so will get you punished. When you join a normal religion, your highest commitment is to your understanding of its core beliefs, not to its current leadership, because you do not conflate the two. Cults fuse their $\mathbb{SR}$ meaning and values with $\mathbb{S}$ purpose, and they demand obedience, whereas normal organizations are led by temporary leadership who accept that their actions are choices, not immanent manifestations of the ultimate will.

But how do we separate the definition of the `ultimate` purpose from group meaning in $\mathbb{SR}$, how do we find an anchor for our values on a firm, durable, and valid base?

The only part of our mind that is built to comprehend transcendent meaning is $\mathbb{S}$, a subset of $\mathbb{CS}$ that is almost certainly more ancient than those parts of $\mathbb{CS}$ that support language. Transcendent ideas are just that, overarching ideas that subsume all physical, social, and psychological ideas under a greater idea that spans realities and still connects directly to our archetypal values. Transcendent ideas exist to answer whatever questions you might ever want to ask, they are `loopbacks`, constructs whose function is to quell overactive thoughts, to calm doubt, to put questions to rest.

When tragedy inevitably strikes, L0 and L2 react by seeing all reality as tragic. $\mathbb{S}$, on the other hand, tends to calm hyper-emotional ideas down until they begin to come into perspective with other long-range ideas. $\mathbb{S}$ contains constructs that do recognize tragedy as more heartbreaking than other events, certainly, but, it provides a larger viewpoint from which all life events can be seen in proper perspective, as being natural, and not entirely unexpected. $\mathbb{S}$ frames all experience in perspective with the ultimate, however it conceives of it, and gradually demotes new experiences from being seen as the ultimate tragedy to end all tragedies, to being just another life event, however painful, however horrible the loss.

A successful three point solution requires that a global maximum be extrapolated from group and personal doctrines in such a way that it is sufficiently above personal and group interest to have the promise of holding true for our personal eternity, and not be invalidated either by current events, group actions, or any historical test.[1]

The structure of a statement on a global value maximum is tightly constrained by the limitations of $\mathbb{S}$, since the belief has

---

[1] See *The Structure of Truth* for a complete discussion of what truth is and how it is determined on the various cognitive levels.

to universally calm anxieties below its level of importance. Casually phrased beliefs, of the sort tried out by post-adolescents every few months, for example, do not meet the requirements of $\mathbb{S}$ for a fully functional loopback, and are not stored there, and so are not long remembered. $\mathbb{S}$ statements are pithy *antswers*, a neologism meant to suggest the class of answers that are formulated in advance (*ante-*) of any questions, and applied to questions without reference to their class or content. Examples of this abound: "It is God's will", "It's fate", "To everything there is a season", etc. The intelligentsia sneer at these primitive formulations, and then promptly come up with their own equally vacuous bromides: "If we look at this rationally", "Reason can always . . . ", "That's not logical", etc.

Meaning is found in the act of extending the self in $\mathbb{SR}$, beyond the boundaries and imagination of our specific $\mathbb{CS}$ self, but there is more to finding purpose than merely accepting a group's creed. Just accepting a group's creed without extrapolating transcendent values from it only enhances our personal value structure, it does not add the transcendent meaning to it that durable purpose requires. The difference between the two is that personal values disappointed by experience lead only to frustration and despair, while transcendent meaning encompasses both value and tragedy together in an integrated whole, where neither is belied by the other, but each actually helps to explain the other.

Super stupidity co-locates the ultimate value point with the group's creed, thus reducing the self-other-ultimate aspirational vector to just the simple two point group membership relation. This emasculation of our ability to align our cognitive space and chosen semantic realities with a principled, abstract concept of the ultimate, leaves us dependent on the group for our moral compass. It brings us down to the level of concentration camp guards who were 'just following orders'.

Surrendering an ability as awesome as the power to define the ultimate to a power-hungry group merely aids and abets the group's tendency to become tyrannical, and makes us unintelligent, uninteresting, and weak. It makes us partners us with, and enablers of, tyranny.

Blocking Intellectual Progress

Super stupidity blocks intellectual progress because it:

- replaces education with erudition;
- makes intergenerational progress in $\mathbb{SR}$ impossible by fusing the `ultimate` and the `other` points.

By conflating ultimate and group values, the super stupid elite destroy the concept and purpose of education and replace it with the degraded goal of erudition. Erudition is only ever about fitting into a group in a way that benefits the self, thus limiting the purpose of higher education to goals no higher than mere ambition.

When universities formed themselves as finishing schools whose only mission was to prepare the privileged to strut their stuff in their chosen hierarchy pageant, instead of being focused on becoming true educational institutions, this condemned intellectualism to forever wallow in the barnyard of interest-based values when it should have been seeking to extend knowledge into the unknown.

The only meaning that exists in the collapsed self-other join relation is ambition: ambition in the mission of the group, ambition to achieve status in, and to secure resources from, the group hierarchy. The only value, therefore, of training (no need for education) is to prepare one to enter the group on an advanced level, and to equip one to climb higher and faster than one's competitors. Thus, the university's only mission, from the start, has been to manifest the erudition fallacy.[2]

Erudition and education are mutually exclusive. Erudition is based on agreement, because it is essentially a social activity focused on learning to form alliances and navigate in $\mathbb{SR}$, so you learn the language, attitude, and actions you need to know in order to blend smoothly into a group. Pretending that studying the humanities and soft sciences teaches you to think and to analyze is ridiculous. If that is what you wanted to learn, then you would take classes in formal language pattern manipulation,

---

[2]See appendix E.

not waste your time in classes mucking about in internal thought obliquely exercising pattern manipulation skills in an informal, non-reproducible form.

Yes, education is built on language mastery, starting with the informal native language, but, where erudition continues to focus on the social-verbal model, education moves on as soon as practicable to tackling formal languages, such as the various mathematical and scientific disciplines, as well as various executable languages. Further education requires that lessons in model-oriented reasoning be introduced early, followed by higher level exposure to the principles and practices of faceted model-oriented reasoning.

It is only through understanding the laws of model-oriented reasoning that one can deliberately enter the realm of exploration and discovery of the unknown. Education is the process of learning how to explore the unknown in a disciplined manner that maximizes the opportunities for discovery. Erudition is nothing more than learning to talk good.

Even in the formal fields, the only thing that universities offer is training, not education. The individual genius with the will and the means to go beyond the mundane to produce original, significant work is hindered, not helped, by the pedagogical practices of the institution. The flower of genius will never be exactly common, but it could flourish in educational institutions in numbers that are unimaginable in today's erudition factories.

The replacement of education with erudition changes the focus of the higher learning process away from striving to master the discipline of structured exploration of the unknown, towards to the mastery of competitive, rhetorical reasoning that is limited to the self-other relation. Worst of all is that, without an independent, properly defined point positioning the ultimate where we can see, but not reach, it, progress in tackling pinnacle questions is not possible, because no one can position themselves to take up where we leave off. All effort is then local to an arbitrary group peak in $\mathbb{SR}$, and there is no path from it to a stable ultimate, so there is no path that can be extended to further the progress towards a universal goal.

When super stupidity fuses the ultimate to the group value point, thus reducing the self-other-ultimate vector to the simple self-other join relation, it does more than just damage the ability of a $\mathbb{CS}$ to build a balanced, purposeful psyche, it also destroys education and humanity's potential to solve pinnacle problems.

Causing Unbounded Loss

In order to understand how super stupidity has the inherent capacity to cause devastation in all of the internal and external realities, we first have to review two fundamental concepts: the self, in both its specific and extended forms, and the formal definition of evil. Once we have these concepts firmly in hand, then we can begin to understand how the flaws built into the group structures created by the super stupid elite always lead to destruction, sometimes on a massive scale.

Self

Imagine that you were trying to code a simulation of cognitive entities so that you could see and test how behavior arises from the different levels of intellects in the model. That done, you now ask yourself how you are going to represent groups so that you can test behaviors in a social context. The natural starting point — at least for anyone with a background in object-oriented languages — seems to be to think of the group as a *thing* with certain attributes. The problem is, once you start coding it up, you pretty quickly confront the question, *where is the group?*

We are evolved, organic creatures, our reality starts in the genes that express themselves in producing structures and processes in a body, but the group has no genes, it has no physical form. So, it's not an object so much as it is an association. But, is it an association *between* individuals, or *from* an individual to a network of other individuals? Since a network is a set of links and nodes, which, in this case, means that the links are messages and actions that occur in $\mathbb{R}$, but whose value is set by the recipient node, it seems reasonable to use the latter model.

But, this brings us to the question, what is the motivation for an individual to join a group? Is it an entirely new motivation related only to grouping, or is it just an extension of standard individual concepts, considerations, and actions used in self-interested seeking and choosing which incorporates some portion of *other* into an expanded concept of *self*?

Since the simulation already validates the L0-L2 model of:

L0: perceive, evaluate, retreat, approach, ignore;

L1: remember, recognize, learn, compare, react;

L2: patternize, contingent branching, anticipate, plan;

then it seems likely that, simply by making the sense of self flexible enough to include others in its calculation of survival interests, grouping behavior can be entirely accounted for with the concept of an `extended self` that expands the range of the cognitive awareness of the interests of the `specific self` to include others.

One of the observations that informed the development of this model is the almost routine selfless heroism of those in the armed forces who have deliberately given their own lives to save others. (It is repulsive how the educated elite scorn ideals of valor and heroism because their own malignant ideology does not have room for positive ideals, but this is just a symptom of super stupidity, not an argument against the good.)

The normal behavior of parents is a near universal validation of the concept of the extended self because of the way that they prioritize the safety of their loved ones over themselves. Likewise, when it's time for animals to raise a new generation, the fact that many species chase their adolescent offspring away, is evidence of the flexibility of the extended self, showing that it can be expanded or contracted as circumstances require. Honor killings is a particularly grisly human example of the extended self instantaneously shrinking.

Combining the concepts of the specific and extended self with the model of a group as a network of individuals linked by messages and actions gives us a complete working model of human groups that can be parameterized with message physics to simulate groups from friends to families to nations to fanatical hordes.

Evil

The smart set scoffs at the notion of evil, dismissing it as a primitive superstition because they *know* there is no supernatural force of evil, and they also *know* that everything is relative and that what is evil to one is good for another.

Now, some errors are mistakes, some are simple, some are vile, but some are evil, and dismissing the existence and importance of evil actually *is* evil.

In *Xiom*[3] the technical definition of evil will be fully worked

---

[3] *Xiom* is the next volume planned for this series. It is intended to be a sketch of $\mathbb{SR}$ physics. It is currently in progress.

out into a general formula that will be useful in predicting and understanding the genesis and course of an evil surge well before the postmortem analysis has to take place.

For now, understand that we are not discussing evil as some dark, sinister force that compels us to sin. The model we are exploring focuses on modeling internal structures to account for observable actions and messages that appear in $\mathbb{R}$, the reality between us. So, when we model evil, we are looking for relations among model elements that can explain and ultimately predict evil actions.

Thus, the side of evil that we are discussing is its visible aspect; the internals of it are only interesting in so far as they help us to model visible actions. Keep this in mind while we are discussing the internals that manifest as evil actions because, as with all models, the mechanisms we are explaining are only as true as the predictions they produce.

Since our focus is the visible evidence of evil, we have to define what evil looks like. Despite modern, blushing protestations to the contrary, this has never been hard to do, because evil is not that hard to spot. For instance, we know that the commandment is "you shall not murder", not "you shall not kill", so that alone should tell us that killing is not always evil, but we knew that already, because self-defense is a good thing when minimal sufficient force is used. So, if it is not the action itself that is necessarily evil, then it must be the motivation behind

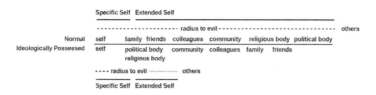

Figure 11.5: The radius to evil.

the action because that is what determines the scale, frequency, and avoidability of the deed, and these are the attributes that separate accidental or justifiable actions from negligent or deliberately malevolent ones.

But, how can we objectively determine motivation, which is an internal feeling? Easy, we do it from the outside by assessing the scale, frequency, and avoidability of the deed and inferring the motivation. Of course, motivation must be assessed on a scale, probably with a range extending from pure accident to carelessness to negligence to deliberate actions to unprovoked sadism. For our purposes, we can just assume such a scale has already been determined and proceed to show the basic concepts that make the quantification of evil practical and useful.

In figure 11.5, the **Normal** line indicates that the extended self begins with family, and extends as far as we want to include some or all of: friends, colleagues, community, religious group, and nation.

Notice the difference between the **Normal** and the **Ideologically Possessed** line below it: the order of items in the extended self is altered to prioritize the ideological group over any other normal association. This represents the fact that cults can, and sometimes do, demand that the novitiate cut ties to their friends and family in order to maximize their commitment to the cult. The community item is placed after the cult body to represent how schisms can split cults into competing factions.

The key concept in this model of evil is that the propensity to evil grows as the radius to evil (the dotted line), the distance between self and others we care nothing about, shrinks. The ideologically possessed pull the **others** boundary all the way into the cult boundary, which puts all of the rest of humanity outside of the range of protection defined by the bubble of the extended self. Furthermore, cults tend to label all outsiders as enemies, and often develop a narrative where they are always being threatened by their enemies. This creates a specter of an ever-present source of danger and threat, the imminence of which sanctions the most extreme measures against outsiders without any further provocation.

The two essential component evaluations that combine to produce evil are:

- propinquity: how far does the extended self reach beyond the specific self, or, how close to the specific self is the boundary where **otherness** begins?

- identity: what combination of hostility and alienation does one feel to **other**, either in general, or in a specific case?

The answers to these two questions will determine an individual's *propensity* to evil. The reasoning is that, the more of the world one feels alienated from, or injured by, the more likely one is to approve of, or participate in, predation just for the joy of it, which is the response at the extreme end of the evil motivation scale.

Propensity for evil does not, of course, equal commission of evil, for this requires an act, not just a proclivity, but propensity is important for two reasons: 1) it makes the act more likely, and 2) it eliminates the chance that you would correct your behavior after seeing the damage your actions have caused.

What goes for extreme cults also applies to psychopaths, sociopaths (those who have no extended self), and anyone else who have convinced themselves that their own needs and fears count more than the interests or rights of anyone or anything else.

We can now formally define evil:

Evil: having extreme indifference about, or taking joy in, inflicting wanton, unwarranted pain and loss on others.

The greater the damage, the more wanton the act, the greater the evil. Evil can be identified both in intent and in actions, and the above definition refers to evil acts, so what about evil intent? Whence does evil arise? Can the propensity to evil be calculated? If so, then we would know both who is more likely to commit evil acts, and what evil acts actually look like. The calculation of the tolerance of, or proclivity to, evil is fairly straightforward and arises naturally from the universal cognition model:

$$eq = \frac{|\texttt{other}|}{|\texttt{extended self}|} \cdot |[a, -, n]_o| \cdot ag \cdot en \cdot init \cdot iq \quad (11.1)$$

eq = evil quotient

$|\texttt{other}|$ = magnitude of other

$|\texttt{extended self}|$ = magnitude of extended self

$|[a, -, n]_o|$ = level of hostility and alienation to other

ag = constitutional aggression level

en = constitutional entitlement level

$init$ = constitutional initiative level

iq = constitutional intelligence level

This formula calculates one's propensity to evil, one's evil quotient, with these factors:

- The first term is the ratio between the magnitude of how one defines the **other** segment of existence and the magnitude of one's extended self. The more that **other**ness dwarfs the part of reality one can relate to, the more of reality one is indifferent to, or alienated from.

- The second term ($|[a, -, n]_\circ|$) defines how one feels about **other**, as represented by the anti-self and non-self components in the evaluation of **other** (which may be at a general, or a specific group, level, depending on the subject of interest). The more negatively one feels about, and the more alienated one feels from, the **other**, the more motivation there will be either to accept, or initiate, depredations on them.

- The last four terms are constitutional levels of aggression, entitlement, initiative, and intelligence. The more aggressive and entitled one is, the more natural it is to view the interest sphere belonging to an **other** as fair game to plunder. The more initiative one has, the more likely that plans and intentions will become actions. The more intelligence one has, the more inventive one can be in improvising ways to accomplish a nefarious (or any other kind of) goal.

Super stupidity arises from the debris of rejected traditional values, and it ascends on the imbalance of values between narcissism, ambition and irresponsibility on the one hand, and all of the other realities on the other. When this turning away from good joins with an ideological possession, it creates a noxious combination whose only natural offspring is evil intent. Just as it is not a surprise when a rock dropped from the hand falls to the ground, so neither is it a surprise when emboldening and

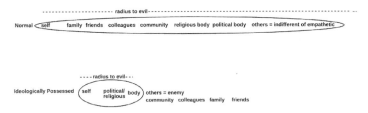

Figure 11.6: Super stupidity, ideology, and the radius to evil.

releasing one's inner demons of envy, resentment, and avarice into the collective fury pouring from one's ideologically indoctrinated brethren inevitably wreaks havoc on the greater good. To the truly envious, tearing others down is even better than building oneself up.

* * * *

Volitionally mobile creatures are built to consume or attack food and enemies; the more of one's world one others, the more of it falls into the consumable/attackable category. Figure 11.6 shows the stark difference between the inner world views of normal people on the one hand, and ideologically possessed super stupid people on the other. The acceptance and benevolence of normal people tends to stretch towards the horizon, at least, while those possessed by a super stupid ideology shrink their world of us to just their inner circle of true believers, and enemize everything else as other. The super stupid reduce all other to an exploitable, or expungeable, resource; only initiative needs to be added to reify evil intent into evil action.

As amply demonstrated in the numerous manifestations of communism, super stupidity has a nearly unbounded capacity to destroy. Its destructive power springs from loosening the moral and cultural ties that have traditionally held evil back for long enough for large bubbles of prosperity and relative peace to develop over time around the globe. The current prosperity bubble has brought the majority of the world's population out of abject poverty in just the last quarter century or so.

Super stupidity others everyone and everything not at the center of one's cult, and gives cult members a virtual license to kill — both in a literal, as well as figurative, sense — any outsiders they don't like. Super stupidity knows it can't be wrong, it knows that its morality is the most highly evolved, and it knows that its intellect has framed the subject in exactly the right way to exclude the possibility of error. This lack of humility breeds a vicious intolerance.

At a very early age, we learn to lean into turns when riding a bicycle, but we also automatically know to straighten ourself out right after we finish the turn. That is, we learn that under certain circumstances we have to perform actions that would unbalance us in normal conditions, but that can keep us upright in other situations. The same rule holds true in semantic space: we can temporarily bend our attention away from the other reality planes in order to focus our effort in a particular plane to achieve a goal. This tactic becomes super stupid, though, when we elevate a tactic to a fundamental belief, when we decide that the solution to all of our problems is *always* to lean in a particular direction, regardless of how circumstances otherwise change.

Super stupidity spreads stupidity by leveraging the lossy narrowing typecast from the pattern to the belief object as a strength, rather than a weakness. In elevating feelings above evidence, super stupidity eagerly washes all evidence out of opinion objects as quickly as possible in order to fix their ideas as permanent, universal truths. Thus, not only are super stupid ideas not self correcting, they cannot be corrected by anyone else either, because their truth is unassailably ensconced in a $O(1)$ complexity belief truth object in core doctrinal beliefs stored in $\mathbb{S}$, and so are immune to factual attack.

Super stupidity's commitment to tilt semantic reality in its favor, regardless of other reality concerns, acquires a fanatical religious fervor when it is joined to an oppressor/oppressed ideology. To the super stupid, nothing outside of the doctrine in $\mathbb{SR}$ matters, not people, not nature, not reality. In the name of maintaining the core $\mathbb{SR}$ truth of his religion/ideology, an ideologue will consider all costs borne by other, less important realities to be reasonable, no matter how onerous. Super stupid ideologues do not care if their policies lead to the death of hundreds of millions of victims, because, in their world, outsiders' lives are of no importance compared to the truth of their ideology.

The dearest cost of super stupidity is that it arrogantly and insistently pronounces a local truth to be a global truth, with devastating effects:

- The urbane sophisticates — who are really just cult members — wind up promoting the most narrow-minded, obtuse ideologies as being modern, enlightened, and broad-minded, when they are actually primitive, narrow-minded, and medieval tribal systems.

- In failing to create an external definition of a trans-generational, cross-cultural, transcendent goal, super stupidity guarantees that no progress towards resolving pinnacle questions can even begin.

- Since their focus is always on a local $\mathbb{SR}$ truth, the educated elite have neither interest in, support for, nor tolerance of the possibility of disruptive discoveries that might threaten the worshipped status quo.

Some $\mathbb{SR}$s, such as commercial enterprises, strongly interact with external realities, whether in $\mathbb{SR}$, $\mathbb{R}$ or both, and this inhibits the inclination towards getting too far into super stupidity. Although the unrecognized and unresearched barrier between $\mathbb{R}$ and any $\mathbb{SR}$ creates significant communication and conceptualization problems, nevertheless, the employees of lumber companies, mining companies, and the like, are subject to having their silly, internal ideas rebuked by an indifferent $\mathbb{R}$ on a daily, if not hourly, basis. Even the employees working in companies that only trade with other companies in a shared $\mathbb{SR}$ have their ideas tested and often crushed by their independent $\mathbb{SR}$ partner.

The academic world, however, stands apart, in that, at the faculty level, their ideas never need to be tested (indeed, most are not even testable) unless they choose to make the effort. Since reward is in publication, not testing, rigorous testing rarely happens outside of the hard sciences.

Since super stupidity obviates the possibility of fixed, higher goals — precluding even the hope of achieving progress towards any aspirational purpose — it has an inherent directionlessness that makes both indifferent and negative results equally likely. Super stupidity condemns humanity to a future in which any resolution of pinnacle questions is simply impossible.

Ideologies created by the super stupid elite are, by nature, prone to evil because they reject the significance of $\mathbb{R}$, they are immune to criticism, they **other** everyone and everything outside of their small $\mathbb{SR}$ bubble, they reject traditional limits and values, and they know they are right with a greater conviction than the most narrow-minded bigot.

The super stupid ideologues in academia have effectively recreated a rigid, intolerant, prudish, medieval religion that is potentially more destructive than the religions that were actually around in medieval times ever were.

Part III

The Future

Chapter 12

Solutions

Where do we go from here? How can we leverage the universal cognition model, and our new knowledge of structural cognitive limits to make an impact both on our personal lives, and on the current and future health of our society?

Ultimately, of course, the way forward will be found on an educational path that develops our self-programming skill, while also supporting the advancement of the science of quantitative modeling of subjective realities, extends the UCM, and develops the physics of $\mathbb{SR}$, etc., all while holding onto the good that we already have. But, 'ultimately' is a little ways away at the moment, so we still have to address the rather more practical questions: what do we no now, what do we do first?

This final section will address different options we have,

some more immediately practical than others. In chapter 13, Stop the Bleeding, the focus will be on stopping the damage currently being done to our society by the sororities of the super stupid. In chapter 14, Coping Strategies, the focus will be on how we, as individuals, can reorient ourselves to our realities in a way that leverages the concepts discussed here. Finally, in chapter 15, ASPICS, we will introduce a final model of who and what we are at a level above the specifics of our individuality or species.

There are many things large and small, immediate and remote, that we can begin to do now to start to bring our life vector into alignment with whatever self-other-ultimate value vector we define for ourselves. Some actions can be done today, with just the knowledge gained from this book, while others would take years of education. In the remaining chapters, a large number of ideas, tips, and suggestions will be provided to give the reader a variety of starting points they can consider, but it is up to each individual to pick and choose, or to invent, their personal project and path forward.

Chapter 13

Stop the Bleeding

Although the question, "What do we do first, what do we do *now?*" is more impulsive than reasoned, this question does have some gravity due to the fact that our civilization is currently bleeding from countless wounds inflicted on it by a super stupid educated elite hell-bent on imposing their ideological idiocies on us through the bureaucracies they control.

Since there actually is an urgent need to stanch the bleeding from these injuries before surgery can become a reasonable option — let alone before we can even begin to dream about moving forward — this chapter will list a number of things in a handful of subjects that we can begin to work on right now. These suggestions fall into one of two categories: "stop doing this" or "start doing this". The **stop** category is just emer-

gency first aid steps to slow the rate at which we are bleeding
out, while the **start** category is more a list of things to consider (maybe think of them as suggestions for research projects).
Keep in mind, though, that the underlying intent of this chapter
is not to offer a prescription for a radical new social engineering
program, but is just intended to help the reader flesh out their
understanding of the ideas we have already discussed with easy
to understand, practical illustrations.

Reasoning

Story problems in math class had to be the bane of the average
junior high schooler's existence. Groans would fill the classroom
when verbal problems appeared on a test, because everyone
knew that, not only would they have to solve an equation, but
that they would first have to try to figure out how to pull the
equation out of some stupid little story. Even those of us who
were good at math would groan a little, because we knew that
we would have to shift gears from calculation to analysis mode
and back again, and that this would take extra time that we
didn't have a surplus of during tests.

But, imagine how much worse it would have been if we were
not only presented problems in verbal mode, but also had to
solve them in verbal mode without equations and without variables. If we weren't able to convert words into an easy to solve

equation, we would just have to reorganize the words and then calculate the solution in clumsy, ambiguous, confusing words. This nightmare actually has a name, and it's called *rhetorical algebra*, and it was the only form of algebra available until about 1500 CE.

It is no accident that the scientific revolution didn't begin until after rhetorical algebra was replaced by symbolic algebra. Rhetorical algebra was a clumsy early point in the development of useful mathematics. Once the key discoveries of symbology and variables in algebra were made, the world just opened up for a tsunami of progress to commence.

It's easy for us to shake our head in wonder at how primitive scholars used to be, but before you feel too superior, you might want to take a moment to realize that we are **still** stuck using *rhetorical reasoning*. That is, outside of the little we might do in formal languages, we still do all of our reasoning in words. What's the alternative? Just as the alternative to rhetorical algebra is symbolic algebra, so the alternative to rhetorical reasoning is symbolic reasoning.

The problem with symbolic reasoning, the reason that attempts to solve subjective problems with it have all failed so far, is that it only applies to quantitative subjects, and historically, subjective problems simply did not qualify. At least, they did not qualify until now.

Faceted model-oriented reasoning[1] applied to the evolutionary cytomodel is the advancement that opens up the subjective world to formal methods for the first time by allowing us to quantize subjective phenomena to prepare them for formal reasoning methods. Faceted model-oriented reasoning gives us a verifiable methodology that can externalize internal knowledge. The externalization process applied to an evolutionary model can express internal thoughts and feelings in a format suitable for expression in a formal language. This is the same system we have been using in this book to explain normal and super stupidity, concepts that clarify so much about how our cognitive abilities work, and what their limitations are.

What to Stop

- We have to stop using rhetorical reasoning to try to solve complex problems. Rhetorical reasoning is so cumbersome and imprecise that it actually does qualify as serious reasoning, since it does not even support calculation and verification. Complex problems can only be solved with powerful, precise tools, not with ambiguous, imprecise verbal narratives full of untestable, implicit assumptions.

- It is past time to stop premature simplification. As explained in *The Structure of Truth*, the ternary truth form (true/false/unimportant) is only useful in the transition

---

[1] See *Ultrareasoning*.

phase between reasoning and action, because it is actually derived *from* the basic decision language, a language so simple it only has three basic terms: approach, retreat, ignore. It's the carryover from this primitive movement language that makes us inclined to think that all truth can be reduced to right/wrong/don't care form. It is a mistake to think that this reduction to simplicity is the path to finishing or understanding a thought. We unconsciously assume that the good/bad/unimportant judgment captures the true meaning of the idea. In reality, if we want to optimize our reasoning ability, we should save the agree/ disagree/meh reduction strictly for deciding how to act, not how to think.

- It is past time to stop using one-dimensional thinking since there are no subjective problems that only have one dimension: there are always at least the various realities, cognition levels, inputs, outputs, and stakeholders, and it is an error to summarily exclude any of them from consideration. Every $\mathbb{SR}$ problem requires multivariate analysis. In fact, the only concept that can be expressed in one dimension is personal preference. Highly impassioned ideologues will invariably declare entire complex systems to be right or wrong based on a single thought, dimension, number, or narrative, and we can no longer pretend that there is any $\mathbb{R}$ validity in this approach, that it is anything but super stupid.

- It is past time to reject the idea that the simple right/ wrong truth structure has universal application: while it is essential for decision-making, it has very little application beyond that.

- It is past time to stop thinking that ideology has anything to do with $\mathbb{R}$, because its only function is to energize and strengthen group bonds. Ideology *only* has $\mathbb{SR}$ truth, and *no* $\mathbb{R}$ truth (accidental alignment with $\mathbb{R}$ is purely coincidental). Ideology cannot explain reality because the composite container object we use to conceptualize it generalizes the opinion object which only *sorts* facts, it does not *rely* on, or explain, facts.

- It is time to stop basing reasoning on narrative threads, because such threads are just links to a $\mathbb{CS}$ value context, links to our distortion field, and are not related to $\mathbb{R}$ at all. The fundamental property of all $r_i \in \mathbb{R}$ is *specificity*, a characteristic that makes each fact independently testable and falsifiable or verifiable. The truth in a narrative thread is a native $\mathbb{CS}$ value truth which manifests through messaging in $\mathbb{SR}$; it is not specific, and is not relevant to $\mathbb{R}$.

What to Start

- Learn how to use different reasoning with different truth functions for different types of discussions: decision, exploration, progress, bonding, etc.

- Learn how to shift gears between $\mathbb{SR}, \mathbb{R}, \mathbb{CS}$ and $\mathbb{S}$ when thinking about different problems.

- Learn how to think in $\mathbb{S}$ using L3, or at least L2, instead of just L0.

Identify and Respond

The key symptom of super stupidity is the twinned phenomenon of disrespect and arrogance: a disrespect of tradition, dissenting opinions, and of $\mathbb{R}$ itself, and an arrogant infatuation with the infallibility of one's own ideas and reasoning ability. Super stupidity stems from the narcissistic love of internal knowledge above everyone and everything else. We must begin to recognize super stupidity in the wild, and learn how to respond to it.

What to Stop

- Stop pretending that super stupidity is anything else, don't treat it like it's a thoughtful argument.

- Stop accepting unquantified, untested ideas as valid concepts, they are sham thoughts whose only purpose is to feed the speaker's ego while they try to draw adherents into their sphere.

- Stop accepting anything that any scientist or expert says that is outside of their field or not backed up with sound, verified numbers. Realize that the instant they mention value or policy they are outside of their area of expertise, and have less than no idea of what they are talking about, since they don't even know they are already lost in the swamps.

- Stop seeing arguments that engage your emotions as being in any way intellectual: discussions about $\mathbb{R}$ are restricted to specific, verifiable facts, not generalities, not affective rhetoric.

What to Start

- Start to appreciate that super stupidity is perfectly appropriate in group building discussions in areas not critically dependent on the specifics of $\mathbb{R}$.

- Start to figure out how to respond to the inappropriate appearance of super stupidity in group settings where you cannot leave and the outcome in $\mathbb{R}$ matters to you.

Opinion

Opinions sort facts into agree/disagree categories so that we can maintain an equilibrium between our sense of self, our values, and our social relations.[2] Opinion *discussions* have nothing to do with facts, they are entirely about social bonding between the participants. If you are concerned with social bonding, then use opinion discussions, but, if you are concerned with realities that ultimately manifest in $\mathbb{R}$, then do not.

Surely, everyone has noticed that if we change our opinion on a big topic, such as life, politics, or religion, we will generally have to change our circle of friends and associates, too. We all know that opinion discussions are about social bonding, because we all know that their goal is *agreement*, not understanding or discovery. The goal is for the participants to validate each other with the explicit or implicit declaration that, "I'm with you!" These discussions succeed when harmony is maintained, and agreement, or at least acquiescence, is achieved. We know this because the function of the opinion object itself is to process information in a way that maintains identity and values, and this is the stuff of which social bonds are made.

We craft our opinions, those which we do not inherit from one or more groups, by defining and modifying an archetype proposition in a given value arena. This *feels* like reasoning,

---

[2]See appendix D, or *Ultrareasoning*, chapter 23.

like rational thinking, but it's not, it doesn't reach that level. It's actually just a transformation of values, experiences and relations into a statement that can be used as a basis of comparison for processing message input into the anti-self, pro-self, and non-self buckets.

The goal of crafting an opinion is to create a standard that will allow us to keep our balance and to properly identify friend and foe.

What to Stop

- Stop seeing opinions as intellectual constructs.
- Stop participating in opinion debates except when the objective is strictly social, to compete for position, or to persuade others to join the group.
- Stop thinking of your own opinions as correct; they work for you if they keep you balanced and maintain your group relations, but that's all they do.

What to Start

- Start looking for anomalies in your opinions where they unexpectedly vary from $\mathbb{R}$. Then, instead of glossing over them, relentlessly pursue them until your opinion requires a major adjustment.
- Start observing how you process information through an

opinion. Try to catch the moment when the opinion object sorts the message into the appropriate bucket and then note the subtle, but real, emotional satisfaction and validation that occurs. See if you can catch what happens next: you no longer care about trying to learn something from the message, because the focus has now shifted from processing the message to validating that you already knew the answer.

Evidence

Facts are neither fun nor sad, they just are, because the defining attribute of all $r_i \in \mathbb{R}$ is specificity: things have a position, events have a time, forces have a vector. When a phenomenon, p, is evaluated in terms of $\mathbb{R}$, the result is numbers; when evaluated in terms of $\mathbb{CS}$, the result is value; when evaluated in terms of $\mathbb{SR}$, the result is meaning.

While we care about things with value, and things with meaning have real or potential effects that we care about, facts themselves are just facts until we invest them with value or meaning.

What to Stop

- Stop adducing facts in opinion discussions unless they have rhetorical value.

- Stop mixing $\mathbb{SR}$ debates with fact-based discussions.

- Stop making or allowing the mistaken claim that certain evidence in $\mathbb{R}$ leads to the logical conclusion that a particular policy in $\mathbb{SR}$ must be right.[3]

- Stop expecting that evidence will lead to one absolute truth in philosophical or political discussions.

What to Start

- Start to demand multidimensional thinking when unidimensional facts are introduced as evidence supporting a social or political point.

- Start to object to the use of comparatives and superlatives in fact-based discussions, and require verified numbers always be used instead.

- Start to think of evidence as test results that challenge or support your model, and begin to expect that additional evidence will often be available that will require you to modify your conclusions.

- Start to isolate decision discussions (where value and meaning are applied to facts from a particular interest perspective) from evidence discussions. Both are important, but they shouldn't be mixed together.

---

[3]See chapter 30, Subjectivity Conjecture, in *Ultrareasoning*.

Debate

We are using the term `debate` to refer to any public conversation whose intent is to persuade participants and listeners to agree with one of the speakers. This covers everything from speeches to panel discussions to Q&A sessions, and everything in between. What all these different formats have in common is they degrade intellectual discourse by using rhetorical reasoning to attract followers instead of using quantitative reasoning to consider or explain issues, options, and trade-offs. In other words, debates use rhetoric to persuade listeners that a particular rhetorical reasoning narrative is the "truth."

What to Stop

- Stop accepting rhetorical displays as something serious, substantive, and worthwhile, since they are nothing of the sort.
- Stop conflating emotional engagement with intellectual understanding.
- Stop accepting truncated data sets as a legitimate basis for reasoning.
- Stop accepting unidimensional analysis from speakers.
- Stop accepting ideology as an argument about $\mathbb{R}$.

What to Start

- Start to demand that policy debates explicitly use the optimization formula.[4]

- Start working on learning how to see rhetorical debates as anti-intellectual grouping exercises.

- Start working on learning how to see that the subject of debates is rhetorical reasoning on $\mathbb{SR}$ physics, not $\mathbb{R}$ facts, or even $\mathbb{S}$ morality.

- Start to demand that fact-focused debates be restricted to discussing an enumerated list of facts with evidence, and nothing else.

- Start to demand that the non-self evaluation of debate evidence be defined in advance and fixed, and prohibit devaluation by participants.[5]

Education

Academia is currently overrun with poorly educated dullards who, in their ideological possession, have decided that power is the only truth, and that $\mathbb{R}$-truth does not matter. Post-modernists use this reasoning to justify both doing anything to increase their own power, and doing anything they want with

---

[4]See appendix F, or *Ultrareasoning*, chapter 30.

[5]While we are each free to decide that some idea or event is not important, this is an invalid argument in a debate since it is universally true that the truth value of any statement doesn't matter if the statement itself is given zero importance.

whatever power they have, no matter how heinous.

The creators of postmodernism half stumbled upon a fragmentary awareness of the concept of $\mathbb{SR}$ and the definition of $\mathbb{SR}$ truth. But then, rather than pushing forward to build on this small insight to discover the multiplicity of realities and other wondrous things discussed in this volume, instead they chose to turn away from the bright light of discovery in order to build a dark ideology that feeds on their resentments and justifies their inadequacies. Instead of challenging both the individual and society to confront, and take responsibility for, their failures, they took the lesser path that follows the tradition of murderous socialist/Marxist philosophies: they opted to don the cloak of the oppressed, so that they could righteously point the finger of blame away from themselves, and towards some class of people whom they would destroy for the imaginary sin of causing all of their psychic and economic misery.

While the destruction of education with the worship of erudition is by no means a new crime, yet the vigor with which it is being prosecuted today in the name of postmodernism threatens to overwhelm even the previously secure bastion of the exact sciences. No longer is merit a requirement for inclusion, no longer is incompetence a cause for dismissal, no longer is objective truth something to be valued, on the contrary, fealty to the ideological cause is now the only truth, and anyone foolhardy enough to suggest otherwise is punished with disgrace and banishment.

Super stupidity is born anew in every generation when the pursuit of erudition is reaffirmed as the primary objective of learning, and actual education is rejected yet again. This generational renewal of super stupidity places a hard cap on the power of reasoning, and limits it to the minor role of a crude tool in the competitive struggle to improve or protect one's position in the hierarchy.

The majority of damage done by the super stupid battalions is done by academics who arrogantly and ignorantly fail to recognize or respect any reality outside of their own little arid domain. They deliberately elevate an unbalanced assessment of the relative importance of the internal and external realities to be a core tenet of faith in their religion in order to gain an unwarranted sense of status and importance in their $\mathbb{SR}$ group.

If we simply reduce the rate at which higher education produces ideologically possessed graduates groomed only to be vocal advocates of super stupidity, this will go a long way to slowing the bleeding. Once we do that, we can get on with the hard work of creating the knowledge infrastructure necessary to support the effort to extend the scientific revolution into the subjective sphere.

What to Stop

- Stop supporting the academic priesthood, a profane cloister in which professors act as gate keepers to the inner rings of $\mathbb{SR}$ power.

- Stop public funding of humanities and pseudo-sciences degree programs.

- Stop offering tenure, since it doesn't even stop the zealots from purging moderates who resist their religion.

- Stop offering indoctrination classes that teach that the only answer to every question is Grievancism.

- Stop using the humanities to teach pattern manipulation reasoning.

What to Start

- Start to develop the $\mathbb{SR}$ physics research discipline.

- Start requiring that all courses generate reproducible results, and demote anecdotal courses to survey classes, eliminate them altogether, or move them to optional evening discussion groups where they belong.

- Start new programs that offer degrees or certificates in para-science, para-math, and para-technology so we can replicate experiments cheaply, and minimize the need for PhD supervisors.

- Start to pair colleges across institutions to create teams that will reproduce all of each other's published work to verify or challenge it.

- Start teaching faceted model-oriented reasoning, and organize first years' studies around the prerequisites for it.

- Start teaching the subjectivity conjecture[6] and the role that the optimization formula plays in framing all subjective problems.

- Start to reorganize the curriculum to eliminate grievance studies courses, as well as all other classes with non-reproducible results.

  - Move internal knowledge specialties to teachers' colleges.

  - Move theology courses to theological institutions.

- Start a required $\mathbb{SR}$ orientation curriculum.

- Start to teach pattern assimilation/manipulation directly in their own courses.

Politics

What to Stop

- Stop public funding of media.

- Stop pretending that there is any truth in campaigning or reporting on campaigns other than $\mathbb{SR}$ truth.

---

[6]**Subjectivity Conjecture**: all subjective problems can be expressed in the optimization formula (see appendix F), see *Ultrareasoning*, chapter 30.

- Stop pretending that political solutions are `right` or `wrong`, since they are only suggested solutions to some application of the optimization formula.

What to Start

- Start limiting new spending/redistribution laws to a limited term, after which they must satisfy specified performance requirements to be renewed.
- Start to apply formal reasoning and requirements to political debates.
- Start to use the optimization formula for the basis of all legislation, so that all known trade-offs are explicitly predicted.
- Start to require all laws to have milestones, timetables, and sunset/cancellation criteria

Postmodernism

Postmodernism is the current spear tip of the super stupid movement — it is the purest form of super stupidity that has ever been developed — so if we hope to slow the bleeding, it must start here. We have already addressed it in several of the previous topics, but we must now address it directly.

The problem with critical theory and postmodernism is that its creators stumbled upon the fact that $\mathbb{SR}$ exists, but rather

than seeing it as a new reality in the set of realities, they fool-
ishly, and without any justification whatsoever, concluded that
$\mathbb{SR}$ is the **only** reality, and that $\mathbb{R}$ is somehow just a construct of
our society. Thus, their cynical, myopic claim that only power
matters, was born. Where a competent, healthy reasoner would
grok that it really means that the cardinality of the set of realities is greater than one,

$$|\mathfrak{R}| > 1$$

they somehow came to the ridiculous conclusion that $\mathbb{SR}$ being
real somehow invalidates the reality of $\mathbb{R}$, and then completely
missed the pseudo-realities of $\mathbb{CS}$ and $\mathbb{S}$.

Devaluing other reality dimensions to maximize returns in
one, incurs a mortgage on our future that must be paid back to
restore balance. Unfortunately, as history amply demonstrates,
with sufficient power and privilege, the beneficiaries of such dis-
tortions can often assign the accrued debt to be paid by others
less powerful than themselves, and by those as yet unborn.

While it is true that super stupidity is often a product of
moral failure, not even that means it always achieves a bad end.
Super stupidity is a way of concentrating power in a single point;
whether or not this is a good thing is a value judgment. My
particular objection to its position as the primary ruling force
in academia is because it precludes the possibility of us ever

making progress towards solving any of the pinnacle questions, and since doing exactly that has been my life's work, you might understand that I take this personally. To have the people who run the education establishment deliberately do everything they can to sabotage education, to have the people who supposedly want to mitigate injustice and human suffering do everything they can to exacerbate and perpetuate it, is just infuriating.

Chapter 14

Coping Strategies

Many paths to a better future are open to us, and it is up to us to choose which ones we want to explore, but the skills we bring to the table and how we prioritize problems will limit which paths we are equipped to explore successfully.

Learning cannot change inherited structures, of course, so no epiphany or stroke of genius is ever going to erase organic cognition's inherent limitations. Structural limitations are just that: the very structures that enable us to perceive and interpret experience are the same ones that limit the cognitive process. Fantasizing that we would benefit from eliminating them is kind of like thinking that we could swim further in a pool if only we knocked down its sides, when, in reality, no sides to the pool means no pool, just as no limits to cognition means no cognition.

So, what can we do to cope with our built-in limitations? The long-term answer, of course, is to build out faceted model-oriented reasoning with theoretical foundations and practical mathematical and executable solutions, and to entirely revamp the educational system to support and leverage these efforts. In the meantime, though, there are a number of very practical things that we can already begin to do, even without having to do a lot of extra studying first.

This chapter will focus on individual strategies we can employ sooner rather than later, actions that we are nearly or actually ready to take right now. These are things that we can begin to do simply by bringing in some model elements to inform and improve our interactions with $\mathbb{SR}$ and $\mathbb{R}$, and to balance our reasoning in both $\mathbb{CS}$ and $\mathbb{S}$.

In §Traditional Strategies, we will discuss how to mine religion and cultural mores for elements of meaning that we can use to weave our own self-other-ultimate value vector.

In §Creative Strategies, we will discuss new ways to think about, interact with, and interrogate normal forms of social interaction and messages.

In §Practical Tips, we discuss a handful of tips about different ways we can restructure the foundations of our knowledge and opinion webs to make them more consistent with the cognition limits. The goal of this restructuring is to be able to see our familiar world with new eyes.

Traditional Strategies

We can revive and update the traditional solutions by leveraging our new awareness of our cognitive limits to tailor familiar strategies to fit our own needs, interests, abilities, and experiences. But, before we begin crafting innovative ways to cope with our limitations, let us first look at religion with a fresh eye to see how we can use its demonstrated power and potential, despite its flaws, as a starting point.

Religion

It is time we start to understand and value religion in a proper perspective: evolution invented the socket that god plugs into, so we can be sure that *something* will get plugged into that socket, regardless of whatever facile, sophomoric ideas we have about the irrelevance of religion and god.

The obvious modern alternative to religion is scientific atheism, the major manifestation of which is Marxism, a religion that managed to murder roughly 100M people in the twentieth century alone. That's a rate of one million murders a year, a far greater rate of slaughter than any traditional religion has ever caused, yet intellectual atheists still preach that people should overthrow traditional systems and replace them with their own.

Brilliant.

Social justice warriors have followed the postmodernist creed and created a religion which is nihilistic, intolerant, racist, anti-Semitic, destructive, prudish, and on top of that, both profoundly anti-rational and anti-science. Yet, the atheists still urge us into this dead end, apparently because they just discovered that God $\notin \mathbb{R}$, and they urge us to follow them with all of the smug arrogance their erudition and rhetoric can ooze.

It is an unfortunate sign of the times that we must remind everyone that traditional solutions, solutions which have worked — admittedly, some better than others — for thousands of years, are still largely valid. Even after a religion's ideas about realities in $\mathbb{R}$ are exposed as false, the $\mathbb{CS}$ and $\mathbb{SR}$ parts of its solution might still be perfectly serviceable, and capable of providing a guide for both the individual and the community about how to live a healthy, constructive, and ordered life.

The major religions seem to follow something like a standard life arc from the moment they are created, to when they grow, to when they mature, to when they begin to whither away. The transition phase of this arc that connects the stage where the focus is on political goals to the stage that focuses on purely spiritual and community goals — where it goes from concentrating on control and domination to concentrating on the internal and communal spiritual aspects of its creed — is what separates reformed religions from imperialistic or primitive ideologies.

Reformed religions have learned to surrender the fantasy that internal thoughts and feelings have the power to dominate $\mathbb{R}$, while orthodox religions still cling to the dream of making their inner magic dominate external reality. In general, unreformed religions or groups will deny the errors and contradictions in their doctrines in order to strive for hegemony in their semantic sphere of interest. These groups value their $\mathbb{SR}$ truth over any other, and are content to blithely ignore blatant contradictions between scripture and $\mathbb{R}$, because, under certain circumstances, doing so can make the group stronger.

The first step that a modern, sophisticated person can take to meaningfully engage with a reformed religion or ideology — even though they consciously believe it to be mostly or wholly man-made — is to identify aspects of its aspirational goals that they find inspiring. Next, they will selectively choose or prune the acts and sayings down to a shape that enables the accepted goals to be integrated into their life in a meaningful way.

The justification for pruning religious doctrine is that, historically, congregations put continual pressure on the clergy to add more actions, rituals, and stories to the creed so that the believers can festoon their lives with their choice of observations and apothegms until they are effectively insulated from the harsh reality of having to make decisions. Such amendments (e.g., death penalty for wearing a combination of fabrics, the here-and-now doesn't count, lying is okay, etc.) bear the heavy imprint of human hands, and can generally be put aside without concern, since doing so nearly always restores, rather than diminishes, the original doctrine.

The fact is that we have to take responsibility, not only for everything we think and do, but also for everything we believe. This means that, rather than accepting a doctrine unquestioningly, we have to select such parts of a traditional one that are meaningful and valuable. One of the very first things we have to do is to define, or accept, a very high level aspirational goal that:

1. is eternally laudable and worthwhile;

2. is beyond the grasp of a lifetime. We should be able to approach, but not achieve, it (selecting an achievable goal, such as a career milestone, guarantees a midlife crisis as soon as it is achieved);

3. cannot be achieved by an already known or obvious path (if the means to achieve a goal are known, it is merely a task, not a meaningful goal).

Obviously, since most readers with the education and interest to read this book will have long since abandoned organized religion, this whole discussion undoubtedly seems ridiculous, if not repellent. However, that's not a valid objection, it's just one of the problems you have to figure out how to solve on your own (by the way, you don't have to join a congregation or attend meetings to connect to a system of values, but you can if you like the cookies).

Academics and intellectuals have reacted to the decline of religion's authority in $\mathbb{R}$ in the most unfortunate way possible, but this was discussed in detail in chapter 8. Societies that we like to think of as modern, enlightened, sophisticated cultures have been persuaded or influenced by a diabolical cabal of educated charlatans to devolve from having a spiritual/religious/service focus to being entirely consumed by hedonistic/materialistic/ hive goals. Striving for ultimate meaning has been replaced by an urgent impulse to seek satiety in avarice and sensation, and safety in group acceptance.

While the range of solutions available in any high-level optimization problem, such as the problem of how to successfully define the meaning of life, is truly infinite, it provably does not include hedonistic materialism in the set of potentially successful pathways. The obvious way to avoid such identifiable errors as going down that path is to start building our own coping strategy by selecting a religious/philosophical solution template that has a well-documented history of success.

An attitude of piety towards your chosen religion/belief system is only useful for the recalcitrant masses that the controllers need to keep in line, it is not appropriate for either the explorer or the controller. So, if blind acceptance of doctrine is not a viable option for the you, then you must selectively choose only those doctrinal offerings that do, or should, appeal to you, and then integrate them into your life in such a way that they will help to guide you in a path that is both within the cognitive limits, and yet open-ended enough to allow for individual development in the direction you choose. But, here's the critical point: choose, then commit. Choosing principles and morals without being willing to work to respect them over the longterm is hypocritical and a waste of time.

Extracting ideas from existing systems to craft your own image of a god who can fit into the traditions, values, and mores of your system of choice, is, of course, a perfectly valid option, but only so long as you avoid inventing a whole new religion yourself. You don't want to do that, since the probability that it wouldn't be a disaster would be effectively zero, while a somewhat customized version of a long-tested traditional system has a much greater chance of not being much worse than the original system.

Create a Personal Code

To illustrate how one might go about this doctrinal customization, table 14.1 shows one of the many ways that the Ten Commandments, the Seven Virtues, personal life lessons, and the Cognition Limits can be distilled and combined together into a personal code that respects both internal and external realities.

Cognitive or Life Lesson	Virtue
external realities exist	respect
we know realities through very incomplete internal models	humility
we assign value to, and construct meaning for, our mental models	responsibility
focused, persistent work is required to accomplish goals	diligence
relationships survive by decision and effort	commitment
knowledge boundaries are expanded through exploration	imagination

Table 14.1: Strategies map to virtues

It is not an accident that each cognitive/life lesson couples with a traditional virtue, since it is the reality orientation of traditional values that has preserved societies over the centuries. Let us review them one by one:

RESPECT is paired with acknowledging that external realities exist, because being able to accept that we aren't the center of everything puts us in a position to respect the significance of the realities that exist outside of our personal needs and values.

HUMILITY is paired with understanding that our internal mental models are very approximate and incomplete, because understanding our cognitive limitations requires a profound sense of humility. The inability to recognize that all internal thoughts are personal has been the great weakness of traditional societies, but even this can be redressed by humility, but not humility in respect to authority, rather, humility with respect to external realities.

RESPONSIBILITY pairs with the understanding that it is up to us to define the value and the meaning in our life. We must accept all the responsibility for fulfilling or shirking this duty, both the credit and the blame. Since it is we who will pay the price for failing to find/define meaning in life, we deserve the blame for it, too. Assigning value and constructing meaning properly is its own reward, but a nasty, unhappy, unfulfilled life awaits all of those who shirk the responsibility to set their own moral and ethical values and goals.

DILIGENCE aligns with the understanding that endless work is required to achieve worthwhile results. Since we are volitionally mobile creatures, we must move ourselves and other objects every day in order to further our mortal purpose, else we will not long survive this fragile existence.

COMMITMENT and relationships go hand in hand, because hardly a day goes by when it wouldn't be easier to leave a relationship than to stay in it (and that's the good ones, to say nothing of the bad ones). We have to work to make our way on our own, and when we couple with another we multiply not only our power, but also our problems, so we both have to work to make the union succeed over time. (It's not a relationship if only one party is committed, so if we find ourselves in such a situation, the responsible thing to do may well be to move on.)

IMAGINATION is the only reliable path to discovery. Unfortunately, since everyone still thinks that L2 pattern processing is the highest form of thought, and they don't even suspect that the L3 query engine exists, their imagination is artificially and fatally limited. Against all evidence, people still think that discovery is achieved simply by linking known pattern blocks together in novel combinations. This misunderstanding of the locus and mechanism of discovery explains why we just accept that strokes of genius are highly unpredictable, extremely rare experiences, when, in fact, once you get the hang of L3 reasoning, you can actually schedule them.

Obviously, even without knowing anything about the cognitive limits, anyone who follows the traditional values is already pretty far down the road to respecting them. All we need to learn is the difference between internal and external reality, and then our ethics will not only respect reality, but also support the possibility of discovery.

Creating an enhanced traditional solution is a much safer alternative than trying to create an entirely original one on your own. The good news is that one can undertake this effort right now, even without undertaking the heavy task of studying faceted model-oriented reasoning and its related disciplines (calculus, discrete math, linear algebra, physics, computer science, as well mastering a library of great books of the western world, etc.).

Creative Strategies

We can go beyond just tweaking traditional solutions by identifying various parts of the cognition model that we are already comfortable with, and then using them to form the basis of a collection of reasoning tools that we might be able to use in our daily life. For example, the insight that we tend to see each other as $(\xi_{you}, \mathbb{CS}_{me})$, instead of $(\xi_{you}, \mathbb{CS}_{you})$, has the potential to help us see that we are literally projecting our own self-concept onto everyone we interact with. This little insight, while not original, by itself gives us a fulcrum we can use to pry open some very important questions that cannot but help move us forward in our efforts to better understand social interactions.

Also, knowing about $\mathbb{SR}$ and the different truth functions used by different intellect levels for different realities should enable every reader to finally understand why, oftentimes, lies not only don't seem to matter, but actually work better than what we are sure we can prove is "the" truth.

Ambitious readers thus already have a broad range of options at hand that can be explored in an effort to achieve innovative progress in matters of importance to them. To give the reader a head start on this project, we will examine six different enhancement topics to reveal a plethora of tips and ideas that can be readily applied to real life situations.

Statement

It cannot be overemphasized how important it is to grok the implications of the technical definition of `statement`:

`statement` = [context] + content + [goal].

The first step to grasping this insight is to realize that this definition is descriptive, not prescriptive. The assertion is *not* that this *ought* to be the definition of `statement`, but that this *has always been* the actual, working definition of `statement`. In normal conversation, our dim awareness of the implicit components of a statement is forced to the surface whenever the substitution of the listener's context and goal for the speaker's version produces a result so absurd as to crash the conversation into a dead end. These conversational disruptions are so common as to be an everyday event. This anomalous, but entirely common, breakdown in normal communication should provoke anyone who pays attention to such wrinkles in reality to acknowledge that, deep down, we have always known that every statement has these hidden components.

Simply grasping that a statement is so much more than a string of words should be a game changer for understanding our experience of relationships and the reasoning process. With this one definition, we can not only greatly increase our understanding of why informal communication fails so often, but we can open entirely new avenues for more effective communication with the skillful application of formal and semi-formal methods.

The reason we had to invent science and formal languages was to create a framework that requires both context and goal to be both explicit and external. This is what differentiates *testable* statements about external reality from subjective statements about hidden, internal feelings.

It isn't hard to see that statements are the actual links that bind us together in semantic realities, and that the strength of our bond to the speaker and their group is defined by the context and goal *we* choose to attach to the statement content.

Listening Perceptively

Conversation is the social milieu of statements, the written or spoken interactive exchange of messages between two or more

CSs. Conversations can be of a social or a task-oriented type. Task or technical conversations occur in situations that usually make the context and goal of each statement more or less explicit. They are unambiguous to the extent that argot is used over informal rambling, and to the extent that the goal is defined and kept in focus. All other conversations, regardless of the raiment they don, are informal interactions whose primary function is social, not intellectual, intercourse. In fact, there is no such thing as an intellectual conversation in an informal language.

Lectures and speeches may seem different than a conversation, but they are really just conversations in which the audience side of the interaction generally internalizes, rather than expresses, their responses to the speaker (except for the cheering or booing encouraged by the speaker's rhetoric). Duplex personal conversation is a social mechanism that is responsible for creating, modifying, extending, or breaking the links that tie ξ units together into a semantic reality; any other purpose piggybacked onto it is just a poor attempt to overload a primitive social coordination function beyond its limits.

This startling conclusion about the nature and limits of conversation, speeches, and debate, actually applies to all nonformal communication. This shouldn't be a surprise to anyone who actually grasps that the nature of semantic reality is that it is an association of individuals bound to together solely by the

messages exchanged between them for the purpose of maximizing centralized benefit. The bottom line is that **conversation
is primarily a semantic graph link maintenance mechanism**.

Language has a definitional meaning but, like a bullet, it also
carries the marks of the barrel that fired it, as well as the scars
of what it hits. By listening for clues about the assumptions,
intentions, and truth functions explicitly or implicitly packed
into the messages we hear, we can know a lot more about the
speaker's expectations and limitations than their mere words
reveal. Words that assert sincerity can be belied by their hidden
context and goal.

Normally, we try to decipher the meaning hidden in language
by combining our understanding of the words, the speaker's
background and interests, and his body language. We can
achieve a quantum jump in our ability to interpret speech perceptively by adding the new insights we've gleaned from the
layered cognition model to our perceptive listening skill base.

Following is a short list of examples that show how we can
learn to listen beyond the narrow boundaries of the content of
social conversations to see how much of the unspecified context
and goal components are actually supplied by the structures
that hold the data and truth values associated with the conversation type. The list is merely suggestive, not exhaustive, and
is only meant to illustrate how much more you can know about

a conversation even before you begin to look at its manifest content.

Conversation types embed, so this means that as the types switch back and forth, our analysis has to switch, also (for example, making plans in $\mathbb{R}$ occurs in task conversations most commonly embedded in social conversations).

When you hear: friendly conversation
Understand that: the speaker is seeking to strengthen and affirm whatever bond you already have with them. They are NOT looking for an intellectual conversation that ignores their feelings. Like a bee repairing part of the hive, they are striving to strengthen the bonds that holds this part of their semantic reality together.

When you hear: hostile conversation
Understand that: they think that they are right from a non-negotiable, absolute truth perspective. This means that you are wrong, and that, since their self-interest is engaged, facts are not a defense. Convincing them that you are on their side (which is the only thing they are interested in at the moment) will require somehow reaffirming you both belong to the same interest group whose goals govern you both. The other alternative is to accept being adversaries.

When you hear: do you agree?
Understand that: they are asking, "are you with us?" The

subject is group commitment, not the statement content. If you agree, you are accepting that you both see the same facts in the same semantic reality, and you are both on the same team. This applies no matter how frivolous or serious the subject matter is.

When you hear: x is [right|wrong|true|false]

Understand that: they are asking, "Are you friend or enemy?" because the only three values supported by the absolute truth data structure are: pro-self, anti-self, non-self. If the initial statement is impassioned, then the L0 survival mechanism is fully engaged, and agreement means you are a friend, disagreement means you are an enemy. If the initial statement is more tentative, then it can be interpreted as a question, which opens up other alternatives.

When you hear: x is true (by experience)

Understand that: it means that in their world it's true. How flexible someone is about hearing other options depends on their personality and commitment to this particular idea. The point to understand is that they have stopped considering the idea, since they have found an acceptable solution to the problem at the powerful L1 level.

When you hear: "it makes sense," or "it's logical"

Understand that: they are saying that the idea makes them comfortable because they have processed it in a way that balances with their interests and temperament. Unless you are shown the formal proof, *logical* never means what they think it means, it really just means that they have reconciled an idea with part of their opinion web.

When you hear: "<insert opinion here> is right."

Understand that: they are asking you to follow their lead, to join their group, to give them a feeling that they are properly situated in a problem space. The level of their attachment to the opinion determines how much freedom you are being given to disagree, or to just have your own ideas. The subject here is how they see the world, how they have processed some information, not the content of the opinion.

When you hear: A value statement follows from a scientific fact

Understand that: the speaker doesn't know anything, regardless of whether or not they are actually a scientist or an expert. No statement in $\mathbb{R}$ can dictate a unique solution in $\mathbb{SR}$.[1] Scientists who make this mistake do not understand the fundamental principle of science, and since they can't become public figures unless they are willing to make this mistake on cue, then almost none of the scientists you hear in the media actually understand science, let alone the policy they are promoting.

When you hear: scientific rationality explains everything

---

[1] Every solution in $\mathbb{SR}$ is produced by the optimization formula, which has no unique solutions (see appendix F, or chapter 30, *Ultrareasoning*).

Understand that: the speaker is an intellectual who is claiming feudal privilege. He is claiming that his exalted position in the cognoscenti puts him in a position of authority above you, and that you should defer to him. Since what he thinks of as science only addresses $\mathbb{R}$, and doesn't even acknowledge the greater $\mathbb{SR}$, all this means is that his position in a privilege bubble allows him the delusion that he as gained dominion over the joy, tragedy and malevolence of life. Bubbles beg for puncture.

When you hear: a prepared sequence of questions

Understand that: the interviewer is not listening to any of the answers. This means that the conversation is little more than a clown show.

When you hear: formal language

Understand that: as long as it remains value-free, you may be hearing an intellectual or technical conversation. Conversely, any conversation held in an informal language is NOT an intellectual or technical conversation, but likely just an opinion-based $\mathbb{SR}$ maintenance exercise.

Questions

Questions occur in conversations, so they either reflect or influence the type of the conversation. Since they are often leading indicators of the ultimate direction that the conversation will take, it is best to ferret out their significance earlier, rather than later.

Whenever you hear a question, before you even begin to answer it, you should determine whether:

- it is just attention-seeking device;

- it is actually seeking information, or just agreement;

- the answer is going to be used to attack you;

- it is born from curiosity, or prejudice;

- the question is competent;

- the interviewer is competent to understand a nuanced answer.

Prejudiced, attacking questions, of course, can be dismissed out of hand, just like any question asked by someone too stupid to understand the answer. We have learned from politicians and entertainers that the best way to deflect undesirable questions is simply to take them as opportunities to talk about some other favored topic. This is also a valid tactic to employ whenever questions are being asked in bad faith.

Questions do not impose any obligation on the interviewee to address the content if doing so furthers a malign purpose. In fact, it's usually more effective to respond to the intent or limitation of the question, rather than to allow oneself to be manipulated into trying to sincerely answer the content of an insincere question.

When formulating an answer to a question, it is helpful to remember that only very rarely does anyone ever actually want to know what is going on inside your personal cognitive space. Everyone is generally consumed by the sturm und drang roiling inside their own reality. The general purpose of any question is to secure some kind of benefit to the questioner in return for the effort. Frequently, questions are an attempt to determine whether the hidden part of your mind, your internal reality, is likely to externalize something that will impact the interrogator.

Thanks to the purblind defect, we live in the delusion that our ξ equals our $\mathbb{CS}$, and that our $\mathbb{CS}$ is fully immersed in $\mathbb{R}$ as a first class object, as an actor who sees, knows, and understands its surroundings. Part of this delusion includes the unspoken assumption that our questions are formed in the same plane in which the physical objects in our environment exist. But, we now know that this is not true in any sense.

Questions come from a particular place in our mind, but they don't all come from the same place, rather, different types of questions come from different layers in our mind, and each one pairs with a truth function from its own layer. In order to understand the intent and limitations both of a question and the person asking it, you must first identify the question's associated truth function, and use this knowledge to identify the mental layer behind the question. Several examples follow:

Absolute truth, or interest-based questions come from L0, and therefore, require a simple ternary truth value, and do not support or recognize either detail or nuance above that level.

Experience, grouping, or how to questions come from L1, and therefore relate to a specific context. Answers that reference another context are inappropriate and are interpreted as rejecting the question's thesis.

Pattern assimilation or extension questions are from L2, and are only subject to internal validation since they implicitly devalue experience. They are invariably part of an opinion conversation, so discordant answers can shake the questioner's sense of well-being.

Comparison, recognition, or categorization questions are also from L2, and thus do not support any kind of innovative or original answer. The only way answers to these questions can even be processed by the questioner is by comparing them to the standards referenced in the question.

Probing, open-ended, questions can be from L3 if and only if the questioner integrates the first answer into a transformation of the question to open the path for the next question. (You will likely never hear this happen in your lifetime.)

Comparison, Refutation, Probing Questions The difference between these types of questions is stark: comparison questions seek only so much information as needed to compare an idea to the known. Refutation questions are asked by interviewers who already know the truth and just need a word from you to prove you are wrong. Probing questions are of the form: so, if x, then y? where the question about y is an hypothesis formed on the spot to build out a speculative model of what you are thinking. Probing questions are the unicorn of questions, a hypothetical fantasy that might be nice to imagine, but that you'll never hear in real life. As a practical matter, all you are ever going to hear are belief, experience, comparison, and refutation questions.

Formal and Informal Language

Learning to create quantitative models that can be exercised with formal languages takes quite a bit of effort, and might be better tackled as part of a degree program, but since no such program exists yet, for the moment we will just consider the subject from a very high level to get to the gist of the problem.

You might wonder how you could learn to express subjective experiences in a fully specified formal language, but it is easier to do than you might expect. The insight that we do not, in fact, have an infinite range of emotions makes the problem of modeling our emotional reactions tractable, since it means that we can validly represent emotional responses with simple functions that take parameters which are limited to discrete values within a relatively small range.[2] After that, all we have to do is switch from wondering how to express subjective responses in formal language to asking ourselves how we can test the effect that each of the values in the range will have. Once we understand this, we are off to the races.

So, instead of trying to formalize how you feel about something, first you calibrate the level of feeling, and quantify it. Next, since by nature L2 idea constructs are inherently predictive in form, convert the statement to the normalized L2 form of: given situation x, action a will produce result y with a z level of certainty. In natural language, the statement would be: "I [suspect | think | know | am sure] that y is happening because someone did a in situation x." This statement can be tested across the range of allowable values to produce a result set. Then, iteratively, the output of the model can be compared against historical data, more parameters added and tuned, and so on, until the model behavior begins to align with historical data. Finally, we can start to use the model predictively, and then continue to enhance, modify, and tune it until its predictive accuracy achieves a useful level.

It helps, of course, to have first studied faceted model-oriented reasoning[3], and to have worked on approaching problems with

---

[2] See *Xiom.*
[3] See *Ultrareasoning* and *The Structure of Truth.*

the habit of switching from facet to facet to mature the model: from a verbal model that provides a high level, informal sketch, to a semi-formal visual model that helps define relations and set containment, to a mathematical model that formally defines relations, to an executable model that automatically tests everything, and so on.

Using the Truth Matrix

It is more important to understand that there is a truth matrix (see chapter 5, Lesson Four) than it is to become immediately adept in using it. Just knowing that the simple [true/false | right/wrong] paradigm is really only appropriate for use in the final steps of the decision making process, and that it is usually destructive when used prematurely in higher level reasoning, is a bracing first step on the road to injecting discipline into the reasoning process.

Table 14.2 shows how the truth matrix can immediately be used with some of the more commonly seen real life problem types.

Problem Type	$\mathbb{CS}$	$\mathbb{SR}$	$\mathbb{R}$
Internal	✓		
Work		✓	✓
Social		✓	
Resource		✓	✓
Hierarchy		✓	✓
Existential	✓	✓	
Physical		✓	✓

Table 14.2: Applied truth matrix

Let's examine each problem type in the left column to understand how using the matrix can both open our minds and focus our efforts on the right problem.

INTERNAL: Internal problems include all problems that trigger an emotional response in us, regardless of whether or not there is an external component. Internal truth, the [a,p,n] value that we assign to an evaluation, is the truth of internal problems, which means that $\mathbb{CS}$ truth is subject to change whenever our evaluation changes for whatever reason.

This level of truth is entirely personal and subjective, so, apart than calling it out as separate from the other types of truth calculation, there isn't much of interest to say about it. All statements can involve a $\mathbb{CS}$ component if we choose to accept personal responsibility for part or all of a problem, but since this is an internal reality (we evaluate the thing, we judge how we feel, we decide when we are satisfied), we own the consequences of our more or less arbitrary decisions and evaluations.

WORK: The table shows that work problems have a solution in both $\mathbb{SR}$ and $\mathbb{R}$: this means that work problems *always* have two different solutions with different truth values. It is up to us to choose which one to focus on, or how to apportion our efforts. The $\mathbb{SR}$ component is the political aspect of the work authority hierarchy, while the $\mathbb{R}$ component is the set of changes or consequences the problem will have in physical reality.

When your boss suggests a really bad idea in a meeting, what is the *right* thing to do? First of all, get rid of the concept of *right*, and switch to the matrix to see the dual dimensions of the problem. Then, ask yourself how sure you are of: the inevitability of the mistake's consequences; the cost of the mistake (trivial or severe); and the superiority of your alternative. Then weigh the cost to you of embarrassing your boss in front of his bosses. Finally, look for ways to contribute to the discussion that maximizes your benefit, which may or may not include a duty to the company, or the public, as your ethics dictate.

The key concept to grasp is that both $\mathbb{SR}$ and $\mathbb{R}$ truth functions legitimately apply. It's easy to focus on our feelings about the $\mathbb{R}$ dimension and deplore the 'politics' of the $\mathbb{SR}$ dimension, but that attitude is simply wrong because it is shaped by our historic failure to understand the existence and importance of $\mathbb{SR}$.

SOCIAL: In contrast to work problems, social problems are confined to semantic reality, and the truth of their solutions is measured by the $t \propto \frac{|G'+m|}{|G'|}$ relation. It is our choice, of course, whether the G' we are considering is restricted to our personal beneficial group relations alone, or whether it more expansively includes the interests of the whole, or just part, of the larger group.

The question in social problems is, how should we act to bend the semantic reality space in a way that is advantageous to our specific or extended interests? Since social problems are always optimization problems,[4] and since only the $\mathbb{SR}$ truth function applies, we know there is no question of absolute right and wrong beyond our own internal belief structure.

RESOURCE: Resource allocation problems are always two dimensional, because, beyond coming up with parameters for the optimization formula that will allocate resources ($\mathbb{R}$) favorably to our interests, the work in achieving the change will invariably involve group action ($\mathbb{SR}$).

The only time the L0 truth function enters into a resource problem discussion is after all research, discussion, and

---

[4]See *Ultrareasoning*, chapter 30.

testing have been done and we are down to the point of making a decision of choosing `this` or `that`. Introducing it earlier in the discussion is just a ploy to short-circuit the investigative phase of the process, which may be perfectly valid for securing a preferred outcome, but it is not consistent with the intention to rationally consider alternatives.

HIERARCHY: Hierarchy issues are essentially work problems with an explicit $\mathbb{SR}$ component focusing on self-interest, and, invariably, some component that will impact entities in $\mathbb{R}$. At the highest levels, there seems to be an implicit assumption that the self-interest of the primary competitor (us) is identical to the interest and benefit of the larger group. This is not always true.

EXISTENTIAL: Existential problems relate to the meaning and purpose of life. Since meaning is an $\mathbb{SR}$ construct that must be instantiated with a value parameter, and value is a $\mathbb{CS}$ construct, then existential problems are two dimensional, with both a personal ($\mathbb{CS}$ and $\mathbb{S}$) and a group ($\mathbb{SR}$) component.

As previously explained, looking to $\mathbb{R}$ to solve an existential problem is just plain silly, while seeking to find a solution exclusively in $\mathbb{CS}$ can keep us running around in circles for a while, but cannot ultimately succeed until we include $\mathbb{SR}$.

Ultimate solutions to existential problems must be aspirational, not achievable, otherwise they cease to motivate and guide us. Thus, the $\mathbb{SR}$ component. The $\mathbb{CS}$ component is our conceptualization of what we need to do to fix the $\mathbb{SR}$ component in the firmament ($\mathbb{S}$) of our internal reality in such a way that we will never lose sight of it.

PHYSICAL: Physical problems will be two dimensional if we need group help to realize our objective. If, for example, our intention is to build a garden shed, while some of us can do the work ourselves, almost all of us will rely on the economy for a building supply outlet, as well as some kind of network for knowledge reference. In this case, we can generally take the $\mathbb{SR}$ component for granted, and focus all of our attention of the $\mathbb{R}$ details of building a sturdy structure (within code, or we're back to explicitly involving $\mathbb{SR}$). In underdeveloped areas, the $\mathbb{SR}$ component would likely be more significant in figuring out how to compensate for the lack of stores of materials.

Scientific and technical problems fall into the physical problem type, and our focus is generally on the scientific or technical component in $\mathbb{R}$. Of course, all scientific and technical solutions depend on a strong semantic reality to support and transmit the wherewithal to find and propagate new solutions.

In all multi-dimensional problems, we choose how to apportion our attention and concern for the various dimensions, anywhere from 100/0 to 50/50, etc. The purpose of this analysis is to identify the components of the problem, not to prescribe any particular solution one should seek.

Understanding Conversations

Conversations are the vehicle that creates, modifies, extends or destroys the links that tie semantic realities together. Conversations occur in $\mathbb{SR}$, not a vacuum, and $\mathbb{SR}$ is the antithesis of a disinterested space, since interest-based value links are what define it.

Because conversations occur between two or more $\mathbb{CS}$-backed ξs pursuing their own interests within the context of a local $\mathbb{SR}$, the encounter is governed by the same rules that apply to every other encounter between volitionally mobile beings: each participant evaluates the other to assess the degree to which they are a threat, an opportunity, or a non-entity, and then they react accordingly. The only difference between us and squirrels is that our language faculty gives us a larger set of possible responses in $\mathbb{SR}$.

A conversation is a set of message links that create and sustain a relationship (which can be either an ephemeral or a durable small $\mathbb{SR}$) between the conversants within a larger semantic reality. The fact that the two end points of each link are people should make it apparent that the primary purpose of a (non-task) conversation is social bonding, not information processing.

Technical/task conversations do have a high level of information value and focus, but even high-information conversations have both formal and informal dimensions. The formal, $\mathbb{R}$, dimension is constrained by the governing technical language, while the informal, $\mathbb{SR}$, dimension is only concerned with group formation, either ephemeral or durable, and the power dynamics involved in hierarchical decision making.

We can enhance what we already know from our personal experience with conversations by asking some important questions about every important conversation we join:

Is the context explicit? Are the necessary terms and assumptions explicit and sufficient? If not, then how can the conversation be productive when its context and assumptions are undefined and unexpressed?

Is the goal of the conversation explicit? Is the content related to the goal? If not, then how can all the participants work together to a common purpose?

Do the context and goal match the content? Is all of the necessary background, vocabulary, and option history consistent with the message content being discussed? Does the content have the capacity to achieve or support the goal? (For example, if boss's goal for a conversation is to make a decision, then it will be a mistake for you to focus on exploring the problem, since he thinks we're already past that stage.) If either one or both are misaligned, success is almost impossible.

What is the domain of the conversation? Personal feelings ($\mathbb{CS}$), group dynamics ($\mathbb{SR}$), or physical reality ($\mathbb{R}$)? If the participants don't agree on the domain, then all talk will likely be at cross purposes.

Do the context and goal have the same domain? If they do not, the conversation cannot be neither coherent nor productive.

What is the level of the conversation? The level equals the lowest level being used by any participant. The level of work conversations is normally controlled by a competent moderator. It is quite common to speak at the L2 level, but to object at the L1 or L0 level.

What truth is being asserted? At any point, the conversation's level and domain can be changed by a truth assertion with a different level and domain.

Does the current configuration support the goal? Level, domain, and truth function all have to agree in order to successfully support a specific goal.

Can the conversation be transitioned? Can one bring a conversation back to the necessary configuration to achieve the original goal, or do we just have to try again another day?

Furthermore, by listening to the language cues in the conversation, we can know even more. Here are a few examples of how to map what you hear to what it tells you about the nature or boundaries of the conversation:

Cue: passion or conviction $\rightarrow$ The speaker is belief-committed, they are invested in an L0 truth, and are not readily amenable to compromise.

Cue: reference to experience $\rightarrow$ The speaker is relying on practical knowledge in $\mathbb{R}$, or traditional knowledge in $\mathbb{SR}$.

Cue: tendentious reference to logic $\rightarrow$ The speaker is relying on L2 pattern language grammar validation, and, unless proven otherwise, may not have any supporting proof in $\mathbb{R}$. Likely will disrespect L0 truths and L1 experience.

Cue: doubt, waffling $\rightarrow$ The speaker is L2-bound, adrift from L0 and L1 knowledge, values, and experience, and therefore pliable and uncomfortable making decisions.

Cue: tangible facts $\rightarrow$ The speaker may be focusing on a reality-oriented task conversation that has the potential to be productive.

Cue: intangible facts $\rightarrow$ See 'tendentious reference to logic' for the base type. If passion is involved, then it is really a 'passion or conviction' conversation, or if waffling is key, then it is a waffling conversation, etc.

Cue: group dynamics → The speaker is pushing for a resolution in their interest in an $\mathbb{SR}$ conversation.

Once we identify the level of the conversation from the verbal cues, then we can figure out which level of data structure is being used. Knowing all of this gives us a very practical advantage since it tells us almost everything we need to know about what is possible, necessary, and to be avoided in this and similar conversations.

If the level of the conversation is inappropriate for your objectives, it is unreasonable to expect your conversants to understand the ideas you want to talk about. Your choices at this point are either to walk away, to continue the argument at the identified level, or to try to induce a change in the thought level by, for example: depersonalizing the language, retreating from decision-making mode, or suspending the conversation for long enough (10-20+ minutes) for everyone's mindset to shift to neutral ground.

Practical Tips

In a nutshell, our parting advice to the conscientious student is:

You should be able to cope pretty well with normal, structural stupidity if you add knowledge-humility to the traditional virtues, and try to re-

strict certainty to the decision-making process.

Admittedly, knowing the finer points of the universal cognition model might help you get further, but with just this single tip, you should be able to hew close enough to the upward path to avoid suddenly stumbling into the abyss.

However, with just a little bit of extra effort, you can exceed this very modest goal of just merely coping *pretty well*. Incorporating an awareness of cognition limits into your normal thought process will help you to enhance your life, and the lives of those around you, by helping you to be more effective in your work by reducing the number of avoidable reasoning mistakes you routinely make.

Rules of Thumb

The remainder of this chapter is devoted to some simple rules and tips that are meant to be readily applicable to normal life. This is just a grab bag of different applications of the cognition limits, please feel free to pick through it and take anything you find useful.

- `Because` and `therefore` are two very troublesome words. The problem is caused by the patina of respectability they gain from being terms in faux (informal) logic:
    - in informal conversations, `because` is almost always used only as a false-cause conjunction, i.e., a link

between a result and a cause that can usually be summarized as: "because of *reasons*." `Because` invariably assumes either knowledge beyond our reach, or imputes a teleological structure to reality.

– in informal conversations, the term `therefore` is a bridge to stupidity. So rarely does the adduced evidence support the conclusion that it is safer to reject it out of hand.

- As explained in *Ultrareasoning*[5], opinions are not what we think they are, they don't work like we think they do, and their function is fundamentally unrelated to what we think it is. When used in conversations, opinions can be an invitation to join or affirm, or an invitation to some level of conflict. Opinions are not in any sense intellectual, or correct in $\mathbb{R}$.

- In interpersonal communication, if one person sees the conversation domain as $\mathbb{CS}$ (i.e., feelings), and the other sees it as $\mathbb{R}$ (i.e., facts), then nothing good can come from it.

- Facts do not imply or prove values; value is applied to facts. Facts $\in \mathbb{R}$, value $\in \mathbb{CS}$, which are disjoint sets.

- A personal conversation between two or more people defines a local $\mathbb{SR}$ that prioritizes the link between the participants over the message content.

---

[5] *Ultrareasoning*, p375ff

- An impersonal, formal or semi-formal conversation will prioritize the goal desired by the $\mathbb{SR}$ authority center over anything else.

- It is important not to make the intellectual's mistake of equating indecision with wisdom. Wallowing in endless analysis and hypotheticals vitiates our ability to make a decision, and this is a weakness, a flaw, not a strength.

- Humility is necessary, arrogance is abhorrent, but decisiveness is required.

- Intellectuals and academics do not yet understand that the current state of science only defines an idea's relation to $\mathbb{R}$, not to $\mathbb{SR}$. Defining an idea's relation to $\mathbb{SR}$ requires mastery of two disciplines they do not know even exist: faceted model-oriented reasoning, and the universal cognition model.

Tip 1: Solid Foundation

As long as we are wise enough to start with a sound foundation of traditional values, it is not that hard to cope successfully with the structural cognition limits that make us normally stupid. The following values are similar to those held by many believers already, and they would provide a solid foundation for a worthwhile life:

- RESPECT: respect external realities, both $\mathbb{R}$ and $\mathbb{SR}$, and accept that your ℂ𝕊 is just an internal, personal reality with an undefined relation to external reality. Create or accept a concept of the ultimate that you respect enough to make it work as your polestar throughout your life.

- HUMILITY: accept that what we know about anything is always less than what we don't, and be humble enough to limit certainty to the decision and action phase of the reasoning process.

- RESPONSIBILITY: step up to your responsibility to define value and meaning in your life, but base it on sound, tested values and beliefs, not hubris, whim, or fashion.

- DILIGENCE: whatever it is, it won't happen if you don't do it, so focus your efforts on the important, shirk not your duty, and persevere.

- COMMITMENT: positive, productive relationships do not just happen, and they do not thrive without careful attention.

- IMAGINATION: the domain of the unknown is infinitely larger than that of the known. While not everyone needs be, or can be, an explorer, more of us than we realize have some potential in the field. Disciplined, persistent, open questioning, and endless studying are the primary keys to discovery.

Tip 2: Knowledge-Humble

The issue of being being knowledge-humble, of not being too certain about too many things, is tricky because traditional systems have never done this very well, since they have tended to emphasize certainty in their doctrine. An excess of belief-certainty has actually been the greatest error of traditional systems because, while it helps with group cohesion, it inhibits the development of knowledge about $\mathbb{R}$, and is used to justify religious wars. The difficulty we encounter in correctly using certainty is caused by our misunderstanding of the need to balance $\mathbb{R}$ and $\mathbb{SR}$ truth appropriately for different circumstances, since certainty is helpful in some places, but harmful in others:

- Certainty is generally beneficial in $\mathbb{SR}$, since there is a correlation between certainty on group doctrine and the group's power to secure enhanced resource allocation. Certainty is the glue that holds groups together and makes them strong.

- However, certainty is generally detrimental in dealings with $\mathbb{R}$, since $\mathbb{R}$ is never wrong, and our knowledge of it is never complete.

Tip 3: Settling

How satisfied any one of us should be with a traditional solution is a complex question that turns on how our experience of our inner reality relates to the encompassing dominant semantic reality. To calculate this, if we let $\mathbb{CS}$ be the unmeasurable totality of one's inner reality as previously defined, and let ξ be the negotiated public persona that participates in a specific $\mathbb{SR}$, and, finally, let ξ_i be our variable, conscious inner sense of self, then we can say that an individual will be content with a traditional society to the extent that:

$$\frac{\xi_i}{\xi} \to 1 \tag{14.1}$$

That is, the closer our variably defined inner sense of self aligns with our negotiated public self, the happier we will be functioning in an $\mathbb{SR}$ functioning as ξ. The larger the variance, the more likely it is that we should consider making our own way, or changing $\mathbb{SR}$s.

Tip 4: Realities

Sure, $\mathbb{SR}$ is built on $\mathbb{R}$, but just as in our evolved mind L2 depends on L0 and L1, the lower levels in an evolutionary accumulation do not, and cannot, have any awareness at all that the higher levels even exist, and just so is $\mathbb{R}$ oblivious to $\mathbb{SR}$. Yes, L2 knows about L0, and $\mathbb{SR}$ knows about $\mathbb{R}$, but the only things that exist in $\mathbb{R}$ because of us, because of our efforts, are the results of our physical actions (both messages and movements), and none of our private, internal agonies amount to the smallest speck of dust either in $\mathbb{R}$ or $\mathbb{SR}$.

Tip 5: Explorer

The explorer is separated from the follower by his relationship to his conception of the ultimate: the explorer is a god wrestler, while the follower is a servant or a slave to their god. The principle of responsibility requires that we take full credit, blame, and ownership of our relationship with the ultimate, and this involves not deferring responsibility for any part of it to any other person or authority. It is important not only to have a relationship with the ultimate, but to *own* that relationship, to know everything about it and its opportunities and costs, because we cannot explore any of those parts of the unknown that we forbid to ourselves.

Chapter 15

ASPICS

Experience-based societies devote most of their energy to the struggle to survive, and, in the process, they tend to develop a system of values consistent with a world view that keeps them on a path towards both their material and aspirational goals. The practical kind of truth they learn, however, has never been enough for our super stupid educated elite, the self-impressed snobs who have always tried to supplant well-tested, successful ideas with harebrained notions fermented in their isolated hothouse of privilege.

In the middle of the last century, the intelligentsia's misguided, never-ending quest for modern, sophisticated philosophies stumbled upon the obvious insight that, since

$$\{\texttt{value, meaning}\} \notin \mathbb{R}$$

therefore, meaning must be an idea we extract from our social milieu, and its value must be something we determine ourself. From this rather self-evident truth, they used their meager reasoning — blunted to dullness by the millennia-long failure of the university system — to come to the ridiculous conclusion that $\mathbb{R}$, physical reality, is therefore the reality that is somehow **not** real, and that $\mathbb{SR}$ gravity/power is the only real truth.

The rest of us, those who do know how to think, can now understand how to define what a `reality` is, and grok that `meaning` (both in the philosophical as well as in the lexical sense) only can arise in $\mathbb{SR}$ through physical message transmissions through $\mathbb{R}$, and that `value` can only be determined in each individual $\mathbb{CS}$. The confusion that has befuddled the literati for so long now instantly disappears, because we see that, even though the set of realities is much more complicated than we previously suspected, nevertheless, each reality in the set of realities — even the pseudo ones (in their own *cogito, ergo sum* way) — are most definitely real.

More sophisticated and balanced minds can learn to appreciate that each reality has its own truth, that each one is important in its own way, and that each one has its own limitations. Only a mind infected with the primitive Marxist duality paradigm of the oppressor/oppressed archetype, would ever even think to react to the partial, poorly visualized discovery of $\mathbb{SR}$ by enthroning it in the ascendant, and consigning $\mathbb{R}$ to the vanquished, position.

Clearly, by the very definition of reality, both $\mathbb{R}$ and $\mathbb{SR}$ are separate, real, and not in competition with, or validated by, the other. The very definition of a reality states that it comprises an isolated set of elements and forces, so it doesn't take much effort to work out that limits, both relating to components and to isolation, are the crux of reality. This means that it is just ridiculous to think, even for a second, that conceptualizing a new reality has any impact whatsoever on other realities.

We live in at least two pseudo-realities and two actual realities, all of which are built on one of them, $\mathbb{R}$, and all of which disappear the instant that their anchor in $\mathbb{R}$ is severed. From a naive point of view, it may seem ironic that the two pseudo realities often seem to be much more real, much more consequential, than either actual physical reality or the abstract reality of relationships built out of word messages, but it makes sense, because our consciousness is immersed in our internal realities, and it is only *through* them that we vaguely experience the external, verifiable realities.

Class oriented philosophies, such as Marxism and neo-Marxism, suffer from several categorical flaws, not the least of which is the problem of premature simplification. Two classes? Really? All of history can be understood by dividing all of humanity into just two classes, oppressors and oppressed? Really? Aside from the fact that Marxism is an unholy alliance of

Christian mythology (Garden of Eden, Utopia/end of history) and Victorian mechanical metaphors (determinism, clockwork of history), it is the ultimate example of an institutionalized preference for the simplicity of the L0 binary truth data structure over the multidimensional complexity of either semantic or physical reality.

What we haven't had the tools to understand before now is that Marxism is simultaneously both true and powerful in $\mathbb{SR}$, and false and stupid in $\mathbb{R}$. Students, intellectuals, and academics are Marxists precisely because it allows effete intellectuals to feel brave and powerful in the rarefied domain of the educated elite.

The Marxist urge to reduce individual $\mathbb{CS}$ potential and capability to a class-level conceptualization of generic needs and rights entirely misses the fact that the nature of the unknown's fractal problem space dictates that the only possible way forward in solving pinnacle questions is by means of independent exploration. It is through the failure of the many expeditions that the success of the one is even possible.

A shared flaw of the best of traditional approaches and the worst of the modern idiocy is that both center their reasoning on L0 binary truth, and seek to solve the problem of the unknown by using either L1 traditional knowledge, or by combining and extending L2 pattern structures. The academic approach pretends to rely on self-validating L2 idea systems, but, ultimately, it, too, relies on the same emotional L0 belief truth that the most primitive religions use.

Both modern and traditional philosophies base their concept of reasoning on an unexamined truth structure. What they fail to take into account is that none of the cognitive levels below L3 is capable of exploring and discovering the unknown. This explains why insights and innovations have always been rare, serendipitous events that cannot be triggered on purpose, or accomplished on a schedule. Routinizing exploration and discovery requires predictable access to the L3 querying mechanism, otherwise, insight is relegated to the rare lightning flash that strikes the random genius every few generations or decades. It is, however, now possible (albeit not easy) for us to open the nondescript door to L3 on purpose, and to make exploration and discovery in the vastness of the unknown a regular, even mundane, occurrence.

The unknown, where the explorer blindly probes for discoveries, is a dark, irregular space of unknown extent, topography, and elements; everything in it can be a surprise, including even the occasional episode of recognition and familiarity. The unknown is a *fractal* space: an irregular space with unpredictable variations that repeat across scales of resolution. Traversing such a space feels oddly similar at the highest levels of abstraction as it does at increasingly fine levels of resolution. The distinctive characteristic of an unknown space is unpredictability: knowing the first three steps on a path does not help to predict, or find, the fourth. This, of course, makes sense, inasmuch as we know everything by means of discrete models, and discrete models of the unknown include only so much as we have discovered and understood, and nothing else.

L2 pattern processing skills are unhelpful in exploring such a space, because the resolution of the pattern object is far too low to support probing of an unknown area at the required fine level of resolution. The only way to predictably explore the unknown is with the fractal L3 query mechanism that supports using a full spread of independent queries iteratively to find unpredictably configured and placed local maxima. Only by collating the results from a large set of such queries can we work our way towards finding better and better models that verifiably bring dark areas of the unknown into the light of working knowledge.[1]

The key to our future is not to be found in a philosophy, an ideology, or even a religion, but in the nature and structure of evolved organic cognition, because we are more than mere humans, we are ASPICS, and this is what makes us capable of finding, inventing, and creating whatever future we are willing to make real. ASPICS are:

A Autonomous

---

[1]See *Pinnacle Reasoning* for a more experiential presentation of this topic.

SP Self-Programming

I Interactive

CS Cognitive Spaces

From the point of view of the universal cognition model, the fact that we are humans is just an implementation detail, and a fairly unimportant one, at that. What counts is that:

- we are `autonomous`: we move under our own power in whatever way we **decide** is in our best interest;

- we are `self-programming`, this means that we can modify, or add to, the idea graph in our brains involved in cognition, evaluation, and action, so we have the ability **to change** how we think and act;

- we are `interactive` (a very broad term as it is used here), meaning that we **interact** with other beings and objects in our environment, as well as with each other to develop and maintain social ($\mathbb{SR}$) structures;

- we are `cognitive spaces`, meaning we **interpret** our perceptions in order to understand them from the point of view of *our* mortality interests.

`Autonomy` is the manifestation of free will, however limited the scope of our choices may be, because most of those limitations are subject to modification by us, they are not predefined by the nature of any external reality.

`Self-programming` is the ability of a cognitive entity to modify and extend its own cognitive and behavioral control code. This is why 'what we are' and 'what we can be' are such very different things. The reach and implications of self-programmability have not even been glimpsed yet, because we are, even today, still trying to understand and modify our own behavior using the primitive verbal models of psychology, religion, and philosophy. Even though most of us do appreciate the limitations of philosophy and religion, most of us have simply not even begun to realize that the verbal constructs underlying psychology are simply not *true* in any sense, but are just primitive, imprecise, largely anecdotal, unscientific models.

Interactive is a generic term that covers both interacting with things and with people, including the interactions that create and maintain complex $\mathbb{SR}$ grouping structures.

Cognitive Spaces, $\mathbb{CS}$, are biased conceptualizers of internal and external realities, a bias that favors its own conceptualization of its specific and extended self-interest.

As ASPICS, we are able to learn about all realities, and those of us with an activated L3 intellect are able to discover previously unknown aspects of them. Even before we master discovery learning, by respecting traditional virtues, and understanding the limits of evolved, organic cognition, we are already able to choose to value our responsibility to hew to a path of meaning which we define for ourselves, a path that propagates both our kind, and our queries, well into the future.

We are fully capable of making responsible choices today: in

most situations, we can choose to balance our needs in each reality; we can borrow from the future when needed; we can invest
in the future when required to guard against future misfortunes.
The more balanced we are in our approach to interrogating and
understanding all of the realities, the less likely we are to inad-
vertently starve any of them badly enough to damage our future
interests.

$\mathbb{S}$ is our built-in compass, its job is to guide us to whatever
true north we designate, but it is up to us to calibrate, and
then use it diligently to keep us on a worthwhile path. Intellectuals who reject the evolutionary structure of $\mathbb{S}$, and all of
its capabilities, forfeit the ability to keep themselves oriented
to worthwhile, distant goals, and instead consign themselves to
having to use situational ethics to forever wend a meandering
path to no ultimate purpose.

Therefore, prudence would suggest that we use the utmost
care when we define the ultimate, our pole star, so that it will
always be consistent, not only with our needs and fears, but
with our community's, with life's, and with cognition's goals.

How do we choose our northern star? The universal cognition model suggests that cognition, itself, already has a de
facto purpose: elaboration. A cognitive population that finds,
or creates, circumstances of svelte abundance can live in an elab-
orating, extending, growing state. Such populations can evolve
towards unbounded, robust complexity as their $\mathbb{SR}$ structures

grow richer, more complex, and more resilient, and thereby create meaning that has value throughout the reality stack.

Figure 15.1: ASPICS can reprogram themselves.

Appendices

Appendix A

Laws

Laws

The fundamental axiom of the universal cognition model is that it is impossible for cognition to evolve anywhere in our universe in violation of the following laws.[1]

1: Reasoning Occurs on Structures

On what material substrate could thinking possibly occur, if not on evolved structures? It is natural, I suppose, for one to think of reasoning as a process more than as a structure, but since the reasoning capacity is inherited, it must be largely describable as a structure with related processes, rather than as

---

[1] Edited from *Ultrareasoning*, chapter 2.

a set of processes independent of any structure. Since the reasoning capacity is the product of evolution, and since primitive reasoning is observable in simpler creatures, reasoning had to have evolved in steps, and some of those stages must still be present in our more highly evolved minds.

The purblind defect prevents us from perceiving that our reasoning is a composite of more primitive and more advanced structures and processes, that it is, in fact, an emergent property that is more or less functional depending on how many lower level functions are active and effective at any given time. We know that our thinking suffers when we are impaired by illness, fatigue, intoxication or emotional stress, but we rarely appreciate how this reveals the emergent nature of thought. Impairment strikes our perceptual/cognitive apparatus unevenly, eroding some functions utterly while leaving others untouched, which often leaves us unable to recognize or acknowledge our abnormal or degraded mental function.

The consequence of the purblind defect is that we tend to labor under the misapprehension that our 'mind', *as a unit*, 'thinks'. We are oblivious to the various divisions of the mind, with their distinct functions and responsibilities that developed independently along our lengthy evolutionary path. Therefore, it might not occur to most of us that, rather than being a process that the mind does as a whole, reasoning is the product of many smaller functions that may coordinate, but actually operate independently on the various structures that evolved at different times in our mind throughout the development of our species.

Higher level cognition is a whole that is an emergent property of various independent functionalities; there is no single 'reasoning' structure or function in the brain, rather, 'reasoning' is a just a lazy term our minds use to refer to the aggregate product of many unrelated, unorchestrated functions that each do their own work independently, and without regard to each other, or to the end product.

When considered from this evolutionary perspective, it might be easier to understand that, of course, earlier parts of our mind must use simpler structures to execute simpler functions related to self-preservation, while more recently evolved parts of our minds use more complex structures to support such functions as language and abstract thought. This implies that some of our thoughts come from our most primitive mental functions, while others are produced by more evolved structures, yet we don't differentiate between them, nor do we acknowledge that the earlier parts of our minds cannot understand our more sophisticated thoughts, since they aren't built to handle them. The purblind defect means that we are not naturally equipped to anticipate what will happen when our self-preservation mind tries to handle a language concept it has no way of processing.

So, the first law of model-oriented reasoning: 'all reasoning is executed by, and specific to, evolved structures', states it is not possible to have reasoning without an organic structure to support the process (the asomatous psyche that will be discussed later will be able to reason without organic structures, but it was originally created by an organism), and the structures involved have evolved over time. This means that thoughts must be encoded into evolved structures, so thoughts produced by structures that evolved later cannot be processed by predecessor structures except through a lossy, narrowing typecast (conversion), and since we have no faculty that equips us to avoid these costly forays up and down our evolutionary structures, the only way we can limit this degradation of our knowledge is by learning to use intellectual constructs to compensate for the purblind defect. Only by mastering higher level concepts will we be able to gain an articulated level of understanding of what happens in our mind as we think and feel.

2: Reasoning Occurs on Models

By the first law, we know that reasoning executes on evolved structures. These structures exist in our brain, so in order for us to respond to an external event with anything more than a nervous flinch, we have to convert sensory impulses into charges on evolved brain structures before we we can reason on them in order to eventually generate an appropriate response. These structures are elementary models, and we reason only on them, not on whatever external phenomenon reflected the light, generated the sound waves, or emitted the aromatic molecules that assaulted our senses.

This process of charging internal structures to match external experience may be summarized as:

$$P(x) \to m_i \in \mathbf{M}_0$$

That is, the perception process, P, maps any external event, x, to an internal model, m_i, which is an element of the set of all models, $\mathbf{M}_0$, belonging to the zeroth cognition level.

The second law is not that we *ought* to reason against a model, but that all reasoning is the process of comparing, analyzing, generalizing, adding, subtracting (and so on) the values in heritable attribute arrays to arrive at the basis for making self-significant decisions. The point is that there is no reasoning without a model:

Reasoning is the process of performing operations on models to produce conclusions that form the basis for the definition and execution of self-significant actions.

Essentially, model-oriented reasoning is the set of all operations that map a model from a set of models into itself or a different model in the same set. Because of the evolutionary nature of our composite mind, it is possible for a higher intellect to instantiate a model in its domain with a model from a lower intellect, but the limitation remains that a given intellect maps models in its domain back into it, just as addition maps integers in $\mathbb{Z}$ to $\mathbb{Z}$. The origin of this limitation should obvious to anyone who reflects that each level of intellect had to function for eons before the next level began to appear.

Model Types

The set of all models in a given intellect level, $\mathbf{M}_L$, equals the union of the set of formal models $\mathbf{M}_F$ and the set of informal models $\mathbf{M}_I$ in that level, L.

$$\mathbf{M}_L = (\mathbf{M}_F \cup \mathbf{M}_I)_L$$

A mixed model is simply an informal model with some formal bits mixed in, so if you think of the above definition as recursive, a mixed model is just an early union of formal and informal models. The practical difficulty with mixed models is that we invariably overestimate the size of the formal element in order to endow our informal thought with undeserved authority.

Formal models are expressed in formal terms. 'Formal' means that both the context and the goal of each statement, as well as the content, are explicitly defined in unambiguous terms in a formal symbolic language. Formal models support independent tests by disinterested experimenters, and in addition, can be expressed in any sufficiently complete modeling language of the verbal, visual, mathematical and executable type.

Informal models can only be expressed in informal terms, and any translation to any other formal or informal terms cannot be verified for accuracy and completeness. The essence of an informal model is *subjective incompleteness*, that is, they lack of any mechanism to objectively assign any particular attribute or function either to the set of included or excluded elements. In this work, we call informal models *mudball models* on the principle that they contain an indeterminate mix of whatever happens to be around each time they are expressed, a hodgepodge of vague notions that will differ every time it is assembled or referenced.

Of course, there are many ways to partition the set of all models that can exist on any particular intellect level, but this partitioning of models into the formal and informal subsets is useful for our purposes of understanding the limits and capabilities of these two very different kinds of models.

Formal models are implemented either as continuous functions or discrete models. Continuous functions describe an infinite number of points, while discrete models have a finite number of data points, regardless of how many measurable points might exist in the referent. The miracle is that our minds are able, by creating internal images with a handful of data points, to model externalities that effectively have an uncountably infinite number of measurable dimensions, and to model them so well that we survive long enough to prosper and proliferate. There is no need for us to include every point from the referent into our model, but this truncation does dictate that there is always more that we don't know about something than what we do know.

$$\forall \ m_i \in \mathbf{M}_L, |P_m| \ll \infty_c \qquad\qquad (\text{A.1})$$

The cardinality of the set of testable points in a discrete model, $|P_m|$, is a lot less than a countable infinity. In more practical terms, the number of testable points is more likely on the order of 10^n for a small n since every point in the formal model has to be added by a finite mind in a finite amount of time.

3: Reality Referents Have Unlimited Data

$$\forall \ r_i \in \mathbb{R}, |measurements_r| \approx \infty_u$$

The number of points in a given entity in reality, r_i, is effectively a countable infinity, but the number of *measurements* possible actually is an uncountable infinity when precision is unbounded or when the number of indeterminate states is included. Counting, at the limit, is comprehended by a countable infinity (think: integers), but measurement is comprehended by an uncountable infinity (think: real numbers). If we are modeling a tree, we can say it has n cells, where, although large, n is a countable number. However, since all things in reality, $\mathbb{R}$, are characterized by dimension or magnitude, and since these are *measurable* characteristics, then each entity/force in reality involves an uncountably infinite number measurements each of which may have an unbounded fractal measurement.[2]

Let's just say that reality ranges from the incredibly small to the immensely huge, and tends to the impossibly numerous at every level, and can be measured in an uncountably infinite number of ways. We must keep this nature of the referent in mind whenever our model of reality is discrete, that is, when it is based on a small number of specific data points, rather than on a continuous function.

4: Only Formal Models Are Testable

A test is a formal, reproducible procedure that produces a measurement of the variance between the statements made on a formal model and observable reality. A statement on a model can properly be viewed as a prediction that the referent of that

---

[2]See "How Long Is the Coast of Britain? Statistical Self-Similarity and Fractional Dimension" by Benoit Mandelbrot, *Science*, 1967.

model has a particular characteristic. That is,

$$\forall\, m_i \in \mathbf{M}_{F_L}\, \exists\, t_{m_i} \in \mathbf{T}\ :\ t_{m_i} \to r_i \Rightarrow |m_i - r_i| < \epsilon$$

That is, for every formal model, m_i, there exists one or more tests, t_{m_i}, that produces a real[3] number measurement, $|m_i - r_i|$, that quantifies the variance between the predictions in that model and observable reality. The essential characteristic of a formal model is that it can be expressed in abstract, quantitative terms that have technical definitions that allow independent researchers to precisely reproduce the experiment, without recourse to the original experimenter, to determine a measure of the variance between the model and reality. Every model can be used to generate one or more tests for each testable point in the model.

5: Model Validity is Test Dependent

$$v_m = |T_{m_v}| / |r_\mathbb{R}|$$

The validity of a model m, v_m, is proportional to the ratio of verified tests of m, $|T_{m_v}|$ to the number of testable points in the model referent, $|r_\mathbb{R}|$. Since the number of testable points in a reality referent is effectively an uncountable infinity, the validity measure of discrete models, while critically important, is a very

---

[3]The measurement could be a complex number, but for most purposes, a real number will probably suffice.

small number. We should be humbly awed that, through the miracle of cognitive faculties that only use a tiny number of points to model infinite realities, we can conceive in our heads workable models of reality. It's a miracle that we can know anything, not a disappointment that we don't know everything.

While using a model with, for example, only 5 verifiable test points of the uncountable infinity its referent contains may chasten us, yet there is all the difference in the world between that model and another of the same phenomenon that only has 2 verifiable test points, or a mudball model that has none.

The question, "How many testable points does a discrete model need to have in order to be considered a valid representation of a continuous referent?" cannot be answered in real life for a fairly obvious reason. Consider:

$$min(p)_m = n * |d_{interest}|$$

That is, the minimum number of points, p, in a model equals n times the number of dimensions of interest. If we want to map a reef in the ocean to allow shipping to avoid it, do we need a fractal map of all the concave and convex shapes in its outline down to the picometer level? No, of course not, and in all likelihood, we would be satisfied with a simple polygon larger than the reef by some comfortable margin of error. This illustrates the point that a discrete model is *not* modeling reality, but rather, it is modeling the profile of our *interaction* with reality. Ultimately, our very mortality posits that we have a rather parochial interest in reality, so our discrete model only needs enough tests to validate that, based on current information, we likely won't have an unfortunate experience with the model referent. When new information adds new risk or opportunity points to our data set, then we will probably find it necessary to extend our model accordingly.

So, the minimum number of testable points in a valid model is whatever number we are personally willing to bet our life on; no more, no less.

6: Validity of Informal Models Is Near Zero

$$v(m_i \in \mathbf{M}_I) \cong 0 \cong v(m_j \in \mathbf{M}_I)$$

Since informal models have no tests, the validity for any of them is undefined or approaching 0, (depending on how you look at it). Therefore, logically, any informal model can be substituted for any other informal model without any loss of verifiable correspondence to reality, $\mathbb{R}$. Thus, all informal models can be considered equivalent because they have the same validity measure relative to any $r \in \mathbb{R}$.

But, what about those cases where we actually have some evidence or a test or two for a couple of points in an informal model, does that matter? Mixed models that combine an equation or an experience-verified fact or two with opinion represent such a case, and as does practice in the technical trades. The essence of testability is reproducibility, and, while it may lack a numerical or theoretical facet, one worker showing another what happens when he strikes or pushes something, still falls into the realm of externalized, reproducible knowledge. In these cases, the reproducible parts can be confirmed, but the surrounding framework is still just unreliable noise.

In many cases, we actually do have physical bruises from bumping into reality, or we have learned that by avoiding it we stay unbruised, so that many mudball models have some experiential verification validating parts of them, but this is both unquantified and largely, if not wholly, unreproducible. So, while we may sometimes know something, we rarely can be sure of what is is that we do know.

As a practical matter, we have to choose one model over many others in our daily reasoning, and there are better and worse ways to make this type of low information decision, but this happens below the level of formal model-oriented reasoning, and is discussed elsewhere.

7: Law of Preservation

Level L_{n+1} can supplement or replace functionality at L_n, the earlier level below it, but it cannot degrade the performance of any preserved function of the lower level. Complex structural changes represent an accumulation of smaller changes, and intermediate changes that impair current function before advanced functionality matures, certainly must pose a serious disadvantage in the struggle to survive. One can expect such changes will generally be culled by natural selection.

Appendix B

Levels

Since our cognitive apparatus evolved over time, and since we can see more primitive versions of our own thought apparatus in all other animals, and since those examples range from the simple to the complex, and since evolution proceeds by editing and extending far more often than by erasing and starting over, there is every reason to expect that our mental model of cognition will have to be layered in order to accurately portray the organic reality it represents.[1]

A specific cognitive level is defined by a heritable data structure and the associated functions that produce an evolutionarily benign or positive capability enhancement over earlier versions in the line. A cognitive level has the following characteristics:

- a segmentation of mental functions defined by a collection

---

[1] Excerpted from *Ultrareasoning*, chapter 4.

of structures and functions that correlates to the evolutionary model.

- idea structures are specific to a certain level. Ideas can be translated from one level to another, but loss of information is certain in one direction (wider to narrower data structure), and loss of meaning is certain in the other (away from the personal to the abstract).

- they are independent, not parallel or coordinating tracks.

Cognitive levels enable us to structure our models so that they mirror and respect the evolutionary process. The concept of levels forces us to design disciplined models that prohibit lower level functions from processing higher level structures (higher levels can instantiate their own model from the data in a lower level model). Violating this stricture would violate the evolutionary process as we understand it.

The model used both in the asomatous psyche simulation and as the basis for this book implements the following layers:

Level Name	Object	Functions
L0	mentacule	avoid threat and seek opportunity with movement; belief and truth
L1	result	learn from experience
L2	pattern	anticipate, plan, and use language
L3	query	explore, discover, innovate

Table B.1: Level Model

Since our intellects evolved over time, each new level of intellect only has to package the model from the preexisting lower level into the model defined by the new, higher level structures in order to add a new level of complex functionality to our mental faculties. This repackaging allows for existing functionality to be preserved and leveraged, instead of having to reinvent it at each new level of development. Note that, by this definition, while higher level intellects can become aware of the lower level intellects in the same way they can become aware of anything, lower level intellects are simply incapable—due to a lack of both wiring and the wherewithal to comprehend—of perceiving or understanding any of the more recently developed structures or functions.

If we look at levels from the perspective of the programmable simulation, then the set of functions $f()$ on any model m in the set of models $\mathbf{M}$ defined by an intellect level, L, will include the initialization function, $init(m)$, that instantiates a model, and all other functions, $g()$, supported on the set of models in a given intellect level, $\mathbf{M}_L$. Note that a model is instantiated with input from a lower-level intellect, $\mathbf{M}_{L-1}$.

$$
f(m \in \mathbf{M}_L) = \begin{cases} init(m) = \begin{cases} Domain : \mathbf{M}_{L-1} \\ \\ Range : \mathbf{M}_L \end{cases} \\ \\ g(m) = \begin{cases} Domain : \mathbf{M}_L \\ \\ Range : \mathbf{M}_L \end{cases} \end{cases}
$$

What the above definition shows is that model-oriented reasoning maps models from the domain of a particular evolved intellect back into the same set. That is, each intellect, each independently evolved reasoning structure, can only process the models native to its structure.[2] Higher levels can wrap lower level models into their native structure. Since both the domain and range of the model-oriented reasoning functions supported by a particular intellect are the same set of models defined by the structures in that intellect, the limit of reasoning at any level is defined by the set of models that characterize the intellect chosen to do the reasoning.

L0, the first level in the cognition model implements the fundamental ability to benefit from the capability of volitional movement by generally moving towards opportunity and away from danger. It is also the seat of anti-self, pro-self, and non-self emotions and the right/wrong/don't care belief system.

L1, the second level, is L0 plus memory that enables it to learn from experience. This means that the data structures for the two levels are different, that L1 initializes with its objects with L0 objects, that L0 knows nothing about L1, that L1 does leverage L0, and that the domain and range for the operations on each level are the set of elements on that level: L0 for L0, L1 for L1.

L2, the next higher level, is the pattern processing engine,

---

[2]L0 instantiates models by pulling from L-1, the level where hard-wired connections tie sensory experiences to response triggers.

and patterns are what is at the heart of language and what we commonly recognize as intelligence, and also gives us the ability to anticipate the future.

The highest level currently known is L3, and it is characterized by the type of chained queries it can execute based on atomically decomposed L2 pattern elements. L3 is known as the discovery intellect because of its unique ability to systematically interrogate the known in order to learn about it by composition of testable elements, rather than by reductionist metaphor, as L2 does.

Regardless of however we choose to model the levels of intellect, it is an important requirement that, once we do have a model, from that point on, we are bound by the laws of model-oriented reasoning. That is, once we have our levels defined, then we are required to define data structures and operations for each level such that these laws are obeyed by the operations that model observable behaviors in the referent. This means that the outcome of processing any thoughts on a particular level must produce more thoughts on the data type in that level.

Narrowing type-casts to reduce higher level ideas to lower level data structures, and instantiating higher models with lower level ideas are both entirely consistent with this restriction. It is easy to see that data will be lost transitioning an idea from a larger to a smaller data structure, but it would be a mistake, commonly made by intellectuals, to suppose that lower level beliefs can be expressed in higher level ideas without a serious loss of meaning and intensity.

Another constraint introduced by the evolutionary model, on which we are building our cognitive model, is that each level must function independently of, and in parallel with, the others, and not sequentially, because the lower level intellects must not only be utterly unaware of the higher levels, but they must be constitutionally incapable of conceiving higher level ideas. The higher levels can observe the function of the lower levels and consume their output to instantiate their own higher level models, and even prepare output that can, by a narrowing type-cast, be reductively consumed by the lower levels, but the lower levels cannot be aware of the higher, later arriving levels at all; they cannot observe, cooperate with, or wait for the higher levels that they do not know exist. The higher levels evolved thousands to millions of years after the design and implementation of the lower level intellects were validated by natural selection, and the lower levels, while they may have been selectively updated, were not rewritten to correspond to the new functionality introduced by the higher levels (unless in your model you can make the case that they were).

Using levels that conform to the evolutionary model while satisfying one's immediate modeling needs imposes a discipline on our thought that opens the way out of the mudball model and into the world of executable, and therefore testable, model-oriented reasoning.

Appendix C

UCM

Universal Cognition Model

Beyond our species, beyond our own tree of life, beyond our galaxy, what do we know of cognition itself? What do we know about the fact, the process, of cognition that evolves in an organic context? If we limit our consideration to the sort of cognition realized in autonomously mobile, cell-based creatures (without presuming to know whether or not any other kind exists), it turns out we actually know a great deal.[1]

Following is a list of a few basic principles that seem to belong to the universal cognition model. As specific cognition models — either the one being discussed here, or another one

---

[1] Excerpted from *Ultrareasoning* chapter 7.

built from scratch by a reader — are elaborated, tested and adjusted, then we should be able to refine and polish the universal model. For now, we will be content with just these few notes as a beginning.

UC1: Cognition Proves Itself

Cognition proves itself and the space it defines. That is, cognition posits the right of the cognitive entity to struggle to survive and multiply. Value is created in the self singularity, and value, meaning, and purpose only exist within the singularity distortion field.

UC2: Basis of Cognition

$$choice \ + mortality \ \Leftrightarrow \ cognition$$

The necessary and sufficient condition required for cognition to emerge from an organic context in a physical universe is achieved when a mortal frame gains the capacity for forming and implementing choice, i.e., evaluating perception and choosing to move in a self-preferential way. By 'mortal', we should understand not just a finite limit to a lifespan, but also the regular need to secure resources from the environment to survive.

UC3: Self

self ⇔ *cognition*

The cognitive function and the atomic self are one and the same. The self is created when the capacity to make and implement choice becomes part of a mortal line. This level of self is rudimentary and functional, and, likely, not self-aware.

UC4: Essential Cognition

$$\forall\, x \in (\mathbb{R} \cup \mathbb{I})\ \exists\, p \in \mathbf{P}\ :\ L0(p) \to e\ :\ AM(e) \to\ a \in \mathbf{A}$$

The expression says: for all x in the union of external and internal realities, there exists a (possibly null) perception, p, in the set of all perceptions the entity can have, such that $L0$ can evaluate it into a form, e, that the action module, AM, can use to specify an action command (possibly null), a, from the set of actions, $\mathbf{A}$, that the creature is capable of.

Another way to say this is that the fundamental function of cognition is to evaluate perceptions of flat space phenomena by mapping them into the curved $\mathbb{CS}$.

UC5: Value

Value is an attribute of curved space. By **UC1-UC4**, we have
the relation:

$$cognition \iff self \iff value$$

Cognition is achieved when choice is added to mortality, which
both defines and presupposes self, and self, by its existence and
function, defines value.

UC6: Periodicity of Cognition

Cognition is not, and cannot be, a continuous function. It periodically processes input into discrete models that can be evaluated. The function of evaluating input into a model requires
some time $t > 0$, and this makes the process periodic.

UC7: Cognition Evolves in Levels

The evolutionary cytomodel requires that higher level functionality be composed of lower level functions that evolve over time.
The first level of cognition, L0 in our model, only supports self-
preferential movement in response to interpreted perceptions,
and we are an example of language-enabled pattern processors,
so this suggests that there have to be one or more levels between
us and L0, as well as the possibility of levels above us.

UC8: Self-Awareness

True consciousness of self requires multiple levels of cognition. The ability to self-name, which is what we identify as self awareness, requires cognition levels that support container and pattern objects.

UC9: Time

The concept of time is not a native cognitive construct, it is a synthetic inference based on the capability to react to the present, recall the past, and anticipate the future (L0-L2). This requires several levels of cognitive evolution. In other words, *time* is an intellectual construct created by cognitive entities at or above lower L2 levels, which aligns our anticipations with resource cycles.

Although `sequence` does exist in $\mathbb{R}$, time, as we conceive it, doesn't, it is an artifact of our cognitive apparatus.

Appendix D

Data Objects

The laws of model-oriented reasoning only require that there be
levels in the cognitive model, and that each level employ its own
data model. The objects we are discussing below come from the
asomatous psyche application, not from the universal cognition
model. These objects were designed for particular simulations,
so do understand that they not meant as a prescription of what
must be, nor of how it should work, they just suit the needs
of the task at hand. The objects used in the specific model
discussed in this book are:

- An *evacule* is the evaluation object, the basic atom of
  cognition. It has three elements: anti-self, pro-self, and
  non-self evaluations.

- A *mentacule* (L0 level) is the basic molecule of cognition, a snapshot of sensory state. It supports evaluation, comparison, categorizing, and update.

- A *situation* (L1 level) is an evaluated snapshot of current memory, a collection of mentacules.

- A *result* (L1 level) is an object that evaluates actions by calculating the delta between the pre- and post action situations. It supports learning from experience.

- A *pattern* object (L2 level) is a single-in, contingent multiple-out structure of patterns that supports planning, anticipation, and language.

Since our senses are hardwired into our cognitive apparatus, this means that the data objects must use positional semantics, that is, an evacule at one position in the mentacule means something different than one at another position. This should be expected since, for example, our optic and auditory nerve outputs have different meaning.

The L2 pattern object is the basis of planning, reasoning, language, and what we think of as consciousness. The power and complexity of this object makes it convenient to identify a number of different versions that are specialized to support the different functionality. Some of the special versions are:

- Language patterns include lexical and grammar patterns.
- Name patterns support reference and indirection.
- Opinion patterns summarize, absorb and disable facts.
- Experience patterns are extensions of result objects.

- Authority patterns prescribe conduct and organize hierarchies.

- Lesson patterns communicate action instructions within a pattern language context.

- Task patterns communicate action steps to fellow workers or underlings.

- Loopback patterns turn off over-excited ideas.

Evacule

The *evacule* (from *eval*(uation) + (mole)*cule*) is the atomic unit of cognition, the transistor on which all cognitive functions are built. Evacules contain three elements: an anti-self value, a pro-self value, and a non-self value. Each position can hold a value in the range of minimum to maximum, and they all three always hold a value when they register a sensation or event, even if it is just the minimum value.

The semantics of the evacule are defined both as an aggregate for the evacule, and contextually, depending on which strand of which sense it is connected to. The way we *know* anything is by registering each of the dimensions of which we are sensible into evacules. For example, if we have dozens of evacules connected to our olfactory senses, then dogs might have thousands, each one of which registers information by combining the three evaluations in the context of a specific connection.

An evacule with the values [5, 3, 0], for instance, where 5 is maximum and 0 is minimum, might, if connected to the magnitude dimension of sight, register a large, potentially threatening object that, at the same time, offered significant opportunities. The same values in an evacule attached to the volume auditory circuits would mean something else in terms of sound, but it would suggest a similar mix of potentially dangerous power and beneficial opportunity. At the other extreme, an evacule with the values [0, 0, 5], would mean the input could be ignored no matter what the context was.

Volitional mobility requires that experience be evaluated in terms of self-interest to support self-preferential movement, and the axes of self interest certainly address the two questions: is this a threat, or is this an opportunity? But these two questions together necessarily posit the third case: if neither negative nor positive, is this an ignorable case, a nullity? The 3-dimensional value structure of the evacule precisely addresses this need by interpreting every dimension of every perception in terms of anti-self, pro-self and non-self significance within a semantic context defined by a particular facet of the organism's sensorium.

Each of the positions in the evacule holds a value in the inclusive range from the minimum to maximum values. In our simulation, these elements are implemented with discrete, rather than continuous values because a fundamental principle of the universal cognition model is that complexity emerges from simplicity, and it seems that the 100 to 1,000 different permutations arising from having just 5-10 discrete values for each dimension will easily cover the full range of human emotional responses we observe since every event is recorded using from one to ten thousand or more evacules at once.

By UC4, we understand that the process of knowing, the process of making sense of something we perceive, is, first, the process of encoding and evaluating perceivable dimensions of input phenomena onto an organic structure, such as a collection of evacules, which translates the internal or external sensory event into self-significant terms in $\mathbb{I}$ where it becomes conceivable and processable by the self. A tripolar data structure implementing positional semantics satisfies this requirement.

Mentacule

The mentacule is an ordered collection of evacules that encodes a snapshot of internal and external sensory input in a way that the mind can process and react to. The mentacule creates a summary evaluation of all of the evacule evaluations it contains.

The process of populating a mentacule with the data from a perception or event starts when the senses are stimulated, but since the senses seem to be, in effect, analog sensors that produce waveforms continuously even in the absence of actual input (we experience some level of sight events in a completely dark room, for one example, or, to use Isaac Newton's example, touching the side of your closed eye can trigger visual experiences), this implies that, at certain times, a snapshot of the current state of this continuous flow of input is grabbed and committed to a mentacule. Either before or after the moment of snapshot, the analog information is encoded in what we are assuming to be a relatively digital form, and encoded into a mentacule.

Think of a mentacule as an array of evacules in which position is not only semantically significant, but actually hardwired to specific sensory connections.

The three necessary and sufficient functions to support interested movement are:

- Categorize: the mentacule has to be categorizable as a threat, an opportunity, or a triviality.

- Compare: the mentacule has to be comparable to other mentacules to determine degree of similarity.

- Update: the mentacule has to be updateable, even in the case of the virtual mentacule.

The very first requirement, categorizability, is needed so that the organism can instantly, even if incorrectly, identify the mentacule's referent as enemy, friend, or nothing of the type animal, vegetable or mineral (for example). The second requirement is needed to support a refined evaluation of exactly how good, bad, or unimportant this referent is. The third requirement, updateability, is needed even in the case of the virtual mentacule because the current memory is inherently updateable, and once an independent mentacule is supported by a memory-capable mind, the values in the mentacule must be editable to support refinement of perceptions as new data becomes available (e.g., as the other being gets closer).

But, what about the data inside the mentacule? Well, the content and granularity of the abstract representation of the perceptual snapshot will certainly vary from species to species, at least, because not all species have the same sensitivity of each sense, and do not even all have the same set of senses. There certainly seems to be a place where a bitmap of the input is stored, since we have the ability to reconsider our memories, and even to notice details we initially dismissed.

One of the general themes of this work is that consciousness and intelligence are not only not God-given blessings, they are not miraculous, and in fact, they are not even very complicated, but rather are actually so simple that coding them up is pretty easy. A program written to the specifications presented in this book up to and including the naming function, should achieve self-awareness after being initialized correctly and allowed to run continuously in a rich environment for a few months.

The mentacule is a simple object that does not pretend to provide the necessary and sufficient conditions for higher human thought. All it does is to provide the necessary and sufficient conditions for effecting interested movement.

Situation

In memory-capable organisms, current memory is modeled as a priority queue of the $7\pm$ most important entities found in the most recent scan of the environment. A *situation* is a snapshot of this current memory that can be evaluated as a whole. The situation object thus supports a higher level understanding of what impact an action has had by making comparisons of the before and after situations of an action possible.

Simple aggregates like the situation object give rise to rich semantics that support sophisticated thought. Where the mentacule in the simplest organisms is adequate to drive movement, by aggregating several of them together, we gain the ability to understand and respond to the gestalt of current reality.

Result

The *result* is the L1 data structure that endows the mind with a concept of the past and the ability to learn from experience. It comprises a pre-situation, an action mentacule, and a post-situation.

L1 implements the ability to store and recall result objects, and to generalize them into type hierarchies that support rapid recall. Learning from experience is then easily achieved by simply extending the evaluation function to cover situations. Notice that, even though the ability to evaluate and learn from experience seems to be a complex mental function, implementing it actually requires a minimal amount of new structure and only an extension, rather than an invention, of the evaluation mechanism.

Pattern

The *pattern* is the L2 data structure that supports language and planning, which together support anticipation of the future. The essential pattern data structure in the asomatous psyche is:

Listing D.1: Pattern Object

```
// patterns are instantiated with results
Result result

// use this pattern when this pattern matches the current
// situation
Situation entryPoint

// action to take
Action command

// branching condition
Condition condition
```

```
// the collection of alternative paths available
// depending on the match level of the situation
// and supports branching logic , rules , etc .
PatternLinks branches

// indicates current position in an active plan
Pattern currentStep
```

This relatively simple structure supports very complex pattern creation and processing. The wonder of cognition is not that it is so complex, but that simple, genetically encodable structures support extremely complex thoughts.

The pattern functions are simple pattern versions of basic cognitive functions such as: compare, add, subtract, generalize and update. The exit selector function compares the post action situation with the exit points and selects the closest match.

The pattern object has a dual nature as both an anticipation and a plan object. Every pattern is an anticipation pattern in that it tells us what the future might look like, e.g., finding fresh scat in this terrain may match a pattern that tells us we may be within a certain distance of a known type of animal. The other side of the pattern object is the plan aspect: patterns record conditional steps to achieve an objective, i.e., they are plans. So, given a situation, we can match a pattern that suggests a possible future occurrence, or given a need or objective, we may select that same pattern and follow the recorded steps to achieve our goal. This dual nature of prescience and prescription is inherent in all pattern objects.

Types of Patterns

Because the L2 pattern object is the basis of language and conditional reasoning, it defines for us what thinking feels like, so we will examine a brief catalog of different types of commonly used patterns to help the reader better grasp the general idea of patterns: what they are, how they work, and what they do.

There are a number of different types of patterns that enhance our cognitive ability in a variety of ways. They are all built on the same template using the same lower level functions, but they are specialized to perform specific tasks to answer particular needs. Since patterns have the capacity to define new functionality, there is almost no limit to the types of patterns possible. We will restrict the current discussion to cover just a few pattern types that, in addition to being illustrative, are germane to our immediate purposes:

- **Language** patterns hold the building blocks of language, ranging from phonemes to syllables, words, etc. Grammar would be implemented in a separate pattern language. Spelling requires archetype patterns.

- **Name** patterns support indirection, i.e., the substitution of a name for a full pattern structure to make mental calculation tractable.

- **Opinion** patterns are named, evaluated, value linked patterns that summarize potentially complex trees of facts, experiences, lessons, beliefs and feelings.

- **Experience** patterns are built from direct experience and value linked to the pain or reward level of the lesson.

- **Authority** patterns are communicated from an authority and value linked to emotional connection to the authority.

- **Lesson** patterns are school lessons, abstract ideas typically drilled into us by teachers as indivisible, unquestionable whole units.

- **Task** patterns comprise a sequence of concrete steps to accomplish a particular task.

- **Loopback** patterns are answers that are independent of, and exist before, any question that can be asked. They function to quiet all nagging questions, fears or anxieties about the future or the unknown, without regard to content or circumstance.

Container Object

One might expect an idea with content to be more powerful than one without, but the container pattern object only has structure, no actual idea content, and it is much more powerful than any single idea. The container object is a meta-idea, an idea that can define relations between ideas. Container patterns *reference* content, but the container itself exists at the level above content, it isn't content itself. The power in this object is that, by structuring elements, it defines *relations* between elements, it creates a new, higher level of thought, one where we can not only think about *things*, but for the first time, we can now think about the *relations between* things. The concept of a relation between entities *a* and *b* is an invention of the container structure.

A container pattern is defined as a pattern object that has:

- A description,

- An evaluation,

- A synchronous action,

- Zero or more sets of elements.

The `description` or name field is actually a name pattern object that supplies a first level of indirection that allows us to reference an idea or collection of ideas as an idea itself. The `evaluation` field is a value link to a value position in the singularity distortion field. The synchronous `action` only adds or deletes patterns from the container object, it cannot operate at a level below the abstraction; selected pattern elements specify their own actions, such as moving the body.

Container patterns can contain normal patterns, or other container patterns that can contain normal patterns or other container patterns, and so on. Thus, container patterns create the capability to define unlimited levels of abstraction. A container may reference a visible set of entities, but its most striking feature is that it supports meta-thought, i.e., thoughts *about* thoughts. Whereas mentacules, results and patterns support thoughts about things, container patterns support ideas *about* ideas. This is where advanced reasoning begins.

Opinion Object

Opinions compensate for the hard constraint in our cognitive apparatus limiting the number of thoughts we can think at any one time by rolling up the evaluation of a set of patterns into the top level opinion evaluation. This facilitates reasoning by chunking facts into manageable blocks, so that, instead of having to include ten ideas in a subjective calculation, we can just use the evaluation in the opinion object that contains the idea, instead of having to examine all of the individual ideas at once.

Opinion objects organize a set of facts to match our temperament, experience, and social ties. The structure of an opinion object, as shown in figure D.1, includes:

- Description: a structured name object providing a verbal reference for the opinion.
- Evaluation: a computed value link.
- Action: a synchronous local call, or null.
- Membership rules: opinions contain a restricted set of facts.

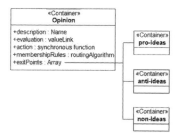

Figure D.1: Opinion Object

- Exit points: pro, anti and non fact categories.

The opinion object sorts facts into the usual three buckets, anti, pro, and non, but these buckets have a special function in this object: pro facts *prove* the opinion, anti facts are *disproved* by the opinion, and non facts are *devalued* by the opinion. The membership rules in the opinion object structure define which facts belong to the pro, anti and non exit points, and so act as a routing algorithm to distribute facts to the appropriate container object for handling.

The result of this structure is that facts are sorted without having any impact on the truth evaluation value of the opinion itself, whether they are anti-, pro-, or non-self facts. Thus, once a fact is compared negatively to the truth archetype in the opinion, it is thereby proven wrong, regardless of how well it may correspond to $\mathbb{R}$.

Opinions only apply to certain types of facts: political opinions to political facts, social opinions to social facts, fishing opinions to fishing facts, and so on. Of course, facts are expressed in an idiom developed by the specific and extended self, so there tends to be a consistent or common style across one's opinions, but there is little to no useful crossover between types.

It is easy to see that opinions have a strange, semi-rational structure: developed opinions are formed from anecdotal evidence (while assimilated opinions are accepted as part of the dues one pays to belong to a group), so one might say they have some vague, undefined relation to reality, but since their truth value is sticky and tends not to vary with accumulating evidence, their claim to a scientific or rational basis is tenuous, at best. Furthermore, the anti fact category of an opinion functions like an opinion disposal unit, capturing and neutering charged facts.

We can think of an opinion as a named evaluation of a set of thoughts, but what it organizes is a set of patterns. That set of patterns can include other opinions, which means that we can have opinions of opinions of opinions, and so on, without limit. In fact, this is how internal reasoning, i.e., reasoning on internal knowledge, actually works: we evolve, from our own experience and our own reasoning, as well as from the opinions we accept from our groups, a web of interlocking opinions that defines our body of knowledge. *All* of our knowledge that is not certifiably external can be described as belonging to a network of opinions, a web of influenced, rolled up evaluations of anecdotal experiences that have an undefined relation to reality.

Appendix E

Fallacies

This is a summary of some of the fallacies explained in *Pinnacle Questions*, chapter 5.

Wisdom Fallacy

The wisdom fallacy is based on the idea that knowledge of arcana in $\mathbb{S}$ insulates us from the dangers of $\mathbb{R}$, that it makes us invulnerable to mortality threats since we know we already have a foot in a transcendent dimension, so that even if the worst should happen, we will go on. This is why our image of the wise man is a picture of someone who is detached, unconcerned, uninvolved, and untroubled by the problems in this mortal world. The beatific smile, the "don't worry, the source of value is elsewhere" attitude, the disdain for gain, the hours spent in solitary meditation, are all symptoms of the wisdom fallacy. They are not indications that actual wisdom lives behind the bland countenance.

In other words, the wisdom fallacy is that, ultimately, $\mathbb{R}$ doesn't count, or doesn't count nearly as much as $\mathbb{S}$. It's a fallacy because everything we are balances on one small point on the physical reality plane, and to deny that in favor of a dream is a dangerous, destructive delusion.

Erudition Fallacy

The erudition fallacy is that learning to think, act, and talk like those at the center of power is the true aim of education. It demonstrates hubris on both the $\mathbb{S}$ and $\mathbb{R}$ realities:

- on $\mathbb{S}$, because the power of our enlightened education frees us from the need to believe in primitive superstitions. After all, since we have been educated in the truths of $\mathbb{R}$, we no longer have any need for a traditional compass to guide our way in the dark.

- on $\mathbb{R}$, because the complex rules of our $\mathbb{SR}$, which we have chosen to join, center us within the highest truth, and with the group's ideology to guide us, we no longer have any need to check our results against something so base as physical reality.

The erudition fallacy is that the only truths that matter are those we have learned from our particular SR. Coincidentally, these truths often stay supreme only so long as we find we can use them to improve our own fortunes.

Being "well-educated" and being "well-bred" amount to about the same thing, unless that education involves the mastery of actual skills. The problem with the erudition fallacy is that it is, at bottom, just a mechanism to enforce the group hierarchy and to teach the less well-bred that only by following their privileged superiors will they get their measly portion. The erudition fallacy confuses *manners* with competence, and that is a fatal mistake. Just because someone dresses well and has good diction does not mean that they are knowledgeable, perceptive, competent, honest, or interesting. It just means they have nice clothes and they learned to speak a certain way.

Erudite comes from the Latin *ex* - from + *rudis* - rough, rude; it means displaying knowledge gained by studying, having the look of someone who has been lifted out of the primitive muck through an education in the company of the elite. The point of this tome is to encourage, not discourage study, so it is not *study* that is the culprit in this fallacy. The erudition fallacy is that study in the academy, by itself, endows one with powers, it makes one *wise*. The truth is that studying a science or technological art in the academy can make one expert in that discipline if everything is done right. But that's not what the fallacy is about, the fallacy is the mistaken notion that being steeped in a cultural tradition in the academy endows one with superior ratiocinative powers, it makes one wise, perceptive, and capable.

Reasoning Fallacy

The reasoning fallacy is based on the idea that a calm demeanor and a measured discussion in the domain specific language of choice can find THE solution to any problem. Generally, each person who engages this fallacy sees himself as the voice of reason who can guide his inferiors, the irrationally impassioned, non-erudite, non-wise disputants into the safe harbor of reason. That safe harbor will be located in the land of philosophy, ideology or spirituality that the leader calls home.

The underlying problem of the fallacy is the delusion that, because of our education, experience, and special gifts, we, more than anyone else, actually see the world for what it is, and so are uniquely qualified to find a reasonable, equitable solution for whatever problem supplicants can bring to us. The difficulty is that those who fall for this fallacy do not understand that the opinion object is only built to sort input according to the rules we establish that preserve our values, interests, and beliefs. They think that their opinions actually describe reality accurately.

The fallacy entails a vast overestimation of the power, reach and importance of L2 pattern processing, to the point that all other realities are devalued down to something to be arranged, ignored, or solved, never recognized or taken into account. The function of opinions is to enable us to manage the incoming flow of information in such a way that we can pluck out the actionable percent and essentially ignore the rest so that we can maintain our sense of orientation, equilibrium and control.

Appendix F

Optimization Formula

In the current version of the model, L3 does not have a memory, just a data structure and the operations that work on it.[1] This is consistent with my experience that discovery structures do not retain charge over time, not even overnight, really. They always have to be refreshed in most branches to regain the charged state that supports insight and discovery. This is also consistent with the evidence that the inventions of L3 can only be communicated to others as L2 patterns that can be followed, not as discovery trees with the charged leaves that make L3 so powerful.

So, where does L3 start its work? With L2 patterns, of course, but it cannot work with patterns as patterns, since their structure hides the most important details of the ideas inside,

---

[1] Excerpted from *Ultrareasoning*, chapter 30.

so the first thing L3 has to do to convert patterns to fractal discovery structures is to decompose the patterns into constituent
parts, and position the parts of interest into the developing discovery tree. Another way to say the same thing, is that L3
has to *expand terms* hidden in patterns into *measurable* concepts, and express relations in a *testable* format that supports
an *iterative* development process.

Formally, the class of subjective problems can be defined
as the tuple: $(\vec{r}_0,\ \vec{a},\ \vec{r}_1)$. If we use the convenience term
circumstance to mean a set of one or more situations, then $\vec{r}_0$
represents the initial circumstance vector, $\vec{a}$ represents an array of actions, and $\vec{r}_1$ represents the post-action circumstance
vector, which, by definition, is intended to evaluate as greater
than the pre-action vector.

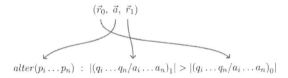

$$(\vec{r}_0,\ \vec{a},\ \vec{r}_1)$$

$$alter(p_i \ldots p_n)\ :\ |(q_i \ldots q_n/a_i \ldots a_n)_1| > |(q_i \ldots q_n/a_i \ldots a_n)_0|$$

Figure F.1: Expanding the subjective problem into an L3 solution.

Figure F.1 shows one way in which the subjective problem
can be expanded to support an L3 solution. Reading from left
to right, it says that:

- if $p_i \ldots p_n$ are the processes that generated the original,
  unsatisfactory state of affairs, $\vec{r}_0$, then our set of solutions

actions will be modifications to those processes that will generate

- an ending state, $\vec{r}_1$, that is intended to have a higher evaluation than
- the beginning state, $\vec{r}_0$.

In any given situation, there are many processes $p_i \ldots p_n$ in the set of all processes $\mathbf{P}$, that influence the situation. Those processes each have outputs $q_i \ldots q_n$ in the set of outputs $\mathbf{Q}$. Those outputs impact the participants $a_i \ldots a_n$ in the set of participants $\mathbf{A}$, where participants can be either different beings, or just different elements in our awareness attribute array. The optimization problem states that we must alter one or more of the processes, p_i in such a way that the benefits $q_i \ldots q_m$ received by the important participants $a_i \ldots a_m$ increase. Converting these words to expression form gives us this:

$$alter(p_i \ldots p_n) \ : \ |(q_i \ldots q_n/a_i \ldots a_n)_1| > |(q_i \ldots q_n/a_i \ldots a_n)_0|$$

That is, alter some processes such that the benefit to the prioritized parties is optimized.

Combining this with the definition of statement,

statement = [**context**] + **content** + [**purpose**]

we can define the context of the optimization formula as $\mathbf{A}_0$, the initial state of the being's awareness which represents $\mathbf{E} \cup \mathbf{A}'$ where $\mathbf{E}$ is the perceived initial state of the environment and $\mathbf{A}'$

is the initial state of the organism; the content of the statement is: $alter(p_i \ldots p_n)$, and the relative improvement of $\mathbf{A}_1$, the subsequent state, over $\mathbf{A}_0$ is the purpose.

Therefore, the expression form of an internal, subjective statement is:

$$given \ \mathbf{A}_0, \ alter(p_i \ldots p_n) \rightarrow optimize \ (q_{i\ldots n}) \ for \ (a_{i\ldots n})$$

Note that each part of the above expression is both easily quantifiable and testable, and that, therefore, by taking this approach, we can quantify and test any subjective statement using this optimization formula. This means that, for the first time, we could actually have policy debates on the explicit costs and benefits of pursuing any policy we want to consider, and we could do this by strictly focusing on verifiable, measurable calculations instead of on primitive L0 concepts of right (meaning: in my specific and extended perceived self-interest) and wrong (contrary to my specific and extended perceived self-interest).

Note also that this in no way guarantees fairness or efficiency, and that

$$|(q_i \ldots q_n/a_i \ldots a_n)_1| > |(q_i \ldots q_n/a_i \ldots a_n)_0|$$

just explicitly states the cost and benefit shifts expected to be caused to the interested participants by the process changes.

What this L3 solution shows is that the essential problem of subjective experience always reduces to an optimization problem: how can I (specific and extended) minimize my risk and maximize my benefit when responding/reacting to an event, external force or entity?

Discussion

Ask yourself, what should the answer to a resource allocation optimization problem actually look like? It certainly is not the simple $[true|false\ |don't\ care]$ value, or the list of unexecutable actions. Instead, it would have to look something like a spreadsheet that showed the winners and losers with their respective gains and losses, and be executable so that you could run what-if scenarios. It would have numbers, lots of numbers. Why would anyone ever expect we should be able to reliably reduce a complex resource allocation solution to a literal two bit value?

Even though L2 sees them as pattern matching problems, *all subjective problems are resource allocation optimization problems*, as only L3 can conceive them to be. L2 is like a space probe that returns pictures whose pixels are 10 or 100 miles on a side — not necessarily wrong, as far as it goes, but missing a lot of detail due to the lack of precision. L2 *cannot* see problems as resource allocation issues because it lacks the refinement ability to explore and define the problem to that level of detail, because it is limited to responding to circumstances or situations as a whole with a pattern as a whole. Instead of discovering the fractal dimension of the coast of England, L2 would probably call it a dodecagon or icosagon (12 or 20-sided polygon) and be done with it.

L4, whatever that evolves to become, will have a different solution, of course, but inasmuch as the L3 level is our current limit, we can confidently say that, at least, all subjective problems can be expressed as resource allocation problems.

The optimization formula is more of an approach, than an actual formula you can use by substituting values for variables, but that's not actually an issue. The real import of the formula is that debating public policy issues as L2 tuples that evaluate to true or false is both incompetent and dishonest, and everyone knows it. Unless candidates and policy makers can use the L3 optimization formula to calculate and demonstrate the projected gains and losses from the changes for the target groups, they should be booed off the stage. Asking that partisans fill out the specifics of the formula is not only not asking too much, it is difficult to imagine why we would expect any less than this.

This means that we should demand the following from all policy change proponents *before* we agree to take their proposals seriously:

- an executable model of the current situation;
- a list of the important mechanisms, processes and con-

straints to change;

- a projection of the output of each of the changes severally and together;

- a list of the beneficiaries and payers;

- estimated gains and losses to the beneficiaries and payers, respectively;

- an affordable experiment or pilot project design with a given time period;

- an error bound, along with experiment premature termination conditions.

How is expecting responsible officials to do some homework before implementing changes that will cost billions and affect millions of people asking too much of them? And shouldn't all policy changes have projections that include tripwire values to terminate failing changes? It's not asking too much, it's not asking very much at all.

What it is doing, though, is demanding a radical course change to convert from L0/L2 planning (what's right for my extended self is right for everyone) to L3 planning (full scientific method protocol) consistent with the recognition that right and wrong are primitive, inadequate concepts in resource allocation discussions since all of the precision data gained from modeling and scientific measurement is lost in the narrowing typecast down to the L0 data structure. We still need L0 to decide, and to act, but we cannot rely on it to perform, or evaluate, the precise measurements that prove that our ideas correspond to verifiable reality: $|i_i - r_i| < \epsilon$.

Index

$\mathcal{M}$, 74

ξ, 74

action module, 15

antswer, 224

ASPICS, 315

character flaws, 132

    alienation, 143

    cowardice, 144

    disrespect, 133

    hubris, 141

    inconstancy, 143

    irresponsibility, 141

    sloth, 142

cognitive space, 36

compound curved space, 41

conversation, **285**, 302

data objects, 357

    situation, **364**

    container, **368**

    evacule, **359**

    mentacule, **361**

    opinion, **370**

    pattern, **365**

    result, **364**

educate, 188

evil, 231, **235**

    quotient, **236**

evolutionary reality, 53

external reality, 49

formal language, 104, 106, 294

Grievancism, 178

higher education, 186

inculcate, 188

informal language, 104, 106, 294

internal reality, 49

lessons, 99

  one, 99

  two, 101

  three, 104

  four, 109

  five, 114

levels, 59

  L0, 60, 85, 86

  L1, 61, 85, 86

  L2, 64, 85, 86

  L3, 85, 86

limits, 71

  Limit 1, 72

  Limit 2, 74

  Limit 3, 79

  Limit 4, 79

  Limit 5, 84

  Limit 6, 91

loopback, **164**, 223, **368**

lying, **115**, 198, 199, 205

meaning, 49, 224

model layers, **56**

mudball model, 55

normal stupidity, 9, **13**, **18**, 23, 197

Occam's razor, 155

partial function, 16

perception, **13**

physical reality, **30**

principles, 130

  Limit 1, 130

  Limit 2, 131

  Limit 3, 131

  Limit 4, 131

  Limit 5, 131

  Limit 6, 132

pseudo-reality, 50

purblind defect, **17**, 47

questions, 290

reality, 26, 27, **28**

reductive process, 14

religion, 147, **153**, 273

    divine origin, 172

    fundamentalist, 153

    hypocrisy, 170

    reformed, 153

rhetorical reasoning, **251**

rules of thumb, 307

self, 229

    extended self, **69**, 230

    specific self, **69**, 231

self-other-ultimate value vector, **216**

semantic reality, 33, 34, **41**, 78

seven virtues, 95

statement, **283**

stupidity pump, 193

super stupidity, 24, 127, **129**, 197

    cost, 213, 225, 238, 241

    power, 200, **203**

supernatural reality, 161

tips, 309

    1: Solid Foundation, 309

    2: Knowledge-Humble, 311

    3: Settling, 311

    4: Realities, 312

    5: Explorer, 313

truth matrix, 296

value, 38, **48**

Made in United States
Orlando, FL
13 January 2023

28617241R00220